Prologue

In the pursuit of civil services, where the quest for knowledge intertwines w
the UPSC Civil Services Examination stands as a formidable gateway. Aspir
merely an individual ambition; it is a commitment to the collective welfare, an aspiration to contribute meaningfully to the nation's progress.

This collection of essays emerges as a compass for those navigating the challenging landscape of the UPSC Civil Services Examination. It is not just a compilation of words but a reservoir of insights, perspectives, and intellectual explorations aimed at equipping the aspirant with the intellectual dexterity required for the demanding journey ahead.

Each essay within this volume is a lantern, illuminating the multifaceted dimensions of the subjects that constitute the UPSC syllabus. From the intricate tapestry of history to the nuanced contours of governance, from the socio-economic dynamics shaping our nation to the global challenges of the contemporary world, these essays serve as beacons guiding the reader through the diverse terrains of knowledge essential for the examination.

The journey toward becoming a civil servant is not confined to textbooks and rote memorization; it is a holistic odyssey that demands critical thinking, analytical prowess, and a deep understanding of the socio-political fabric. The essays contained herein are not prescriptive answers but invitations to explore, ponder, and engage with the myriad facets of the subjects that define the civil services examination.

In the spirit of intellectual inquiry, this collection encourages aspirants to transcend the boundaries of conventional wisdom, challenge preconceived notions, and embrace a holistic understanding of the issues at hand. The essays are not endpoints but starting points for further exploration, catalysts for the development of a robust intellectual framework that goes beyond the examination hall.

As you embark on this intellectual voyage, remember that the pursuit of civil services is not a solitary endeavour. It is a collective commitment to nation-building, a shared aspiration to contribute to the tapestry of our diverse and dynamic democracy. May this collection of essays serve as a companion, a guide, and a source of inspiration as you navigate the challenges and opportunities that lie ahead in the UPSC Civil Services Examination.

The essays herein are not just about acquiring knowledge; they are about cultivating wisdom, fostering a sense of responsibility, and nurturing the qualities that define a civil servant – integrity, empathy, and a deep commitment to the service of the people. May this collection be a testament to the transformative power of education and the enduring spirit of those who embark on the noble journey to serve the nation through the prism of the UPSC Civil Services Examination.

Introduction

The essay paper in the UPSC civil services exam was introduced in 1989 based on the recommendations of Satish Chandra Committee. The major recommendations can be cited from the following extracts of the original report:

Why there should be an essay in UPSC?

5.0402   During our visits and discussions, we were told by Senior Officers and even Heads of Training Institutes that some of the post-1979 entrants to the higher Civil Services did not have necessary skills to prepare a proper Report or a Report on any specified assignment involving integrated thinking and lingusitic skills, etc. In our view, this is a matter, which deserves some serious attention as officers of the higher Civil Services are expected to prepare policy papers, notes, drafts and memoranda on a variety of subjects. It is true that skills in these areas can be imparted at the Training Institute and also can be

developed with experience in service. But these useful skills, are mostly acquired during the academic career in colleges and Universities. Hence these should be tested in the Main Examination.

5.0403   We are of the view that the Essay Paper in the Main Examination will bring out not only the candidate's linguistic skills but also capacity for comprehension, ability for critical analysis, mental quality for integrated thinking, assimilation of ideas and clarity of expression.   We feel that the two papers on General Studies (600 marks) in the current scheme of Common Examination are not able to do these in a satisfactory manner.

How and on what account will the essay be evaluated?

in any one of the 'Indian Languages'.   To ensure uniformity of standards, we recommend that evaluation of the answer scripts on the Essay Paper should take into account (i) comprehension (ii) originality of thought (iii) clarity of expression and (iv) integrated thinking with assimilation of ideas.   We also recommend evaluation of the answer scripts in the Essay Paper by two independent examiners. In this system, the marks scored by a candidate should be the mean of the two scores.

Creating a basis for Essay writing

Start your essay by doing some rough work along the following directives surrounding the keyword/ phrase given in the essay topic.

- **What?**
- **When?**
- **Where?**
- **Why?**
- **Who?**
- **How?**
- **Issues**
- **Suggestion**

Next, start writing the punchlines, quotes, data sets that correspond to the topic of the essay. Finally, create a rough draft for your introduction, body, and conclusion. In the body of the essay, just think about the start and end of each paragraph. You may combine paragraphs with point formats if you have a lot of disjointed things to say about a particular topic, however, sentences and connectors are the mature way forward always.

What to avoid?

- Be careful about- Race, Religion, Region, Ideology, individuals, etc.
- Avoid closed sentences or sweeping statements.
- Avoid Casual Language and short forms.
- Avoid staggered tones- pessimist, serious, sombre, optimistic and enthusiastic tones should be closely knit.

Selecting an Essay topic

1. Avoid honey traps- find your bases.
2. Competitive edge in a topic- optional, leverage\data, fresh ideas
3. Avoid extremes and abstract.

Before you write decide if....

- The topic is thematic or contextually specific.
- The topic is singular or plural in approach.
- The topic is metaphorical or literal.

The topic is oriented towards the past, present or future [Temporal flow]
The topic is based on the punctuation (?,!,.) as a part of the title- preserve the flavour of question mark/ exclamation mark or the full stop in the end.

Creating a thinking framework

- **Thought framework- What(s) and How(s)**
- **Subject framework- topic driven**
- **Organic framework- life cycle approach**

- **Structural- functional framework**
- **Concentric circle framework**
- **Sensitivity framework**

Creating a writing framework

1. Topic
2. Ideas
3. Paragraphs
4. Analysis- logic, example, facts
5. Examination
6. Layering- vertical aspect
7. Fusion- Horizontal integration
8. Cancellation of weak paragraphs
9. Ordering of ideas and paragraphs – Introduce well and do save something for the last.
10. Linkages and transitions- smooth movement from para to para

Parts of an essay

Introduction – 10%

- Theme setting
- Implicit slightly delayed announcement,
- Define the scope,
- Make it interesting
- Set the tone
- Use- quotes, anecdotes, established fact and/ or universal truth.

Body- 80%

- Para starts with a punchline/ thesis statement
- Analyse the statement in a pre-set tone and stay focused
- Square the circle
- Create a connector/ linker for inter-paragraph movements eg: thus, hence, firstly, secondly, etc. or logical transition- creating an expectation in the mind of the reader.

Conclusion- 10%

- Summary- convey the main points
- Post-scripting the missed dimensions
- Maintain the Tone

- Future perspective – creativity, hope, optimism and humility

PREVIOUS YEARS UPSC ESSAY QUESTIONS

UPSC 2023 Mains Essay Paper

Section A

1. Thinking is like a game, it does not begin unless there is an opposite team.
2. Visionary decision-making happens at the intersection of intuition and logic.
3. Not all who wander are lost.
4. Inspiration for creativity springs from the effort to look for the magical in the mundane.

Section B

1. Girls are weighed down by restrictions, boys with demands- two equally harmful disciplines.
2. Mathematics is the music of reasons.
3. A society that has more justice is a society that needs less charity.
4. Education is what remains after one has forgotten what one has learned in school.

UPSC 2022 Mains Essay Paper

Section -A

1. Forests are the best-case studies for economic excellence.
2. Poets are the unacknowledged legislators of the world.
3. History is a series of victories won by the scientific man over the romantic man.
4. A ship in harbour is safe, but that is not what ship is for.

Section – B

1. The time to repair the roof is when the sun is shining.
2. You cannot step twice in the same river.
3. A smile is the chosen vehicle for all ambiguities.
4. Just because you have a choice, it does not mean that any of them has to be right.

UPSC 2021 Mains Essay Paper

Section A

1. The process of self-discovery has now been technologically outsourced.
2. Your perception of me is a reflection of you; my reaction to you is an awareness of me.
3. Philosophy of want lessness is Utopian, while materialism is a chimera.
4. The real is rational and the rational is real.

Section B

1. Hand that rocks the cradle rules the world.
2. What is research, but a blind date with knowledge!
3. History repeats itself, first as a tragedy, second as a farce.
4. There are better practices to 'best practices'.

UPSC 2020 Mains Essay Paper

Section A

1. Life is a long journey between human being and being humane.
2. Mindful manifesto is the catalyst to a tranquil self.
3. Ships do not sink because of water around them, ships sink because of water that gets into them.
4. Simplicity is the ultimate sophistication.

Section B

1. Culture is what we are, civilisation is what we have.
2. There can be no social justice without economic prosperity but economic prosperity without social justice is meaningless.
3. Patriarchy is the least noticed yet the most significant structure of social inequality.
4. Technology as the silent factor in international relations.

UPSC 2019 Mains Essay Paper

SECTION A

1. Wisdom finds truth

2. Values are not what humanity is, but what humanity ought to be

3. Best for an individual is not necessarily best for the society

4. Courage to accept and dedication to improve are two keys to success

 SECTION B

5. South Asian societies are woven not around the state, but around their plural cultures and plural identities

6. Neglect of primary health care and education in India are reasons for its backwardness

7. Biased media is a real threat to Indian democracy

8. Rise of Artificial Intelligence: the threat of jobless future or better job opportunities through reskilling and upskilling

UPSC Essay Topic WISE: 1994-2018

Administration

1. Politics, bureaucracy and business – fatal triangle. (1994)
2. Politics without ethics is a disaster. (1995)
3. The VIP cult is a bane of Indian democracy. (1996)
4. Need for transparency in public administration. (1996)
5. The country's need for a better disaster management system. (2000)
6. How should a civil servant conduct himself? (2003)

Democracy/India since independence

1. Whither Indian democracy? (1995)
2. What we have not learnt during fifty years of independence. (1997)
3. Why should we be proud of being Indians? (2000)
4. What have we gained from our democratic set-up? (2001)
5. How far has democracy in India delivered the goods? (2003)
6. National identity and patriotism. (2008)
7. In the context of Gandhiji's views on the matter, explore, on an evolutionary scale, the terms 'Swadhinata', 'Swaraj' and 'Dharmarajya'. Critically comment on their contemporary relevance to Indian democracy. (2012)
8. Is the colonial mentality hindering India's success? (2013)
9. Dreams which should not let India sleep. (2015)
10. Management of Indian border disputes – a complex task. (2018)

Economic growth and development

1. Resource management in the Indian context. (1999)
2. GDP (Gross Domestic Product) along with GDH (Gross Domestic Happiness) would be the right indices for judging the wellbeing of a country. (2013)
3. Was it the policy paralysis or the paralysis of implementation which slowed the growth of our country? (2014)
4. Crisis faced in India – moral or economic. (2015)
5. Near jobless growth in India: An anomaly or an outcome of economic reforms. (2016)
6. Digital economy: A leveller or a source of economic inequality. (2016)
7. Innovation is the key determinant of economic growth and social welfare. (2016)
8. Impact of the new economic measures on fiscal ties between the union and states in India. (2017)

Federalism, Decentralisation

1. The language problem in India: its past, present and prospects. (1998)
2. Water resources should be under the control of the central government. (2004)
3. Evaluation of panchayati raj system in India from the point of view of eradication of power to people. (2007)
4. Is autonomy the best answer to combat balkanization? (2007)
5. Creation of smaller states and the consequent administrative, economic and developmental implication. (2011)
6. Cooperative federalism: Myth or reality. (2016)

7. Water disputes between States in federal India. (2016)

Indian Culture & Society

1. The Indian society at the crossroads. (1994)
2. New cults and godmen: a threat to traditional religion. (1996)
3. The composite culture of India. (1998)
4. Youth culture today. (1999)
5. Modernism and our traditional socio-ethical values. (2000)
6. Indian culture today: a myth or a reality? (2000)
7. As civilization advances culture declines. (2003)
8. From traditional Indian philanthropy to the gates-buffet model-a natural progression or a paradigm shift? (2010)

Judiciary

1. Judicial activism. (1997)
2. Judicial activism and Indian democracy. (2004)
3. Justice must reach the poor. (2005)

Social justice/Poverty

1. Reservation, politics and empowerment. (1999)
2. Food security for sustainable national development. (2005)
3. The focus of health care is increasingly getting skewed towards the 'haves' of our society. (2009)
4. Farming has lost the ability to be a source of subsistence for the majority of farmers in India. (2017)
5. Poverty anywhere is a threat to prosperity everywhere. (2018)

Media & Society

1. Misinterpretation and misuse of freedom in India. (1998)
2. Mass media and cultural invasion. (1999)
3. Responsibility of media in a democracy. (2002)
4. How has satellite television brought about cultural change in Indian mindsets? (2007)
5. Role of media in good governance. (2008)
6. Does Indian cinema shape our popular culture or merely reflect it? (2011)

7. Is sting operation an invasion on privacy? (2014)

Environment/Urbanisation

1. Urbanization is a blessing in disguise. (1997)
2. Protection of ecology and environment is essential for sustained economic development. (2006)
3. Urbanisation and its hazards. (2008)
4. Should a moratorium be imposed on all fresh mining in tribal areas of the country? (2010)
5. We may brave human laws but cannot resist natural laws. (2017)

Economic sectors/MNCs

1. Multinational corporations – saviours or saboteurs. (1994)
2. Globalization would finish small-scale industries in India. (2006)
3. BPO boom in India. (2007)
4. Special economic zone: boon or bane? (2008)
5. Are our traditional handicrafts doomed to a slow death? (2009)
6. Is the criticism that the Public-Private-Partnership (PPP) model for development is more of a bane than a boon in the Indian context, justified? (2012)
7. Tourism: Can this be the next big thing for India? (2014)

Education

1. Restructuring of Indian education system. (1995)
2. Literacy is growing very fast, but there is no corresponding growth in education. (1996)
3. Irrelevance of the classroom. (2001)
4. Privatization of higher education in India. (2002)
5. Modern technological education and human values. (2002)
6. What is real education? (2005)
7. "Education for all" campaign in India: myth or reality. (2006)
8. Independent thinking should be encouraged right from the childhood. (2007)
9. Is an egalitarian society possible by educating the masses? (2008)
10. Credit – based higher education system – status, opportunities and challenges. (2011)
11. Is the growing level of competition good for the youth? (2014)
12. Are the standardized tests good measure of academic ability or progress? (2014)
13. Education without values, as useful as it is, seems rather to make a man more clever devil. (2015)
14. Destiny of a nation is shaped in its classrooms. (2017)

Women

1. The new emerging women power: the ground realities. (1995)
2. Greater political power alone will not improve women's plight. (1997)
3. Woman is god's best creation. (1998)
4. Women empowerment: challenges and prospects. (1999)
5. Empowerment alone cannot help our women. (2001)
6. Whither women's emancipation? (2004)
7. If women ruled the world. (2005)
8. The hand that rocks the cradle. (2005)
9. Women's reservation bill would usher in empowerment for women in India. (2006)
10. Managing work and home – is the Indian working woman getting a fair deal? (2012)
11. If development is not engendered, it is endangered. (2016)
12. Fulfilment of 'new woman' in India is a myth. (2017)

Quotes-based/Philosophy

1. Youth is a blunder, manhood a struggle, old age a regret. (1994)
2. Useless life is an early death. (1994)
3. Disinterested intellectual curiosity is the lifeblood of civilisation. (1995)
4. When money speaks, the truth is silent. (1995)
5. Our deeds determine us, as much as we determine our deeds. (1995)
6. Truth is lived, not taught. (1996)
7. True religion cannot be misused. (1997)
8. Search for truth can only be a spiritual problem. (2002)
9. The paths of glory lead but to the grave. (2002)
10. If youth knew, if age could. (2002)
11. There is nothing either good or bad but thinking makes it so. (2003)
12. Be the change you want to see in others. (2013)
13. With greater power comes greater responsibility. (2014)
14. Words are sharper than the two-edged sword. (2014)
15. Lending hands to someone is better than giving a dole. (2015)
16. "The past' is a permanent dimension of human consciousness and values. (2018)
17. Reality does not conform to the ideal, but confirms it. (2018)

Character

1. Attitude makes habit, habit makes character and character makes a man. (2007)
2. Discipline means success, anarchy means ruin. (2008)
3. Character of an institution is reflected in its leader. (2015)
4. Need brings greed, if greed increases it spoils breed. (2016)
5. Joy is the simplest form of gratitude. (2017)
6. A good life is one inspired by love and guided by knowledge. (2018)
7. A people that values its privileges above its principles loses both. (2018)
8. Customary morality cannot be a guide to modern life. (2018)

Globalisation

1. Modernisation and westernisation are not identical concepts. (1994)
2. The world of the twenty-first century. (1998)
3. The implications of globalization for India. (2000)
4. My vision of an ideal world order. (2001)
5. The masks of new imperialism. (2003)
6. Globalizations and its impact on Indian culture. (2004)
7. 'Globalization' vs. 'nationalism'. (2009)
8. Preparedness of our society for India's global leadership role. (2010)

Science & Tech

1. The modern doctor and his patients. (1997)
2. Value-based science and education. (1999)
3. The march of science and the erosion of human values. (2001)
4. Spirituality and scientific temper. (2003)
5. The lure of space. (2004)
6. Science and Mysticism: Are they compatible? (2012)
7. Science and technology is the panacea for the growth and security of the nation. (2013)
8. Technology cannot replace manpower. (2015)
9. Alternative technologies for a climate change resilient India. (2018)

Internet/IT

1. The cyberworld: its charms and challenges. (2000)

2. Increasing computerization would lead to the creation of a dehumanized society. (2006)

3. Cyberspace and Internet: Blessing or curse to the human civilization in the long run. (2016)

4. Social media is inherently a selfish medium. (2017)

International organisations/relations

1. Restructuring of UNO reflect present realities. (1996)

2. India's role in promoting ASEAN cooperation. (2004)

3. Importance of Indo-US nuclear agreement. (2006)

4. Has the Non- Alignment Movement (NAM) lost its relevance in a multipolar world. (2017)

Security

1. Terrorism and world peace. (2005)

2. Are we a 'soft' state? (2009)

3. Good fences make good neighbours. (2009)

4. In the Indian context, both human intelligence and technical intelligence are crucial in combating terrorism. (2011)

Miscellaneous

1. India's contribution to world wisdom. (1998)

2. The pursuit of excellence. (2001)

3. Geography may remain the same; history need not. (2010)

4. Fifty Golds in Olympics: Can this be a reality for India? (2014)

5. Quick but steady wins the race. (2015)

UPSC 2023 ESSAY PAPER SECTION A

Thinking is like a game; it does not begin unless there is an opposite team

Thinking, a fundamental cognitive process integral to human existence, has been compared to myriad metaphors throughout history. Among these, the analogy of thinking as a game stands out, suggesting that the cognitive realm operates much like a contest with an opposing team. In this essay, we explore the nuances of this analogy, drawing on dialectical thinking, philosophical perspectives, and scientific insights to unravel the intricacies of thought processes.

Dialectical Thinking:

Dialectical thinking, rooted in ancient philosophy and further developed by figures such as Hegel and Marx, posits that intellectual progress is achieved through the clash of opposing ideas. According to this framework, the synthesis of conflicting concepts leads to a higher, more comprehensive understanding. Applying this lens to the analogy of thinking as a game, we see that the cognitive process gains momentum when faced with an opposing force. The clash of ideas serves as the catalyst for intellectual growth, pushing individuals to refine and expand their cognitive frameworks.

Historical Perspectives:

Philosophical history is replete with examples supporting the idea that intellectual progress often arises from the confrontation of opposing viewpoints. Socratic dialogues, for instance, epitomize the notion that genuine understanding is born out of dialectical engagement. The method of elenchus, employed by Socrates, involved a question-and-answer format that exposed contradictions in one's beliefs, prompting a reconsideration and refinement of one's thinking.

In the realm of science, the Copernican Revolution serves as a testament to the transformative power of intellectual opposition. Copernicus challenged the geocentric model of the universe, proposing a heliocentric alternative. The clash between these opposing cosmological frameworks spurred a reevaluation of long-held beliefs, eventually leading to a profound shift in humanity's understanding of its place in the cosmos.

Psychological Insights:

From a psychological standpoint, the concept of cognitive dissonance further supports the notion that thinking is most fruitful when confronted with opposing ideas. Cognitive dissonance theory, developed by Leon Festinger, posits that individuals experience discomfort when holding conflicting beliefs. To alleviate this discomfort, individuals are motivated to reconcile or revise their beliefs. This process of cognitive adjustment reflects a dynamic interplay of opposing forces within the mind, akin to the dynamics of a game.

Neuroscientific Considerations:

Advances in neuroscience have shed light on the neural mechanisms underlying cognitive processes. Neuroplasticity, the brain's ability to reorganize itself in response to experience, highlights the dynamic nature of thought. When exposed to new and opposing ideas, neural networks may undergo restructuring, facilitating the integration of diverse perspectives. This neuroscientific perspective aligns with the analogy of thinking as a game, where the opposing team serves as a stimulus for cognitive adaptation and growth.

The Role of Opposition in Creativity:

Creativity, a hallmark of human intelligence, often thrives in the presence of intellectual opposition. The juxtaposition of divergent ideas can spark novel insights and innovative solutions. The creative process, whether in the arts, sciences, or any other domain, frequently involves navigating through the tension of opposing forces. This creative tension, akin to the dynamics of a game, propels individuals towards novel and imaginative outcomes.

Conclusion:

In conclusion, viewing thinking as a game with an opposite team provides a compelling perspective on the dynamics of cognition. Drawing from dialectical thinking, historical examples, psychological insights, and neuroscientific considerations, we find a convergence of evidence supporting the idea that intellectual opposition is integral to the richness and depth of thought. Embracing the challenges posed by opposing ideas not only refines individual understanding but also contributes to the collective progress of human knowledge. In the intricate dance of ideas, the game of thinking unfolds, pushing the boundaries of human intellect and fostering a more profound appreciation of the complex tapestry of thought.

Visionary decision-making happens at the intersection of intuition and logic

Visionary decision-making is an art as much as it is a science. It involves navigating through uncertainty, complexity, and ambiguity to chart a course for the future. In this endeavor, decision-makers often find themselves standing at the crossroads of intuition and logic, where the convergence of these two cognitive processes becomes the crucible for visionary choices. This essay delves into the nature of intuition and logic, exploring how their interplay contributes to the making of decisions that transcend the ordinary and shape the course of history.

Understanding Intuition:

Intuition, often considered a mysterious and ineffable aspect of human cognition, plays a crucial role in decision-making. Rooted in rapid pattern recognition and subconscious processing, intuition enables individuals to arrive at insights that may not be immediately evident through analytical reasoning. This intuitive knowing is often characterized by a gut feeling, a hunch, or an implicit understanding that defies explicit articulation.

Research in cognitive psychology suggests that intuition is honed through experience and expertise, drawing on a vast reservoir of tacit knowledge. Malcolm Gladwell, in his book "Blink," explores the concept of thin-slicing, the ability to make accurate judgments based on a narrow window of experience. This process, he argues, is a manifestation of intuition, where the brain rapidly processes information to arrive at a decision.

However, the ephemeral and subjective nature of intuition often raises skepticism in the realm of decision-making. Critics argue that relying on intuition alone can lead to biased and irrational choices. Therefore, the challenge lies in understanding when and how to integrate intuition with logic to foster visionary decision-making.

Decoding Logic in Decision-Making:

Logic, in contrast to intuition, operates within the realm of conscious reasoning and systematic analysis. It is the process of evaluating evidence, assessing probabilities, and drawing conclusions based on deductive or inductive reasoning. Logical decision-making relies on structured methodologies, data-driven insights, and a rational assessment of available information.

In many organizational settings, decision-makers are encouraged to follow a logical decision-making model that involves defining the problem, generating alternatives, evaluating options, and selecting the best course of action. While this method provides a structured approach, it may fall short in addressing the complexities and uncertainties inherent in visionary decision-making.

The Intersection of Intuition and Logic:

The intersection of intuition and logic represents a dynamic interplay between the conscious and subconscious mind. Visionary decision-makers navigate this intersection skillfully, drawing on the strengths of both intuition and logic to arrive at decisions that transcend the ordinary. This harmonious integration involves a recognition of the limitations and strengths of each cognitive process.

Neuroscientific studies have shed light on the interconnectedness of intuition and logic within the brain. Imaging studies reveal that intuitive processes often involve the activation of emotional centers, suggesting that emotions play a crucial role in intuitive decision-making. On the other hand, logical reasoning is associated with the activation of prefrontal cortex regions responsible for cognitive control and executive functions.

Real-World Examples of Visionary Decision-Making:

Examining historical and contemporary examples of visionary decision-making offers insights into the delicate balance between intuition and logic. One such example is the decision-making process behind Steve Jobs' introduction of the iPhone in 2007. While Jobs and his team meticulously analyzed market trends and technological advancements (logic), the final decision to proceed with the revolutionary device was guided by Jobs' intuition about consumer needs and desires.

Another illuminating example is the Apollo 11 moon landing in 1969. NASA engineers and scientists followed a rigorous logical process to design and execute the mission, considering numerous technical and logistical challenges. However, the ultimate decision to embark on this ambitious endeavor was fueled by a collective intuition that reaching the moon would not only be a scientific achievement but also a symbolic victory in the space race.

Implications for Leadership and Decision-Making:

Leaders in various domains often find themselves grappling with the challenge of visionary decision-making. Recognizing the symbiotic relationship between intuition and logic can inform a more nuanced approach to leadership and decision-making. Effective leaders leverage both cognitive processes, understanding when to trust their instincts and when to rely on analytical rigor.

Furthermore, fostering a culture that values both intuition and logic is crucial for organizations seeking to navigate an ever-changing landscape. Encouraging diversity of thought, interdisciplinary collaboration, and a willingness to entertain unconventional ideas can create an environment where visionary decision-making thrives.

Conclusion:

In conclusion, visionary decision-making is a multifaceted process that unfolds at the intersection of intuition and logic. While intuition taps into the subconscious and draws on tacit knowledge, logic relies on conscious reasoning and analytical rigor. The most profound decisions arise when individuals skillfully navigate this intersection, harmonizing the strengths of both cognitive processes.

Understanding the dynamics between intuition and logic requires a nuanced appreciation of their individual contributions and limitations. Real-world examples, from the introduction of groundbreaking technologies to historic space exploration missions, underscore the importance of balancing these cognitive processes in the pursuit of visionary goals.

As we continue to explore the intricate landscape of decision-making, it becomes evident that visionary leaders are those who recognize the complementary nature of intuition and logic. By embracing both elements, decision-makers can unlock new possibilities and shape a future that transcends the boundaries of the known. Visionary decision-making, therefore, stands as a testament to the human capacity to navigate uncertainty and complexity with a synthesis of intuition and logic.

Not all who wander are lost

J.R.R. Tolkien once penned the famous words, "Not all who wander are lost." These words have since transcended their literary origin to become a mantra for those seeking meaning and purpose in their journeys through life. In a world that often emphasizes direction and destination, the idea that wandering can be purposeful challenges conventional wisdom. This essay delves into the profound implications of this phrase, exploring its philosophical, psychological, and cultural dimensions to understand why wandering, far from being a sign of aimlessness, can be a deliberate and meaningful pursuit.

Philosophical Dimensions

At its core, "Not all who wander are lost" speaks to the philosophical concept of existential wandering, where the journey itself becomes the destination. Existentialist thinkers like Jean-Paul Sartre and Albert Camus argue that life lacks inherent meaning, and individuals must create their own purpose through their choices and experiences. In this context, wandering can be seen as a conscious rejection of predefined paths, an embrace of uncertainty, and a commitment to forging one's own narrative.

Existential wandering also draws parallels with the ancient Greek philosophy of hedonism, where the pursuit of pleasure and personal happiness is considered the highest good. Wandering, in this philosophical framework, becomes a means of exploring diverse experiences, encountering new perspectives, and seeking the pleasures that contribute to a rich and fulfilling life.

Psychological Perspectives

From a psychological standpoint, the phrase suggests a departure from rigid structures and a celebration of autonomy. Psychologists such as Abraham Maslow and Carl Rogers emphasize the importance of self-actualization—the process of realizing one's potential and becoming the most that one can be. Wandering, in this context, can be viewed as a self-directed journey towards self-discovery and personal growth.

The idea that not all who wander are lost aligns with the psychological benefits of embracing uncertainty. Psychologist Mihaly Csikszentmihalyi's concept of "flow" highlights the optimal state of engagement and fulfillment that arises when individuals are immersed in activities that challenge and stretch their abilities. Wandering, as a metaphor for embracing the unknown, can facilitate the experience of flow by encouraging individuals to navigate uncharted territories and confront novel challenges.

Moreover, the concept resonates with the psychological theory of self-determination, which posits that individuals have innate needs for autonomy, competence, and relatedness. Purposeful wandering can be seen as a manifestation of the need for autonomy, allowing individuals to exercise control over their choices and explore the vast landscapes of life on their terms.

Cultural Significance

Culturally, the phrase has found resonance in various artistic expressions, popular culture, and spiritual traditions. It has been embraced by adventurers, artists, and those who seek a deeper connection with the world around them. From the Beat Generation's road trips to Jack Kerouac's "On the Road" to the nomadic lifestyle celebrated by contemporary influencers, the idea that wandering is a valid and purposeful pursuit has permeated cultural narratives.

In spiritual traditions, wandering is often linked to pilgrimage—a journey undertaken with a sacred purpose. The act of pilgrimage involves not only reaching a physical destination but also undergoing a transformative inner journey. The pilgrim, like the wanderer, embraces the unknown, faces challenges, and seeks a deeper understanding of self and existence.

The phrase also challenges societal expectations and norms that prioritize linear paths and predefined milestones. In a world that often measures success by tangible achievements and milestones, the concept of purposeful wandering invites individuals to question these standards and consider alternative ways of finding meaning and fulfillment.

Conclusion

In conclusion, "Not all who wander are lost" encapsulates a profound philosophy that challenges conventional notions of purpose and direction. Philosophically, it aligns with existentialist ideas of creating meaning in the absence of inherent purpose. Psychologically, it resonates with the pursuit of self-actualization, autonomy, and the benefits of embracing uncertainty. Culturally, it finds expression in artistic endeavors, unconventional lifestyles, and spiritual traditions that celebrate the transformative power of purposeful wandering.

Ultimately, the phrase invites individuals to reconsider the value of the journey itself, recognizing that wandering can be a deliberate and meaningful pursuit. In a world that often pressures individuals to conform to predefined paths, the idea that not all who wander are lost serves as a reminder that there is inherent value in the exploration of the unknown and the discovery of one's unique path through the complexities of life.

Inspiration for creativity springs from the effort to look for the magical in the mundane.

In a world often overshadowed by the pursuit of the extraordinary, it is paradoxically within the folds of the ordinary that inspiration for creativity is often found. The magic inherent in the mundane is a potent source of artistic and intellectual exploration, leading individuals to discover new dimensions within the seemingly commonplace aspects of existence. This essay delves into the interplay between the search for magic and the wellspring of creativity, examining how the effort to uncover the extraordinary in the ordinary can catalyze innovation and original thought.

Psychological Perspectives:

From a psychological standpoint, the human mind has an inherent tendency to seek novelty and surprise. Psychologist Mihaly Csikszentmihalyi's concept of "flow" highlights the state of heightened focus and engagement that occurs when individuals are deeply immersed in an activity. The pursuit of the magical in the mundane aligns with this concept, as it introduces an element of surprise and novelty into the ordinary, triggering a cognitive response that can foster creativity.

Moreover, the human brain is wired to appreciate patterns and connections. When individuals actively seek the magical in the mundane, they engage in a process of pattern recognition, connecting disparate elements to unveil hidden beauty or significance. This cognitive exercise not only enhances cognitive flexibility but also serves as a wellspring for innovative thinking, as seen in the works of artists who draw inspiration from everyday scenes or objects.

Philosophical Perspectives:

Philosophically, the pursuit of magic in the mundane aligns with the idea that there is profundity in simplicity. Philosophers like Gaston Bachelard and Maurice Merleau-Ponty have explored the significance of the everyday in shaping our perceptions and understanding of the world. Bachelard's "Poetics of Space" delves into the poetic potential of the ordinary spaces we inhabit, while Merleau-Ponty's phenomenology emphasizes the embodied experience of the world.

By seeking the magical in the mundane, individuals engage in a philosophical act of re-enchantment—a process of imbuing the ordinary with a sense of wonder and significance. This act not only enriches personal experiences but also challenges conventional modes of thinking, encouraging a deeper contemplation of the world and its inherent mysteries.

Artistic Expressions:

Artists throughout history have been masters at extracting inspiration from the everyday. The Dutch still-life painters of the 17th century, such as Jan Vermeer and Willem Claeszoon Heda, elevated the depiction of ordinary objects to an art form. Through meticulous attention to detail and play of light, they transformed commonplace scenes into captivating works of art, inviting viewers to appreciate the beauty in the mundane.

In the realm of literature, magical realism is a literary technique that seamlessly blends the magical with the everyday. Writers like Gabriel Garcia Marquez and Isabel Allende infuse their narratives with fantastical elements, intertwining the extraordinary with the mundane. This literary approach not only captivates readers but also prompts them to reconsider their perceptions of reality and embrace the magical woven into the fabric of everyday life.

Contemporary Examples:

In the contemporary landscape, technological advancements have provided new avenues for the exploration of magic in the mundane. Social media platforms, for instance, have become canvases for individuals to showcase the enchanting aspects of their everyday lives. From viral videos capturing the beauty of a sunrise to photography projects focusing on the intricacies of ordinary objects, the digital age has amplified the visibility of the magical in the mundane.

Moreover, the mindfulness movement encourages individuals to engage in present-moment awareness, fostering an appreciation for the richness of the ordinary. By cultivating a mindful approach to daily life, people can unveil the magic inherent in simple acts, such as savoring a cup of tea or taking a leisurely stroll. This heightened awareness not only enhances well-being but also sparks creative insights by encouraging a deeper connection with one's surroundings.

Conclusion:

In conclusion, the inspiration for creativity is intricately tied to the effort to discover the magical in the mundane. From psychological processes that enhance cognitive flexibility to philosophical perspectives that emphasize the profundity of simplicity, and from artistic expressions that elevate the ordinary to contemporary examples showcasing the intersection of technology and enchantment, the pursuit of magic in the everyday serves as a powerful catalyst for human creativity.

As individuals actively engage with the ordinary, seeking hidden beauty and significance, they embark on a transformative journey that reshapes perceptions, challenges conventional thinking, and unlocks new realms of imagination. In recognizing the magic woven into the fabric of everyday life, we not only enrich our experiences but also tap into a boundless wellspring of inspiration that fuels the creative spirit, reminding us that the extraordinary often lies just beneath the surface of the seemingly commonplace.

Girls are weighed down by restrictions, boys with demands- two equally harmful disciplines

The fabric of societal expectations weaves a complex narrative that significantly impacts the lives of individuals, particularly in terms of gender roles. Girls and boys navigate through a maze of constraints and demands, each bearing its unique set of challenges. This essay seeks to unravel the nuanced dynamics of gender-specific pressures, examining how restrictions on girls and demands on boys, though different, are interconnected and contribute to the broader discourse on gender inequality.

Historical Perspectives:

To understand the contemporary landscape of gendered expectations, it is crucial to examine the historical roots that have shaped societal norms. Throughout history, gender roles have been deeply entrenched, with women predominantly confined to domestic spheres while men assumed roles in the public domain. These historical norms have influenced the current expectations placed on girls and boys, shaping societal perceptions of what is deemed acceptable behavior for each gender.

Restrictions on Girls:

Girls are often subjected to a myriad of restrictions that limit their autonomy and hinder their personal and intellectual growth. Traditional gender norms dictate that girls should conform to specific standards of behavior, appearance, and pursuits. From a young age, girls may encounter limitations on their choice of clothing, hobbies, and even career aspirations. These restrictions extend to education, where girls may face subtle biases that discourage them from pursuing STEM fields or leadership roles.

The weight of societal expectations can impose psychological burdens on girls, fostering a sense of inadequacy and limiting their self-esteem. The pressure to conform to societal ideals of beauty, modesty, and femininity can lead to the internalization of harmful stereotypes, affecting mental health and well-being.

Demands on Boys:

Conversely, boys grapple with a different set of challenges, characterized by societal demands that emphasize traits traditionally associated with masculinity. Boys are often expected to embody strength, stoicism, and competitiveness, suppressing vulnerability and emotional expression. The demand for boys to conform to rigid standards of masculinity can create a toxic environment where deviation from these norms is stigmatized.

The pressure on boys to excel in traditionally male-dominated fields, demonstrate physical prowess, and assume leadership roles can result in heightened stress levels and a sense of inadequacy. The demands placed on boys to conform to narrow definitions of success may hinder their ability to explore diverse interests and pursue alternative paths that align with their individual strengths and passions.

Interconnected Nature of Gender Expectations:

While restrictions on girls and demands on boys may seem distinct, they are interlinked by the broader framework of gender expectations. The perpetuation of traditional gender norms contributes to a reinforcing cycle where restrictive expectations for one gender reinforce demanding expectations for the other. For example, the emphasis on girls as nurturing and caregiving perpetuates the expectation that boys should be assertive and dominant, leading to a reinforcing cycle of restrictive and demanding gender roles.

Impact on Individual Development:

The weight of restrictions on girls and demands on boys can have profound implications for individual development. Girls may internalize societal expectations, limiting their aspirations and potential. The imposition of restrictive norms can hinder the development of critical thinking skills and self-confidence, creating barriers to educational and professional advancement.

On the other hand, the demands placed on boys to conform to narrow definitions of masculinity can impede emotional expression and interpersonal skills. The pressure to meet societal expectations may result in suppressed creativity and hinder the ability to form authentic connections with others. Both girls and boys may grapple with identity formation under the weight of societal expectations, impacting their ability to navigate complex social landscapes.

Societal Progress and Gender Equality:

The perpetuation of gendered constraints and demands not only affects individual development but also hinders societal progress towards gender equality. By confining girls to limited roles and pressuring boys to adhere to narrow definitions of masculinity, society perpetuates stereotypes that reinforce existing power imbalances. Breaking free from these ingrained expectations is crucial for dismantling the structural barriers that perpetuate gender inequality.

Conclusion:

In conclusion, the weight of restrictions on girls and demands on boys represents two sides of the same coin, contributing to the perpetuation of gender disparities. By understanding the historical roots, cultural dimensions, and psychological implications of these gendered expectations, society can work towards dismantling restrictive norms and demanding stereotypes. Empowering both girls and boys to embrace their individual strengths, interests, and aspirations is essential for fostering a more inclusive and equitable society. Breaking free from the constraints of gendered expectations is not only beneficial for individual development but is also integral to achieving progress towards a more just and equal world.

Mathematics is the music of reasons

The assertion that "mathematics is the music of reasons" suggests a deep connection between the abstract world of numbers and the aesthetic realm of music. This metaphor has been echoed by influential figures across various fields, from Pythagoras to contemporary mathematicians and musicians. To unpack this metaphor, we must explore the historical context and the fundamental principles that link mathematics and music.

Ancient Greece: The Birth of Harmonic Science

The ancient Greeks, particularly Pythagoras, laid the foundation for the interconnectedness of mathematics and music. Pythagoras, a mathematician and philosopher, discovered the mathematical relationships underlying musical intervals. He observed that the ratios of the lengths of strings on a musical instrument determined the pitch of the produced sound. This revelation marked the inception of harmonic science, revealing the mathematical order embedded in the audible world.

Pythagoras' exploration of ratios and proportions extended beyond the realm of music, influencing his philosophical ideas about the order of the universe. The Pythagorean theorem, a fundamental concept in geometry, further exemplifies the synthesis of mathematical reasoning and the exploration of harmonic relationships.

The Renaissance: Geometry, Proportion, and Musical Structure

The Renaissance era witnessed a resurgence of interest in ancient Greek philosophy and mathematics. Thinkers like Leonardo da Vinci and Johannes Kepler embraced the idea that mathematical principles could be applied to the study of art and music.

The concept of proportion became a central theme in both disciplines during this period. Artists and architects utilized the golden ratio, a mathematical proportion with aesthetic appeal, to create visually pleasing compositions. Simultaneously, musicians explored mathematical ratios to establish harmonic relationships and create compositions with a sense of balance and symmetry.

The Enlightenment: Unifying the Sciences and Arts

The Enlightenment era brought about a shift in the relationship between mathematics and the arts, fostering the belief in a unified understanding of the natural world. Mathematicians such as Leonhard Euler and Jean le Rond d'Alembert made significant contributions to the study of vibrating strings and acoustics, bridging the gap between mathematical theory and musical practice.

Euler's work on the mathematics of vibrating strings, published in his "Tentamen novae theoriae musicae," provided a mathematical foundation for understanding the physics of musical instruments. This synthesis of mathematics and music contributed to the emergence of acoustics as a scientific discipline.

19th Century: Algebraic Structures and Musical Composition

As mathematics evolved, particularly with the development of abstract algebra, composers in the 19th century began to explore mathematical structures in their musical compositions. The use of mathematical concepts such as symmetry and group theory found expression in the works of composers like Beethoven and Schoenberg.

The concept of musical transformations, akin to mathematical group transformations, allowed composers to manipulate musical themes through inversion, transposition, and other operations. This mathematical approach to composition added a new layer of complexity to music, enriching its expressive possibilities.

20th Century to Present: Computer Science, Fractals, and Algorithmic Composition

The advent of computer science in the 20th century further deepened the connection between mathematics and music. Algorithms, inspired by mathematical principles, began to play a crucial role in musical composition. Composers like Iannis Xenakis utilized mathematical models to generate complex and innovative musical structures.

The exploration of fractals, self-replicating geometric patterns governed by mathematical equations, also found its way into music. Fractal geometry offered a new perspective on the organization of musical material, providing composers with a tool to create intricate and self-similar structures within their compositions.

Conclusion:

The metaphor that "mathematics is the music of reasons" encapsulates the enduring relationship between these two seemingly disparate disciplines. From the ancient Greeks to the present day, mathematicians and musicians have continually found inspiration in each other's realms, uncovering the shared principles that underlie both mathematics and music.

The historical journey outlined in this essay demonstrates the evolution of this metaphor, showcasing how mathematical reasoning has shaped the structure, form, and aesthetics of music. As both fields continue to advance, the synergy between mathematics and music remains a source of innovation and creativity.

In essence, the metaphor invites us to view mathematics as a language of patterns, proportions, and relationships—a language that resonates not only in the abstract world of numbers but also in the expressive and emotional landscape of music. As we delve deeper into the intricate connections between mathematics and music, we discover a harmonious symphony of reason that transcends the boundaries of culture, time, and discipline.

A society that has more justice is a society that needs less charity

In the intricate tapestry of societal dynamics, justice and charity stand as pillars that uphold the ideals of fairness, equality, and compassion. This essay contends that a society that emphasizes and achieves a higher level of justice concurrently experiences a reduction in the necessity for charity. Justice, both as a principle and as a practical manifestation, addresses the root causes of societal disparities, fostering an environment where the marginalized and vulnerable find equitable opportunities for growth and prosperity.

The Philosophical Nexus: Justice and Charity:
At a philosophical level, the relationship between justice and charity is often debated in terms of their moral underpinnings. Justice, as defined by philosophers like John Rawls, is the fair distribution of resources and opportunities within a society. On the other hand, charity is often seen as a benevolent act stemming from compassion and empathy. In a society where justice prevails, the need for individual acts of charity diminishes as systemic structures work to eliminate the root causes of inequality.

The philosopher Immanuel Kant argued for a just society based on moral principles that treat each individual with dignity and respect. In such a society, charity becomes a supplement rather than a necessity, as justice ensures that each person has access to the means necessary for a dignified life. This philosophical perspective suggests that justice, when ingrained in the fabric of a society, acts as a preventive measure against the need for charity by addressing structural inequalities.

Economic Equity and Justice:
From an economic standpoint, justice and charity intersect in the realm of resource distribution. A society that prioritizes economic justice ensures that wealth and resources are distributed in a manner that uplifts all members. Policies that promote fair wages, progressive taxation, and social safety nets contribute to a just economic system.

Conversely, charity often functions as a temporary solution to economic disparities, providing relief to individuals facing financial hardships. However, charity alone cannot rectify systemic economic injustices. By fostering economic justice, a society establishes a foundation where charity becomes a supplementary measure rather than a primary means of support. This perspective aligns with the proverb: "Give a man a fish, and you feed him for a day; teach a man to fish, and you feed him for a lifetime."

Societal Harmony and Justice:
Societal harmony, an outcome of justice, plays a pivotal role in diminishing the need for charity. A just society cultivates an environment where diverse individuals coexist without fear of discrimination or oppression. In such a setting, social capital flourishes, and collective well-being becomes a shared goal.

Charity often arises in response to societal discord, addressing immediate needs created by conflicts, discrimination, or neglect. A just society, by contrast, proactively dismantles the barriers that give rise to these issues. By fostering inclusivity, promoting education, and eradicating systemic prejudices, justice acts as a preemptive force that reduces the instances where charity is required as a remedial measure.

Legal and Institutional Frameworks:
The legal and institutional frameworks within a society play a pivotal role in shaping the relationship between justice and charity. A just legal system ensures that laws are applied fairly, without discrimination based on race, gender, or socioeconomic status. This mitigates the need for charitable interventions to rectify injustices resulting from biased legal practices.

Moreover, robust social institutions, such as healthcare and education systems, contribute to the overall well-being of citizens. In a just society, these institutions operate efficiently, providing equal access to essential services. This reduces the dependence on charity to address gaps in healthcare or education, as justice ensures that these fundamental needs are met for all members of the society.

Conclusion:

In conclusion, the symbiotic relationship between justice and charity within a society is intricate and multifaceted. A society that embraces justice as a guiding principle experiences a natural decline in the need for charity. Justice addresses the root causes of societal disparities, fostering an environment where individuals have equitable opportunities for growth and prosperity.

Philosophically, economically, and sociologically, justice and charity intersect in a delicate dance that shapes the fabric of a society. By prioritizing justice, societies can create lasting solutions to issues that often necessitate charitable interventions. The goal should be to establish a framework where charity becomes a supplementary measure, not a primary means of addressing systemic inequalities. In building such a society, we pave the way for a more balanced and harmonious coexistence, where justice serves as the cornerstone of societal equilibrium.

Education is what remains after one has forgotten what one has learned in school

The renowned physicist and Nobel laureate, Albert Einstein, once remarked, "Education is what remains after one has forgotten what one has learned in school." This profound statement challenges the conventional understanding of education as a finite process confined to the walls of a classroom. Einstein's assertion invites us to ponder the lasting impact of education, suggesting that the true essence of learning extends beyond the memorization of facts and figures. In this essay, we will explore the depth and breadth of education, examining how it shapes individuals' characters, influences their worldviews, and contributes to the betterment of society.

Education as a Lifelong Endeavor:

At its core, education is a lifelong endeavor that extends far beyond the formal education received in schools. While the classroom provides a structured environment for the acquisition of knowledge and skills, the true test of education lies in its application throughout one's life. The ability to adapt, critically analyze, and continue learning is indicative of a well-rounded education that persists long after the textbooks are closed.

One's formal education may fade into the recesses of memory, but the skills acquired and the habits of critical thinking cultivated during the educational journey endure. The ability to learn independently, solve complex problems, and navigate an ever-evolving world is a testament to the enduring legacy of education.

Character Development:

Education is not merely a transfer of information but a transformative process that molds individuals' characters. Beyond the curriculum, schools serve as crucibles where values, ethics, and social norms are imparted. The lessons learned about empathy, teamwork, and resilience are integral components of education that persist in shaping individuals' interactions and relationships throughout their lives.

The development of a moral compass and a sense of social responsibility are outcomes of education that linger long after graduation. Individuals who have received a holistic education are more likely to contribute positively to their communities, engage in civic responsibilities, and strive for the betterment of society. Thus, education becomes a catalyst for personal growth and societal progress, leaving an indelible mark on the character of individuals.

Critical Thinking and Problem-Solving:

The ability to think critically and solve complex problems is a hallmark of a well-rounded education. In a rapidly changing world, where information is abundant and dynamic, the capacity to sift through the noise and discern meaningful patterns is invaluable. The skills honed in the pursuit of education—analytical thinking, research skills, and the ability to synthesize information—are enduring assets that individuals carry into their professional and personal lives.

Education equips individuals with the tools to confront challenges, adapt to new situations, and innovate in the face of adversity. These problem-solving skills become an integral part of an individual's cognitive toolkit, guiding them through the intricacies of the real world long after the textbooks have been shelved.

Cultivation of Curiosity:

Education, at its best, fosters a sense of curiosity and a thirst for knowledge that extends beyond the classroom. The pursuit of learning becomes a lifelong journey, with individuals constantly seeking to expand their horizons and deepen their understanding of the world. The seeds of intellectual curiosity planted in the educational soil continue to sprout, driving individuals to explore new ideas, engage in continuous learning, and contribute to the advancement of knowledge.

The curious mind, cultivated through education, is not confined to a specific domain or subject matter. It transcends disciplinary boundaries, fostering interdisciplinary thinking and the ability to connect seemingly disparate concepts. This broad-minded approach to learning persists as an enduring legacy, enriching individuals' lives and contributing to a more interconnected and innovative society.

Education and Social Transformation:

Beyond personal development, education plays a pivotal role in societal transformation. Informed and educated citizens are the bedrock of a flourishing democracy, contributing to an informed public discourse and actively participating in civic life. The principles of justice, equality, and human rights instilled through education serve as the foundation for social movements and advocacy, driving positive change on a collective level.

The enduring impact of education on society is evident in the ways it empowers individuals to challenge injustice, question established norms, and work towards a more equitable world. Education, when imparted effectively, becomes a catalyst for social progress, dismantling barriers, and fostering inclusivity.

Conclusion:

In conclusion, Einstein's assertion that "Education is what remains after one has forgotten what one has learned in school" encapsulates the profound and enduring nature of education. Far from being a transient process confined to the classroom, education leaves an indelible mark on individuals, shaping their characters, influencing their worldviews, and contributing to the betterment of society. The true essence of education lies not in the memorization of facts but in the cultivation of critical thinking, problem-solving skills, and a lifelong curiosity for knowledge. As we navigate the complexities of the 21st century, it is essential to recognize and celebrate the lasting legacy of education—a force that extends beyond the confines of formal learning environments, enriching individuals and societies alike.

Forests are the best-case studies for economic excellence

"The economy is a wholly owned subsidiary of the environment, not the other way around." - Gaylord Nelson

"Investing in forests is an insurance policy for our planet." - Wangari Maathai

Forests are among the most important natural resources that humanity has, and they play a crucial role in our economic well-being. While their benefits are often considered from an ecological perspective, forests are also a best-case study for economic excellence. They contribute to various dimensions of our economy, including job creation, income generation, export earnings, and climate change mitigation. In this essay, we will explore how forests are the best-case studies for economic excellence by examining the various dimensions that they contribute to.

Job Creation

Forests are important for job creation in many countries, particularly in developing nations where they provide employment opportunities for millions of people. The forestry sector is responsible for creating jobs in forest management, timber harvesting, wood processing, and other related industries. According to the Food and Agriculture Organization (FAO), forestry and related industries support over 86 million jobs worldwide, contributing to both rural and urban economies.

In addition, forests also support informal economies by providing non-timber forest products (NTFPs) such as fruits, nuts, mushrooms, and medicinal plants. These products are often collected by local communities and sold in local and regional markets, providing a source of income for many households. For example, in India, the sale of NTFPs is estimated to be worth over $2 billion annually, providing a vital source of income for millions of people.

Income Generation

Forests are also an important source of income for many countries. The timber industry, which is worth over $600 billion globally, is a major contributor to many national economies. Countries such as Canada, Russia, and Brazil are among the top timber-producing nations, with exports contributing significantly to their GDP.

In addition to the timber industry, forests also contribute to other sectors of the economy such as tourism. Forests are often popular tourist destinations, providing opportunities for hiking, camping, and other outdoor activities. According to the World Tourism Organization (UNWTO), nature-based tourism accounts for over 20% of international tourism, generating billions of dollars in revenue for countries that have forested areas.

Export Earnings

Forests also contribute to export earnings in many countries, particularly those with a significant timber industry. Timber and other forest products such as pulp and paper, furniture, and fuelwood are often exported to other countries, generating billions of dollars in revenue. According to the International Trade Centre (ITC), global exports of forest products were valued at over $300 billion in 2018.

In addition to timber and other forest products, countries with significant forest cover can also benefit from the export of carbon credits. Carbon credits are a market-based mechanism for reducing greenhouse gas emissions, and countries with large forested areas can earn credits for their efforts in reducing emissions through forest conservation and management. For example, the REDD+ program (Reducing Emissions from Deforestation and Forest Degradation) provides incentives to developing countries to reduce deforestation and promote sustainable forest management, generating income through carbon credits.

Climate Change Mitigation
Forests are also crucial in the fight against climate change. They act as carbon sinks, absorbing and storing carbon dioxide from the atmosphere through photosynthesis. According to the Intergovernmental Panel on Climate Change (IPCC), forests currently absorb around 2.4 billion tonnes of carbon dioxide annually, equivalent to around 30% of global greenhouse gas emissions.

In addition to their role as carbon sinks, forests also play an important role in reducing the impacts of climate change. They provide a range of ecosystem services such as regulating water flows, protecting soil, and preventing erosion, which are important for mitigating the impacts of extreme weather events such as floods and droughts. Forests also help to maintain biodiversity, which is important for ecosystem resilience in the face of climate change.

Conclusion

In conclusion, forests are indeed the best-case studies for economic excellence. They provide a multitude of benefits ranging from economic, social, environmental, and cultural aspects. Forests contribute significantly to the global economy through timber and non-timber products, ecosystem services, and tourism. Moreover, they play a crucial role in mitigating climate change, preserving biodiversity, and providing clean air and water.

However, forests face various challenges, including deforestation, degradation, and fragmentation, which threaten their economic, ecological, and social functions. These challenges call for a more sustainable and integrated approach to forest management that balances economic development and environmental conservation.

Governments, private sector actors, and civil society must work together to promote responsible forest management practices that create economic value while preserving the natural resources and ecosystem services that forests provide. This will require increased investment in sustainable forest management, the promotion of responsible supply chains, and the enforcement of laws and regulations that protect forests and their communities. The forests are essential to achieving sustainable economic development and environmental conservation. Their value extends beyond their economic contributions to include their cultural, social, and ecological importance. By investing in responsible forest management practices, we can ensure that forests continue to provide economic, environmental, and social benefits for generations to come.

Poets are the unacknowledged legislators of the world

1. "Poets are the unacknowledged legislators of the world." - Percy Bysshe Shelley
2. "The poet is the priest of the invisible." - Wallace Stevens
3. "Poetry is the spontaneous overflow of powerful feelings: it takes its origin from emotion recollected in tranquillity." - William Wordsworth

The famous English poet, Percy Bysshe Shelley, once said that "Poets are the unacknowledged legislators of the world." This statement has been debated and discussed for centuries, but at its core, it suggests that poets have a significant influence on society and culture, despite often being overlooked or undervalued.

One of the most important prose works of the Romantic era, and a valuable document concerning Shelley's own poetic approach, Shelley's 1821 essay 'A Defence of Poetry' argues that poetry is mimetic: that is, it reflects the real world. In the early days of civilisation, men 'imitated natural objects', observing the order and rhythm of these things, and from this impulse was poetry born.

Reason and imagination are both important faculties in the poet. Reason, he tells us, is logical thought, whereas imagination is perceiving things, and noticing the similarities between things (here, we might think of the poet's stock-in-trade, the metaphor and simile, which liken one thing to another). It is through reason but also through imagination that we can identify beauty in the world, and from such a perception or realisation are great civilisations made. Poets, then, are the makers of civilisation itself.

At first glance, it may seem strange to consider poets as legislators. After all, lawmakers and politicians are the ones who make and enforce the laws that govern society. However, Shelley's statement suggests that poets have a different kind of influence that is just as important, if not more so.

Poets are not bound by the same constraints as politicians or lawmakers. They are not elected officials, and they do not have to worry about the political implications of their words. Instead, they are free to express themselves in a way that is honest and raw, and this can be incredibly powerful.

Through their poetry, poets can capture the essence of the human experience and convey it in a way that resonates with people on a deep level. They can inspire us to think differently, to see the world in a new way, and to act in ways that we might not have considered before.

For example,

- The poetry of William Wordsworth was instrumental in the development of the Romantic movement in England. His focus on nature, the individual, and the emotions helped to shift the cultural landscape of the time and paved the way for new ways of thinking and creating.
- The work of Langston Hughes was influential in the Civil Rights Movement in the United States. His poetry spoke to the experiences of African Americans in a way that had never been done before, and it helped to bring attention to the injustices they faced.
- One of the most famous examples of this can be found in the works of William Shakespeare. His plays are not just entertainment, but are also profound insights into human nature. He explores themes such as love, power, jealousy, and betrayal in a way that is both insightful and poignant. Even today, his works continue to inspire people and shape our understanding of the world.
- Another example can be found in the works of Langston Hughes. He wrote about the experiences of African Americans during a time of great social and political upheaval. His poems, such as "I, Too" and "Harlem", captured the pain and frustration of a generation of people who were fighting for equality and justice. Through his words, Hughes was able to give voice to a movement that would change the course of history.
- Maya Angelou is another poet who used her words to inspire change. Her poem "Still I Rise" has become an anthem for people who have faced discrimination and adversity. Her words are a reminder that no matter what challenges we face, we can rise above them and achieve our goals.

Her poetry has inspired countless people to persevere in the face of adversity and strive for a better future.

- The works of Pablo Neruda provide another example of the power of poetry. His poems, such as "If You Forget Me" and "Tonight I Can Write", capture the beauty and pain of love in a way that is both passionate and haunting. His words have touched the hearts of people around the world and continue to inspire us to love more deeply and live more fully.
- Rumi is another poet whose words have inspired millions. He wrote about the spiritual journey and the quest for enlightenment in a way that is both accessible and profound. His poems, such as "The Guest House" and "This is Love", speak to the deepest parts of our souls and remind us of the beauty and wonder of life.
- Finally, we have the works of Emily Dickinson. Her poems, such as "Hope is the Thing with Feathers" and "Because I Could Not Stop for Death", explore the mysteries of life and death in a way that is both profound and beautiful. Her words have touched the hearts of people for generations and continue to inspire us to live our lives with purpose and meaning.

In these examples, we can see how poets have the ability to shape the cultural and social landscape of their time. They may not have the power to make laws, but they can influence the way we think about and respond to the world around us.

Furthermore, poets often have a unique perspective on society and culture. They are observers of the human experience, and they have the ability to see things that others might miss. This perspective can be invaluable in shaping public opinion and influencing change.

"Law operates in a social setting, a realm where poets play,
Their words imbue the world with hues of bright and darkened grey,
Their verses stir emotions deep, a spark to light the way,
And through their art, they shape the course of what tomorrow may.

For laws are not just rules and codes, but living things that breathe,
And poets with their craft and voice, can plant a hopeful seed,
They bring to life the human heart, that laws may oftentimes impede,
And show us paths to empathy, where justice may succeed.

Thus, poets are the unacknowledged architects of law,
Their words can move the hearts of men, and make the broken whole,
For in a social setting, where the law is but a tool,
Poets pave the way for justice, with their words both strong and cool."

In conclusion, Shelley's statement that "Poets are the unacknowledged legislators of the world" holds a great deal of truth. While politicians and lawmakers may have the power to make and enforce laws, poets have the power to shape the cultural and social landscape of their time. They have the ability to inspire, to challenge, and to influence in a way that is both unique and important. As such, we should recognize the value of poetry and the impact it can have on our lives and the world around us.

History is a series of victories won by the scientific man over the romantic man.

"History is the story of the triumph of the scientific man over the romantic man, a tale of reason and progress winning out over emotion and intuition." - Stephen Hawking

"The great achievements of civilization have not come from government bureaus. Einstein didn't construct his theory under order from a bureaucrat. Henry Ford didn't revolutionize the automobile industry that way." - Milton Friedman

"The scientific man does not aim at an immediate result. He does not expect that his advanced ideas will be readily taken up. His work is like that of the planter—for the future. His duty is to lay the foundation for those who are to come, and point the way." - Nikola Tesla

Throughout history, there has been a struggle between the scientific and romantic ways of thinking. The scientific man values reason and logic, while the romantic man values emotion and intuition. While both perspectives have their merits, the dominance of the scientific mindset has resulted in a series of victories over the romantic way of thinking. In this essay, we will explore the ways in which history has been shaped by the triumph of the scientific man over the romantic man.

One of the earliest examples of this victory can be seen in the Scientific Revolution of the 16th and 17th centuries. During this time, thinkers such as Galileo Galilei and Isaac Newton championed the use of observation, experimentation, and mathematical reasoning to understand the natural world. This emphasis on rational inquiry helped to overturn the romantic idea of a universe governed by mystical forces and supernatural powers. The Scientific Revolution laid the foundation for modern science and transformed our understanding of the world around us.

The triumph of the scientific man continued into the Enlightenment, a period of intellectual and cultural growth that emphasized reason, science, and progress. Thinkers such as Voltaire, John Locke, and Immanuel Kant championed the power of reason to transform society and shape the course of history. This rationalist mindset helped to undermine traditional sources of authority, such as religion and monarchy, and ushered in an era of democracy, individual rights, and scientific progress.

The Industrial Revolution of the 19th century marked another victory for the scientific man over the romantic man. This period of rapid technological advancement and economic growth was driven by the scientific principles of mass production, engineering, and efficiency. The romantic ideal of a simpler, more natural way of life was swept aside in favor of progress, modernity, and the pursuit of profit.

In the 20th century, the triumph of the scientific man continued with the rise of modernism and the rejection of traditional art and literature. Modernist writers such as James Joyce, T.S. Eliot, and Virginia Woolf embraced the fragmented, disjointed style of writing that mirrored the disorienting experience of modern life. This rejection of traditional narrative structures and romantic themes helped to establish the dominance of the scientific, rationalist mindset in literature and the arts.

Today, we continue to see the triumph of the scientific man over the romantic man in fields such as technology, medicine, and environmental science. The power of reason and scientific inquiry has helped us to make tremendous advances in these areas, but at the cost of neglecting the emotional and intuitive aspects of human experience. The romantic ideal of a more connected, natural way of life continues to be overshadowed by the emphasis on progress, efficiency, and economic growth.

In conclusion, history can be seen as a series of victories won by the scientific man over the romantic man. From the Scientific Revolution to the rise of modernism, the dominance of the rationalist, scientific mindset has shaped our understanding of the world and transformed our way of life. While there are many benefits to this approach, it is important to remember the value of the emotional and intuitive aspects of human experience, and to strive for a more balanced and integrated way of thinking.

A ship in harbour is safe, but that is not what ship is for

"A ship in harbor is safe, but that is not what a ship is for" is a famous quote by John A. Shedd that captures the essence of risk-taking and pushing oneself beyond their comfort zone. It suggests that while staying in a safe and familiar environment may provide temporary security, it is not the purpose for which we were created. In this essay, we will explore the meaning of this quote and its relevance in our lives.

At its core, this quote is a reminder that we were not created to stay stagnant or complacent. We were created to explore, take risks, and push beyond our limits. While staying in a comfortable and familiar environment may provide temporary safety, it does not allow for growth, innovation, or progress. It is only when we venture out into the unknown that we discover new things, learn new skills, and create new opportunities.

This quote has particular relevance in our professional lives. Many people are content to stay in the same job or career for years, even when they are no longer challenged or fulfilled. They are afraid to take risks and try something new, even when they know deep down that it is what they truly want. This fear of the unknown can hold them back and prevent them from realizing their full potential.

On the other hand, those who are willing to take risks and venture out into the unknown often find that it leads them to new opportunities and experiences. They may find a career they are truly passionate about, discover a new talent or skill, or develop a new perspective on life. By taking risks and stepping outside their comfort zone, they open themselves up to a world of possibilities.

This quote also has relevance in our personal lives. Many people are content to stay in their comfort zones, surrounding themselves with familiar people and experiences. They may be afraid to try new things, meet new people, or take on new challenges. While this may provide temporary security, it can also lead to a lack of growth, creativity, and fulfillment.

Those who are willing to step outside their comfort zone and take risks often find that it leads them to new experiences and personal growth. They may discover new interests or hobbies, meet new people who inspire them, or learn new skills that enhance their lives. By pushing beyond their limits, they open themselves up to a world of possibilities.

In conclusion, the quote "A ship in harbor is safe, but that is not what a ship is for" reminds us that we were not created to stay stagnant or complacent. We were created to explore, take risks, and push beyond our limits. While staying in a comfortable and familiar environment may provide temporary safety, it does not allow for growth or progress. It is only when we venture out into the unknown that we discover new things, learn new skills, and create new opportunities. So, let's take risks and explore the uncharted territories, and set our sails to reach the horizon, as that is what we are meant to do.

The time to repair the roof is when the sun is shining

The phrase "The time to repair the roof is when the sun is shining" is an old proverb that suggests that it is always better to prepare and act proactively rather than waiting for a crisis to happen. This adage means that it is essential to fix any problems in advance, and not wait until it is too late.

The meaning behind this quote is quite simple: when the weather is good and the sky is clear, it is an opportune time to make any necessary repairs to the roof. In other words, it is always better to address any problems before they become worse. This is a concept that can be applied to many aspects of life. In business, for example, it is important to make adjustments to the company's operations and structure while things are going well, rather than waiting until a crisis hits. The same is true for personal relationships, where it is better to work on any issues when things are good, rather than waiting for a blow-up to occur.

The idea behind this adage is that we should take a proactive approach to life. Instead of waiting for things to go wrong, we should anticipate and prepare for potential problems. This requires a certain level of foresight and planning, but it can save us a lot of trouble in the long run. This is especially true when it comes to our physical and emotional health. We should take care of ourselves when we are feeling well, so that we can better weather any storms that may come our way.

The importance of this saying can be seen in many areas of life. For example, when it comes to maintaining a healthy lifestyle, it is always better to take preventative measures rather than waiting for illness to strike. This can involve regular exercise, a balanced diet, and getting enough sleep. By taking these steps, we can improve our overall health and reduce the risk of developing serious health problems down the road.

Another area where this adage is particularly relevant is in finance. It is always better to save money and invest wisely when we have the means to do so. This can involve setting up a budget, creating an emergency fund, and making smart investments. By being proactive about our finances, we can avoid financial troubles down the road and achieve our long-term financial goals.

In terms of personal relationships, this adage reminds us that we should work on our relationships when things are going well. This can involve communicating openly with our loved ones, making time for each other, and being there for one another during difficult times. By doing so, we can strengthen our relationships and avoid potential conflicts or crises down the road.

In business, this saying holds particular significance. Successful businesses are those that are proactive and adapt to changes in the market. This can involve developing new products or services, improving existing ones, and staying up to date with emerging trends. By doing so, businesses can stay ahead of the competition and avoid being left behind.

In conclusion, the proverb "The time to repair the roof is when the sun is shining" is a valuable lesson that can be applied to many areas of life. It reminds us of the importance of being proactive and acting before problems arise. Whether it is our health, finances, personal relationships, or business operations, it is always better to prepare and act proactively rather than waiting for a crisis to happen. By doing so, we can avoid potential problems down the road and achieve greater success in all areas of our lives.

You cannot step twice in the same river

The famous philosopher Heraclitus once said, "No man ever steps in the same river twice, for it's not the same river and he's not the same man." This quote may seem simple, but it contains a profound and timeless message that can apply to our lives in countless ways.

At first glance, the statement may seem obvious - after all, it's true that no two moments are exactly the same. However, upon closer examination, the statement reveals a deeper truth about the nature of change and impermanence.

The river that Heraclitus referred to represents the flow of life, which is constantly changing and moving forward. Just like a river, life is never the same twice. Every moment is unique, and we cannot hold onto any moment forever. Every experience, every emotion, every relationship, and every decision we make is fleeting and constantly in flux.

Likewise, the person who steps into the river is also constantly changing. We are not the same person we were yesterday, or even a moment ago. We are constantly growing, learning, and evolving. Our experiences, thoughts, and emotions shape us into the person we are today, and every moment we are presented with new opportunities for growth and change.

The message behind this statement is not just about the impermanence of life, but also about the importance of embracing change and letting go of the past. Many of us hold onto our past experiences and relationships, hoping to relive them or keep them alive. However, the reality is that we cannot step into the same river twice - we cannot recreate the past or hold onto something that no longer exists.

Instead, we must learn to let go and move forward with an open mind and a willingness to embrace change. Every moment is an opportunity for growth and new experiences, and by letting go of the past, we can fully embrace the present and the future.

Moreover, the quote also highlights the idea that every experience we have is unique, and therefore, we should approach each experience with an open mind and an attitude of curiosity. We should not take anything for granted or assume that we know what to expect. Just as the river is constantly changing, so too are the circumstances of our lives. By approaching every experience with a sense of wonder and a willingness to learn, we can fully embrace the richness of life.

In addition, the quote also implies that every individual has their unique perspective and experience. Even if two people were to step into the same river at the same time, their experiences of the river would be different. Each person sees the world through their unique lens, and this lens shapes their experience of the world.

Therefore, it is important to approach others with an open mind and a willingness to understand their perspective. We should not assume that we know what someone else is thinking or feeling, but instead, we should listen with empathy and seek to understand their unique experience.

In conclusion, Heraclitus's statement, "No man ever steps in the same river twice, for it's not the same river and he's not the same man," highlights the impermanence of life and the importance of embracing change and letting go of the past. Every moment is unique, and we must approach each experience with an open mind and a willingness to learn. Furthermore, each person's experience is unique, and we should approach others with empathy and a willingness to understand their perspective. By embracing these ideas, we can fully embrace the richness of life and become more compassionate and understanding individuals.

A smile is the chosen vehicle for all ambiguities

A smile is a universal symbol of happiness, warmth, and friendliness. It has been said that a smile is the chosen vehicle for all ambiguities, and this is certainly true. A smile can convey a wide range of emotions and meanings, from joy and contentment to mischief and irony. In this essay, we will explore the many ways in which a smile can be used to express complex and often contradictory emotions.

First and foremost, a smile is a sign of happiness and joy. When we are truly happy, we cannot help but smile. A genuine smile lights up our face and radiates positive energy. It is contagious and can make others feel happy too. A smile can also be a sign of relief, particularly after a difficult or challenging situation. It is a way of saying "I made it through" or "I'm glad that's over."

However, a smile can also be used to hide our true emotions. We may smile to avoid showing our sadness, anger, or disappointment. This is particularly common in social situations, where we feel pressure to appear happy and sociable. A fake smile, known as a "social smile," is often used in this context. It looks genuine, but it is not backed up by genuine positive emotions.

Another way in which a smile can be ambiguous is when it is used to convey sarcasm or irony. A smirk, for example, is a smile that is tinged with sarcasm. It can be used to imply that something is not as great as it seems or that the person speaking is not entirely sincere. A smile can also be used to convey a sense of superiority or smugness. This is often seen in situations where one person is attempting to outdo another or show off their accomplishments.

On the other hand, a smile can also be used to show humility and gratitude. When we receive a compliment or a kindness from someone else, we may smile as a way of expressing our appreciation. A smile can also be a way of showing respect or deference to someone else, particularly in cultures where showing too much emotion is frowned upon.

Finally, a smile can be a way of establishing a connection with another person. When we smile at someone, we are inviting them into our emotional world. We are saying "I am happy to be with you" or "I am glad we are sharing this moment." A smile can also be a way of showing empathy or compassion for another person. When we see someone who is struggling or in pain, a smile can communicate our understanding and support.

In conclusion, a smile is indeed the chosen vehicle for all ambiguities. It can convey a wide range of emotions and meanings, from happiness and joy to sarcasm and irony. A smile can be used to hide our true emotions or to show humility and gratitude. It can be a way of establishing a connection with another person or of showing empathy and compassion. Whatever the situation, a smile is a powerful tool for communication and an essential part of our emotional repertoire.

Just because you have a choice, it does not mean that any of them has to be right

Introduction

The concept of choice is a fundamental part of human existence. We are presented with an endless array of options on a daily basis, from trivial decisions like what to eat for breakfast to major life-altering choices such as choosing a career path. However, just because we have a choice, it does not mean that any of them has to be right. In fact, some choices can be harmful, while others may not lead to the desired outcome. In this essay, we will explore the notion of choices and why simply having options available does not guarantee success.

The Illusion of Choice

We often believe that having a choice is a positive thing, as it gives us the freedom to choose what we want. However, the idea of choice is not always what it seems. In reality, we are often presented with a limited number of options, all of which have been pre-determined by outside forces such as society, culture, and the media. These external factors can greatly influence the choices we make, even if we do not realize it. We may think we are making an independent decision, but in reality, our choices are often dictated by others.

For example, the media can greatly influence our choices by presenting us with a particular image or message. This can be seen in the fashion industry, where certain trends are promoted and others are not. People who choose to follow these trends may think they are making a personal choice, but in reality, they are following a pre-determined path. The same can be said for society's expectations, where certain paths are seen as more desirable than others. For instance, pursuing a career in medicine or law may be viewed as more prestigious than pursuing a career in the arts.

The Pressure of Making the Right Choice

Having too many choices can also lead to stress and anxiety, as we may feel overwhelmed by the pressure to make the right decision. This is particularly true in today's society, where there are endless options for everything from what to eat for dinner to what career path to take. The fear of making the wrong choice can be paralyzing, leading some people to avoid making a decision altogether.

Moreover, the pressure to make the right choice can also lead to regret. Even if we have made a decision that seemed right at the time, we may later question whether we made the right choice. This can lead to feelings of regret and a sense of loss, particularly if the choice we made has led to negative consequences.

The Consequences of Making the Wrong Choice

Making the wrong choice can have negative consequences, which can vary in severity depending on the situation. For instance, choosing to eat unhealthy food on a regular basis can lead to health problems, while choosing to skip school can lead to poor grades and a lack of opportunities. In some cases, the consequences of making the wrong choice can be life-altering, such as choosing to drink and drive, which can lead to accidents and fatalities.

Moreover, making a wrong choice can also lead to missed opportunities. If we choose to pursue a particular career path that does not align with our passions or skills, we may miss out on other opportunities that could have been a better fit. Similarly, choosing to stay in a toxic relationship can prevent us from finding true love and happiness.

The Importance of Learning from Our Choices

While making the wrong choice can have negative consequences, it is important to remember that every choice we make is an opportunity to learn and grow. Instead of dwelling on the negative outcomes, we can use our experiences to make better choices in the future. By reflecting on our choices and the consequences they have had, we can gain valuable insights that can help us make better decisions in the future.

Furthermore, learning from our choices can also help us to develop a greater sense of self-awareness. By understanding our own motivations and thought processes, we can make more informed choices that align with our values and goals.

The Importance of Having Support

Making important choices can be a daunting task, and it is important to have support from others. Seeking advice from trusted friends or family members can help us to gain a fresh perspective and consider factors that we may not have thought of on our own. Additionally, seeking professional guidance, such as from a therapist or career counselor, can provide valuable insights and tools to help us make informed choices.

Conclusion

In conclusion, the concept of choice is complex and multi-faceted. While having options can be liberating, it can also be overwhelming and lead to pressure to make the right decision. However, it is important to recognize that the choices we make can have significant consequences, both positive and negative. Learning from our experiences and seeking support from others can help us navigate the decision-making process and make informed choices that align with our values and goals.

At the same time, we must also acknowledge the limitations of choice. Often, the options presented to us are shaped by external factors such as societal expectations, culture, and the media. We must be mindful of these influences and strive to make independent decisions that are true to ourselves.

Ultimately, the ability to make choices is a privilege, and we should approach every decision with care and consideration. By embracing the responsibility that comes with choice and being mindful of the potential outcomes, we can create a life that is authentic, fulfilling, and aligned with our deepest desires.

Hand that rocks the cradle rules the world

The proverb "The hand that rocks the cradle rules the world" is a testament to the importance of motherhood and the influence of women in the development of society. The phrase suggests that women have a significant impact on shaping the values and character of future generations, and by extension, the course of history. The power of the mother's touch, guidance, and nurturing is thought to extend far beyond the immediate family, influencing the entire society. In this essay, we will explore the origins and meaning of this proverb and examine its relevance in the modern world.

The phrase "The hand that rocks the cradle rules the world" is believed to have originated in a poem written by American poet William Ross Wallace in the mid-19th century. The poem, titled "What Rules the World," celebrates the role of motherhood and the power of a mother's love and influence. Wallace wrote:

"The hand that rocks the cradle
Is the hand that rules the world."

The poem recognizes the critical role that mothers play in shaping the future of society, as they have the power to mold the character and values of their children from a very young age. Mothers are the first teachers of their children, teaching them the values of love, kindness, compassion, and empathy. As such, they have the potential to instill these qualities in their children, who will then carry them forward into their adult lives, influencing their families, communities, and the world.

The proverb has since become a popular expression, used to describe the influence of women on society, particularly in the context of motherhood. It suggests that the work of mothers is not only vital to the well-being of their families but also to the larger community and the world at large. It acknowledges the power of nurturing and caring, and the transformative impact it can have on the people around us.

In many cultures around the world, the role of motherhood is highly valued and revered. Women are often seen as the caretakers of the family, responsible for raising children and ensuring their well-being. This has been true throughout history, as mothers have played a crucial role in shaping the values and traditions of their communities.

For example, in ancient Greece, the concept of "paideia" was central to the education of children. This referred to the upbringing and education of young boys, which was the responsibility of their mothers. The mother was seen as the primary educator of her children, responsible for teaching them the virtues of wisdom, courage, justice, and temperance.

Similarly, in traditional Chinese culture, the role of the mother was considered crucial to the upbringing of children. Mothers were expected to instill Confucian values in their children, such as respect for authority, filial piety, and devotion to duty. This was seen as essential to the development of a well-functioning society, as these values were thought to promote social harmony and stability.

In many societies, the role of motherhood has been marginalized or undervalued, particularly in modern times. Women have been expected to balance their responsibilities as mothers with their work outside the home, often facing discrimination and barriers in the workplace. This has led to a devaluation of the work of motherhood, with many women feeling pressured to prioritize their careers over their families.

However, the importance of motherhood and the influence of women in shaping society cannot be overstated. Mothers have the power to shape the values and beliefs of their children, who will carry them forward into the future. This is particularly important in a world that is facing numerous challenges, including social inequality, environmental degradation, and political instability. The values of love, compassion, and empathy that are instilled in children by their mothers can help to create a more just and sustainable society, one that is based on mutual respect and cooperation.

In addition to the direct impact that mothers have on their children, the proverb "The hand that rocks the cradle rules the world" also speaks to the indirect impact that mothers have on society as a whole. As children grow and become adults, they carry with them the values and beliefs that they learned from their mothers. These values can shape their behavior, choices, and interactions with others, ultimately influencing the course of history.

For example, women have played a pivotal role in many social and political movements throughout history. Women have been leaders in the fight for civil rights, labor rights, and women's rights, advocating for change and inspiring others to take action. Many of these women were mothers, who were motivated by a desire to create a better world for their children and future generations.

One of the most notable examples of the power of motherhood to inspire social change is the Mothers of the Plaza de Mayo in Argentina. During the military dictatorship that ruled Argentina from 1976 to 1983, thousands of people were "disappeared" by the government, including many pregnant women and young mothers. The Mothers of the Plaza de Mayo were a group of mothers who gathered in the Plaza de Mayo in Buenos Aires to demand information about their missing children.

These women, many of whom were grandmothers, became a powerful symbol of resistance and hope during a dark period in Argentina's history. Their courage and determination inspired others to speak out against the government's atrocities, ultimately leading to the downfall of the dictatorship. The Mothers of the Plaza de Mayo continue to be a powerful force for social justice in Argentina and beyond, demonstrating the transformative power of motherhood to create positive change in the world.

In conclusion, the proverb "The hand that rocks the cradle rules the world" is a testament to the power of motherhood and the influence of women in shaping society. The role of mothers in raising children and instilling values of love, kindness, and compassion cannot be overstated. Mothers have the power to shape the character and beliefs of future generations, who will carry these values forward into the world.

Moreover, the indirect impact that mothers have on society through the values they instill in their children and the inspiration they provide to others cannot be ignored. Mothers have been leaders in social and political movements throughout history, advocating for change and inspiring others to take action.

In a world that is facing numerous challenges, the values of love, compassion, and empathy that are instilled in children by their mothers can help to create a more just and sustainable society, one that is based on mutual respect and cooperation. The power of motherhood to shape the future of society is undeniable, and it is essential that we recognize and value the critical role that mothers play in shaping the course of history.

What is research, but a blind date with knowledge!

Research is a process of inquiry that seeks to discover new knowledge or to confirm existing knowledge. It is an essential tool for understanding the world around us and making informed decisions. In many ways, research is like a blind date with knowledge because it involves exploring a subject that one may not be familiar with, similar to meeting a person for the first time without knowing anything about them. In this essay, we will delve into the various dimensions of research and provide real-life examples to illustrate how research is like a blind date with knowledge.

Firstly, research is a process of exploration. When researchers begin a project, they often have a general idea of what they want to investigate, but they do not know what they will discover along the way. This is similar to going on a blind date, where one has little to no information about the person they are meeting. For example, a researcher who is investigating the effects of social media on mental health may have a hypothesis about the relationship between the two, but they may discover unexpected findings during the research process that they did not anticipate.

Secondly, research involves venturing into uncharted territory. It is an opportunity to learn new things and to challenge preconceived notions. This is similar to going on a blind date with someone who has a different perspective or worldview than oneself. For example, a researcher who is studying the history of a particular region may discover new information that challenges their assumptions about the people and culture of that region.

Thirdly, research can be challenging and even frustrating, but persistence and perseverance are key. This is similar to going on multiple blind dates before finding the right match. For example, a researcher who is studying a rare disease may encounter obstacles in recruiting participants or securing funding, but they must persist in their efforts to find answers.

Finally, research can lead to unexpected discoveries and opportunities. This is similar to going on a blind date and discovering shared interests or values that one did not anticipate. For example, a researcher who is studying the effects of exercise on mental health may discover a link between physical activity and improved cognitive function, leading to new opportunities for research and intervention.

In conclusion, research is a complex and multifaceted process that involves exploration, venturing into uncharted territory, persistence and perseverance, and the potential for unexpected discoveries and opportunities. Like a blind date, research can be exciting and unpredictable, but it can also be challenging and frustrating. However, the reward of discovering new knowledge and making a positive impact on the world is worth the effort.

History repeats itself, first as a tragedy, second as a farce.

The phrase "history repeats itself, first as tragedy, second as farce" is attributed to Karl Marx, a German philosopher, economist, and sociologist. This quote is often used to describe the cyclical nature of history, where events seem to repeat themselves over time. In this essay, we will explore the meaning of this quote and examine whether it is an accurate reflection of historical events.
Tragedy and Farce

To understand this quote, it is essential to first understand what Marx meant by tragedy and farce. In the context of history, a tragedy refers to a catastrophic event that has significant consequences and often leads to suffering, loss of life, and destruction. These tragic events can be caused by natural disasters, war, political upheaval, or economic collapse.

On the other hand, a farce is a humorous or absurd event that is often characterized by exaggeration, irony, and satire. Unlike tragedy, a farce is not serious and does not have significant consequences. Instead, it is often used as a form of entertainment or social commentary.

History Repeats Itself

The idea that history repeats itself is not a new one. Many historians, philosophers, and social scientists have explored the concept of cyclical history, where events seem to repeat themselves over time. The cyclical nature of history is often linked to human nature, which remains constant despite changes in technology, politics, and society.

One of the most famous examples of cyclical history is the rise and fall of empires. Throughout history, we have seen countless empires rise to power, only to collapse due to internal strife, external pressures, or natural disasters. The fall of empires, such as the Roman Empire, the Ottoman Empire, and the British Empire, has often been accompanied by tragic events that have had significant consequences for the people living at the time.

However, history also repeats itself in less catastrophic ways. For example, we often see trends in fashion, music, and popular culture that repeat themselves over time. This is often referred to as nostalgia, where people look back to a time when things were simpler or better.

Tragedy and Farce in History

Now that we understand the meaning of tragedy and farce in the context of history, we can examine whether Marx's quote is an accurate reflection of historical events.

One of the most significant examples of tragedy and farce repeating itself in history is the French Revolution and the subsequent rise of Napoleon Bonaparte. The French Revolution, which began in 1789, was a tragic event that led to the overthrow of the French monarchy and the execution of thousands of people. However, the revolution also had farcical elements, such as the Reign of Terror, where the Committee of Public Safety executed people for even the slightest suspicion of opposing the revolution.

After the revolution, Napoleon rose to power and became the emperor of France. His reign was characterized by military conquests and expansion, but it was also marked by farcical events, such as his disastrous invasion of Russia and his eventual defeat at the Battle of Waterloo.

Another example of tragedy and farce repeating itself in history is the Cold War and the subsequent collapse of the Soviet Union. The Cold War, which lasted from 1947 to 1991, was a tragic event that divided the world into two opposing camps and led to the proliferation of nuclear weapons. However, the Cold War also had farcical elements, such as the arms race and the propaganda war between the United States and the Soviet Union.

After the collapse of the Soviet Union in 1991, the world entered a new era of globalization and capitalism. However, this new era has also had its share of farcical events, such as the dot-com bubble and the financial crisis of 2008.

Lessons Learned

The repetition of tragedy and farce in history teaches us several important lessons. First, it reminds us that history is not linear and that events can repeat themselves over time. This means that we must be aware of the cyclical nature of history and learn from past mistakes to prevent similar tragedies from occurring in the future.

Second, it reminds us that the human experience is complex and multifaceted. Tragic events can be accompanied by farcical elements, and humor can be found in even the most dire situations. This complexity reminds us that we should not oversimplify historical events and must strive to understand them in their entirety.

Third, it reminds us that history is not predetermined, and we have the power to shape our future. The tragedies and farces of the past should not be seen as inevitable, but rather as the result of human actions and decisions. This means that we must take responsibility for our actions and work towards creating a better future for ourselves and future generations.

Conclusion

In conclusion, the quote "history repeats itself, first as tragedy, second as farce" is a powerful reminder of the cyclical nature of history. It teaches us that events can repeat themselves over time and that tragedies can be accompanied by farcical elements. However, it also reminds us that we have the power to shape our future and learn from past mistakes. By understanding the lessons of history, we can create a better future for ourselves and future generations.

There are better practices to 'best practices'.

"Best practices" is a term commonly used in the business world to describe the most effective methods for achieving success. These practices are often touted as the gold standard for success, and organizations of all kinds strive to implement them in order to improve their operations. However, there is growing skepticism about the value of these practices. Some argue that there are better practices to follow, ones that are more tailored to the unique needs and circumstances of each organization. In this essay, I will explore this debate, examining the limitations of best practices and offering some alternative approaches that organizations can use to improve their operations.

The Limitations of Best Practices:

One of the main limitations of best practices is that they are often too general to be applied effectively in every situation. These practices are usually developed based on the experiences of successful organizations, and they are intended to be broadly applicable. However, this approach assumes that all organizations face similar challenges and that there is a one-size-fits-all solution to every problem. This is rarely the case, as every organization has its own unique set of circumstances, goals, and challenges.

Another limitation of best practices is that they can be difficult to implement. Even if a best practice is theoretically sound, it may not be feasible for every organization to implement it due to factors such as limited resources, cultural differences, or regulatory requirements. For example, a best practice that works well in a large, multinational corporation may not be practical for a small startup with limited resources. Similarly, a best practice that is effective in one country may not be applicable in another due to differences in laws and regulations.

Finally, best practices can be limiting in that they discourage innovation and creativity. When organizations rely too heavily on best practices, they may become complacent and fail to explore new approaches or ideas. This can stifle growth and limit the organization's ability to adapt to changing circumstances or take advantage of new opportunities.

Alternative Approaches:

Given the limitations of best practices, it is worth exploring some alternative approaches that organizations can use to improve their operations. Here are a few possibilities:

1. Tailored Solutions:

Rather than relying on generic best practices, organizations can develop solutions that are tailored to their specific circumstances. This requires a deep understanding of the organization's goals, challenges, and resources, as well as a willingness to experiment and take risks. By customizing solutions to fit their unique needs, organizations can achieve better results than they would by simply following a best practice.

2. Continuous Improvement:

Rather than seeking a one-time fix, organizations can focus on continuous improvement. This involves constantly monitoring and analysing their operations, identifying areas for improvement, and making incremental changes over time. This approach is more flexible than relying on best practices, as it allows organizations to adapt to changing circumstances and take advantage of new opportunities as they arise.

3. Collaborative Problem-Solving:

Rather than relying solely on internal expertise, organizations can engage in collaborative problem-solving. This involves working with external partners such as customers, suppliers, or other organizations to identify solutions to shared challenges. By bringing together diverse perspectives and expertise, organizations can develop more innovative and effective solutions than they could on their own.

4. Design Thinking:

Design thinking is a human-centered approach to problem-solving that emphasizes empathy, experimentation, and iteration. Rather than starting with a predetermined solution, design thinking involves understanding the needs and experiences of users, experimenting with different solutions, and iterating until the best solution is found. This approach encourages creativity and innovation, and can be especially effective for addressing complex or ambiguous problems.

Conclusion:

In conclusion, while best practices have their place in the business world, they are not a panacea. Organizations that rely too heavily on best practices may find themselves unable to adapt to changing circumstances or take advantage of new opportunities. Instead, organizations should consider alternative approaches that are more

Life is a long journey between human being and being humane.

Life is a journey that we all embark on from the moment we take our first breath. It is a journey that is full of twists and turns, ups and downs, joys and sorrows, and ultimately leads us to our destination, which is the end of our life. Throughout this journey, we encounter different people, situations, and experiences that shape who we are and what we become. One of the most important aspects of this journey is the way we treat others and ourselves. In other words, it is the way we strive to be humane, which makes all the difference.

Being humane means treating others with compassion, kindness, and empathy. It means being considerate of their needs, feelings, and perspectives. It also means being aware of our own thoughts, emotions, and actions, and how they impact others. Being humane is not something that comes naturally to everyone, as it requires a certain level of self-awareness and a willingness to put ourselves in other people's shoes. However, it is something that we can all strive for and cultivate, as it is the key to building strong relationships, creating positive change in the world, and living a fulfilling life.

Unfortunately, many people view life as a competition, where the only way to succeed is by putting themselves first and stepping on others. This mindset is what leads to selfishness, greed, and indifference towards others. It is what drives people to prioritize their own interests above everything else, even if it means causing harm to others. When we adopt this mindset, we lose sight of what truly matters in life, which is the relationships we build and the impact we have on others.

On the other hand, being humane requires us to shift our focus away from ourselves and towards others. It requires us to consider the impact of our actions on others and to strive to make a positive difference in their lives. This mindset is what leads to kindness, empathy, and compassion towards others. When we adopt this mindset, we open ourselves up to new experiences, perspectives, and relationships that enrich our lives and make us better human beings.

One of the most important aspects of being humane is empathy. Empathy is the ability to understand and share the feelings of others. It is the ability to put ourselves in other people's shoes and see the world from their perspective. Empathy is what allows us to connect with others on a deeper level, to build trust and understanding, and to create meaningful relationships. Without empathy, we become isolated and disconnected from others, which can lead to loneliness, depression, and a lack of fulfillment in life.

Another important aspect of being humane is kindness. Kindness is the act of showing compassion and consideration towards others. It can be something as simple as holding the door open for someone or as complex as dedicating your life to helping others. Kindness is what makes the world a better place, one act at a time. It is what creates a ripple effect of positivity that spreads throughout our communities and beyond.

Compassion is also an important aspect of being humane. Compassion is the ability to feel sympathy and concern for others who are suffering. It is the ability to recognize the pain and suffering of others and to take action to alleviate it. Compassion is what drives us to help others, even if it means sacrificing our own time and resources. It is what creates a sense of purpose and fulfillment in our lives, as we know that our actions are making a positive difference in the world.

It is important to note that being humane does not mean that we should neglect our own needs and interests. Self-care is also an important aspect of living a fulfilling life. However, it is important to find a balance between taking care of ourselves and taking care of others. When we prioritize our own needs above everything else, we lose sight of the importance of building strong relationships and making a positive impact on others. On the other hand, when we neglect our own needs and well-being, we become burnt out and unable to help others effectively. Therefore, finding a balance between self-care and caring for others is crucial for leading a fulfilling life and being humane.

Moreover, being humane goes beyond just our interactions with others. It also involves how we treat the world around us. We live in a world that is facing many challenges, such as climate change, pollution, and resource depletion. Being humane means taking responsibility for our impact on the environment and striving to make a positive difference. It means being mindful of our consumption habits, reducing waste, and supporting sustainable practices. It also means advocating for policies and practices that protect the environment and preserve it for future generations.

In conclusion, life is a long journey that is full of opportunities to be humane. It is a journey that is enriched by our connections with others, our experiences, and the impact we have on the world. Being humane requires us to shift our focus away from ourselves and towards others, to prioritize kindness, empathy, and compassion, and to find a balance between self-care and caring for others. It also involves taking responsibility for our impact on the environment and striving to make a positive difference. By embracing these values, we can lead fulfilling lives and create a better world for ourselves and others.

Mindful manifesto is the catalyst to a tranquil self

Introduction
In today's fast-paced world, stress and anxiety have become an integral part of our lives. We often find ourselves struggling to keep up with the demands of our daily routines, which leaves us feeling drained and exhausted. Mindfulness is a practice that has gained significant popularity in recent years as a way to combat stress and anxiety. A mindful manifesto is a set of principles that one can use to cultivate mindfulness in their life. In this essay, we will explore how a mindful manifesto can be the catalyst to a tranquil self.

What is mindfulness?
Mindfulness is a practice that involves paying attention to the present moment without judgment. It is about being fully present in the moment and not allowing your mind to wander to the past or the future. Mindfulness has its roots in Buddhist meditation practices but has since been adopted by various fields, including psychology, medicine, and education.
The benefits of mindfulness are numerous. Studies have shown that mindfulness can reduce stress, anxiety, and depression. It can also improve emotional regulation, increase self-awareness, and enhance cognitive function. Practicing mindfulness can also lead to greater empathy and compassion towards oneself and others.

What is a mindful manifesto?
A mindful manifesto is a set of principles that one can use to cultivate mindfulness in their life. It is a way of living that encourages individuals to be fully present in the moment and to live intentionally. A mindful manifesto can help individuals develop a deeper understanding of themselves and their place in the world.

A mindful manifesto typically includes principles such as being present, being non-judgmental, and being compassionate towards oneself and others. It may also include principles such as practicing gratitude, embracing imperfection, and letting go of attachment.
How can a mindful manifesto be the catalyst to a tranquil self?
A mindful manifesto can be the catalyst to a tranquil self by providing individuals with a framework for living mindfully. It can help individuals develop a greater sense of self-awareness and cultivate a deeper understanding of their thoughts, feelings, and behaviors.

Being present
One of the key principles of a mindful manifesto is being present. Being present means being fully engaged in the present moment and not allowing your mind to wander to the past or the future. Being present can help individuals develop a greater appreciation for the small things in life and find joy in everyday experiences.
Being present can also help individuals reduce stress and anxiety. By focusing on the present moment, individuals can avoid getting caught up in worries about the future or regrets about the past. This can help individuals feel more relaxed and at ease.

Being non-judgmental
Another key principle of a mindful manifesto is being non-judgmental. Being non-judgmental means accepting things as they are without trying to change them. It means letting go of expectations and embracing imperfection.
Being non-judgmental can be a powerful tool for reducing stress and anxiety. When individuals let go of the need to control everything, they can find a greater sense of peace and tranquility. This can help individuals develop a more positive outlook on life and improve their overall well-being.

Being compassionate

Compassion is another key principle of a mindful manifesto. Being compassionate means treating oneself and others with kindness and empathy. It means recognizing that everyone is struggling in their own way and extending grace and understanding to oneself and others.

Being compassionate can help individuals develop a greater sense of connection with others. It can also help individuals feel more at ease with themselves and reduce negative self-talk. By treating oneself and others with compassion, individuals can cultivate a more positive and peaceful mindset.

Practicing gratitude

Practicing gratitude is another principle that may be included in a mindful manifesto. Practicing gratitude involves acknowledging and appreciating the good things in life, even in the midst of difficult circumstances.

Practicing gratitude can be a powerful tool for cultivating a tranquil self. By focusing on the positive aspects of life, individuals can reduce negative emotions such as stress and anxiety. Practicing gratitude can also help individuals develop a more positive outlook on life and increase their overall well-being.

Embracing imperfection

Embracing imperfection is another principle that may be included in a mindful manifesto. Embracing imperfection means accepting that we are all imperfect and that it is okay to make mistakes. It means letting go of the need to be perfect and embracing the process of learning and growing.

Embracing imperfection can be a powerful tool for reducing stress and anxiety. When individuals let go of the need to be perfect, they can reduce the pressure they put on themselves and find greater peace and tranquility. Embracing imperfection can also help individuals develop a more positive and self-compassionate mindset.

Letting go of attachment

Letting go of attachment is another principle that may be included in a mindful manifesto. Letting go of attachment means releasing the need to cling to things and accepting that everything is impermanent. It means letting go of the past and embracing the present moment.

Letting go of attachment can be a powerful tool for reducing stress and anxiety. When individuals let go of attachment, they can find greater peace and acceptance in the present moment. Letting go of attachment can also help individuals develop a greater sense of resilience and adaptability.

Conclusion

In conclusion, a mindful manifesto can be the catalyst to a tranquil self. By providing individuals with a framework for living mindfully, a mindful manifesto can help individuals develop a greater sense of self-awareness and cultivate a deeper understanding of their thoughts, feelings, and behaviors. By being present, non-judgmental, and compassionate, practicing gratitude, embracing imperfection, and letting go of attachment, individuals can reduce stress and anxiety, cultivate a more positive outlook on life, and increase their overall well-being. By adopting the principles of a mindful manifesto, individuals can create a more peaceful and tranquil life for themselves.

Ships do not sink because of water around them, ships sink because of water that gets into them.

The phrase "Ships do not sink because of water around them, ships sink because of water that gets into them" is a powerful metaphor for life. It is a reminder that external circumstances alone do not cause failure or disaster, but rather it is the internal factors that determine one's success or failure. This phrase has been used in a variety of contexts, from leadership and management to personal growth and development. In this essay, we will explore the meaning and significance of this phrase and how it can be applied to various aspects of life.

At its core, the phrase is a reminder that external factors alone are not enough to cause failure or disaster. In the case of a ship, the water that surrounds it is not necessarily a problem, as long as it remains outside the ship. However, if water is allowed to enter the ship, it can cause damage to the ship's structure and ultimately lead to its sinking.

Similarly, in life, external circumstances such as economic downturns, political instability, or natural disasters may be challenging, but they do not necessarily determine one's fate. Rather, it is the internal factors, such as one's mindset, resilience, and ability to adapt to changing circumstances that determine one's success or failure.

One of the key lessons that can be drawn from this phrase is the importance of taking care of oneself and one's internal well-being. In the case of a ship, regular maintenance and inspection are essential to ensure that the ship's structure remains strong and that there are no vulnerabilities that could allow water to enter. Similarly, in life, taking care of one's physical, emotional, and mental health is essential to ensure that one is resilient and able to withstand the challenges that may come.

This is particularly important in the context of leadership and management. A leader who neglects their own well-being is likely to be less effective in leading their team or organization. This is because they may be more prone to burnout, stress, and other negative consequences that can ultimately impact their ability to make sound decisions and lead effectively.

In addition, the phrase highlights the importance of identifying and addressing internal vulnerabilities. In the case of a ship, it is essential to identify any weak points or vulnerabilities in the ship's structure and take steps to reinforce or repair them. Similarly, in life, it is important to identify any weaknesses or vulnerabilities in oneself and take steps to address them.

For example, if one struggles with anxiety, it may be important to seek professional help or engage in self-care practices that can help to reduce anxiety and build resilience. Alternatively, if one struggles with time management, it may be important to develop new habits and systems that can help to improve productivity and reduce stress.

Another important lesson that can be drawn from this phrase is the importance of being proactive and taking preventative measures. In the case of a ship, it is essential to take proactive steps to prevent water from entering the ship, such as ensuring that all hatches are securely closed and that the ship's pumps are working properly.

Similarly, in life, it is important to take proactive steps to prevent negative consequences from occurring. This may involve setting clear boundaries, developing healthy habits and routines, and being proactive in managing stress and other challenges.

In the context of business and entrepreneurship, the phrase highlights the importance of risk management and contingency planning. A business that fails to plan for potential risks and vulnerabilities is likely to be more vulnerable to external threats and more likely to fail.

For example, a business that relies heavily on a single supplier may be vulnerable to supply chain disruptions or price increases. By identifying potential risks and developing contingency plans, businesses can mitigate these risks and increase their chances of success.

The phrase can also be applied to personal growth and development. In order to achieve personal growth and success, it is important to focus on internal factors such as mindset, beliefs, and habits.

For example, if one wants to improve their financial situation, it may be important to examine their mindset and beliefs around money, and to develop new habits and practices that can help to improve their financial situation. Similarly, if one wants to improve their relationships, it may be important to examine their beliefs and patterns around communication and intimacy, and to develop new habits and practices that can help to strengthen their relationships.

Ultimately, the phrase "Ships do not sink because of water around them, ships sink because of water that gets into them" is a powerful reminder that success and failure are determined by internal factors rather than external circumstances alone. By focusing on strengthening our internal well-being, identifying and addressing vulnerabilities, taking proactive measures, and developing risk management and contingency plans, we can increase our chances of success in all areas of life.

Simplicity is the ultimate sophistication.

Introduction

Simplicity is often associated with minimalism, a design philosophy that emphasizes simplicity and functionality. The phrase "Simplicity is the ultimate sophistication" is attributed to Leonardo da Vinci, the famous artist and inventor, who believed that simplicity is the key to achieving great things. This essay explores the meaning of simplicity, its benefits, and why it is considered the ultimate sophistication.

What is Simplicity?

Simplicity is the state of being simple, plain, and uncomplicated. It is the absence of unnecessary complexity, ornamentation, or clutter. Simplicity is often associated with minimalism, a design philosophy that emphasizes simplicity and functionality. Minimalism seeks to achieve the most with the least by eliminating all unnecessary elements and focusing on the essentials.

Simplicity can be applied to many aspects of life, including art, design, technology, and lifestyle. In art and design, simplicity is often used to create elegant and timeless works that communicate a clear and concise message. In technology, simplicity is essential to creating user-friendly and intuitive products that are easy to use and understand. In lifestyle, simplicity can help reduce stress and improve overall well-being by eliminating unnecessary distractions and focusing on the essentials.

Benefits of Simplicity

Simplicity has many benefits, including:

1. Clarity - Simplicity can help clarify our thoughts and ideas by eliminating unnecessary complexity and focusing on the essentials. By simplifying our lives, we can better understand our goals and priorities, and focus our efforts on what is most important.

2. Efficiency - Simplicity can help us achieve our goals more efficiently by eliminating unnecessary steps and processes. By simplifying our workflow, we can save time and energy, and achieve better results with less effort.

3. Sustainability - Simplicity can help us live a more sustainable lifestyle by reducing our consumption of resources and minimizing waste. By living a simpler life, we can reduce our environmental impact and promote a more sustainable future.

4. Happiness - Simplicity can help us achieve greater happiness by reducing stress and promoting a sense of calm and contentment. By simplifying our lives, we can focus on what truly matters and find greater fulfillment in the things that bring us joy.

Why is Simplicity the Ultimate Sophistication?

Simplicity is considered the ultimate sophistication for several reasons. First, simplicity is often the result of a complex and sophisticated process of design and refinement. The simplest designs are often the result of many iterations and refinements that eliminate all unnecessary elements and focus on the essentials. The simplicity of these designs belies the complexity and sophistication of the process that created them.

Second, simplicity is a sign of mastery and expertise. The ability to simplify complex ideas and processes requires a deep understanding of the subject matter and the ability to distill it into its essential components. The simplicity of a design or a process is a testament to the skill and expertise of its creator.

Third, simplicity is timeless and enduring. Simple designs and ideas are often the most elegant and enduring because they are not tied to a particular time or place. They communicate a clear and concise message that can be understood and appreciated by people of all ages and cultures.

Examples of Simplicity

The following are examples of simplicity in various aspects of life:

1. Apple products - Apple products are known for their simplicity and user-friendly design. The clean and minimalist aesthetic of Apple products is the result of a complex and sophisticated design process that focuses on the essentials and eliminates all unnecessary elements.

2. Haiku poetry - Haiku poetry is a form of Japanese poetry that is known for its simplicity and elegance. Haiku poems consist of only three lines and seventeen syllables, yet they can communicate a powerful and evocative message.

3. Minimalist art - Minimalist art is a form of art that focuses on simplicity and minimalism. Minimalist artworks often consist of simple geometric shapes or monochromatic colour schemes, yet they can communicate powerful and profound ideas.

4. Zen gardens - Zen gardens are Japanese gardens that are known for their simplicity and tranquility. Zen gardens often consist of simple rock formations and carefully arranged gravel, yet they can create a sense of calm and serenity in those who visit them.

Conclusion

In conclusion, simplicity is the ultimate sophistication because it requires a deep understanding of the subject matter and the ability to distill it into its essential components. Simplicity is often the result of a complex and sophisticated process of design and refinement, and it is a sign of mastery and expertise. Simplicity has many benefits, including clarity, efficiency, sustainability, and happiness. By embracing simplicity in our lives, we can achieve greater fulfillment and happiness while reducing stress and promoting a more sustainable future.

Culture is what we are, civilisation is what we have.

Culture is an intrinsic part of human existence, shaping our thoughts, beliefs, and behaviors. It is a shared set of values, norms, and practices that are transmitted from generation to generation through various means such as language, art, and religion. On the other hand, civilization refers to the complex social organization and material development of human societies, such as technology, infrastructure, and political systems. While culture and civilization are often used interchangeably, they represent distinct aspects of human existence. In this essay, we will explore the meaning of culture and civilization and discuss how they shape our understanding of ourselves and the world around us.

Culture is a broad and multifaceted concept that encompasses many different aspects of human experience. At its core, culture refers to the shared beliefs, values, and practices that define a particular group or society. This includes everything from language and religion to art and cuisine. Culture is not static but rather evolves and changes over time, influenced by a wide range of factors such as technology, migration, and globalization. Culture shapes our understanding of the world around us and provides a framework for how we interact with others. It helps us make sense of our experiences and gives us a sense of belonging and identity.

Civilization, on the other hand, refers to the complex social organization and material development of human societies. This includes everything from the development of agriculture and cities to the creation of political systems and legal codes. Civilization is characterized by the accumulation of knowledge and technological advancements that allow for the creation of increasingly complex societies. It is often associated with urbanization and the growth of large-scale institutions such as governments and corporations.

While culture and civilization are related, they represent distinct aspects of human existence. Culture is what we are, representing our shared values, beliefs, and practices. Civilization, on the other hand, is what we have, referring to the material and social advancements that allow us to create complex societies. Both culture and civilization are important for understanding human existence and the world around us.

The relationship between culture and civilization is complex and multifaceted. Culture provides the foundation for civilization, shaping our values, beliefs, and practices. Without a shared culture, it would be difficult to create the social and material advancements that characterize civilization. However, civilization also has a profound impact on culture, shaping our beliefs and practices in ways that are often difficult to predict. For example, the development of the printing press in Europe led to a proliferation of books and the spread of knowledge, which in turn helped to shape European culture in new and unexpected ways.

The relationship between culture and civilization is also shaped by power dynamics. The dominant culture often shapes the direction and pace of civilization, while other cultures may be marginalized or excluded. This can lead to cultural conflict and tension as different groups compete for resources and influence. It is important to recognize these power dynamics and work to create a more equitable and inclusive society that values and respects all cultures.

In conclusion, culture and civilization represent distinct aspects of human existence, but they are also intimately connected. Culture provides the foundation for civilization, shaping our values, beliefs, and practices, while civilization allows for the creation of complex societies that can support diverse cultures. It is important to recognize the complex relationship between culture and civilization and work to create a more equitable and inclusive society that values and respects all cultures. Ultimately, it is through a deep understanding and appreciation of both culture and civilization that we can create a better future for ourselves and future generations.

There can be no social justice without economic prosperity but economic prosperity without social justice is meaningless.

Introduction:
The relationship between social justice and economic prosperity is a complex and multifaceted one. Social justice is the fair and equitable distribution of resources and opportunities in a society, while economic prosperity refers to the level of wealth and well-being experienced by individuals and communities. Some argue that economic prosperity is a necessary precondition for achieving social justice, while others contend that social justice is a prerequisite for sustainable economic growth. In this essay, I will argue that there can be no social justice without economic prosperity, but economic prosperity without social justice is meaningless, and I will provide examples and data to support this argument.

Social justice and economic prosperity:
Social justice and economic prosperity are interconnected and mutually reinforcing. Economic prosperity provides the material resources necessary to ensure a basic standard of living for all individuals and families in a society. This includes access to adequate food, housing, healthcare, education, and other essential goods and services. Without economic prosperity, it is difficult if not impossible to achieve social justice. For example, in many low-income countries, poverty and lack of access to basic resources hinder the development of a just and equitable society. According to the World Bank, over 700 million people worldwide lived in extreme poverty in 2015, with incomes below $1.90 per day.

However, economic prosperity alone is not sufficient to ensure social justice. Economic growth can exacerbate inequalities and create social and environmental problems if it is not accompanied by policies and programs that promote equity, inclusion, and sustainability. For example, the high levels of economic inequality in the United States and other developed countries have been associated with a range of negative social and health outcomes, including higher rates of crime, mental illness, and chronic disease.

Examples of the interplay between social justice and economic prosperity:
The interplay between social justice and economic prosperity can be observed in many contexts around the world. One example is the Nordic model of social democracy, which combines high levels of economic prosperity with a strong commitment to social justice. The Nordic countries (Denmark, Finland, Iceland, Norway, and Sweden) consistently rank at or near the top of global indices of economic prosperity, social welfare, and human development. They achieve this through a combination of progressive taxation, comprehensive social welfare programs, and strong labor protections. For example, Denmark and Sweden have among the highest rates of union membership in the world, and all Nordic countries have generous parental leave policies that support work-life balance and gender equality.

Another example is the case of South Africa, which has experienced significant economic growth in recent decades but still faces major challenges in achieving social justice. Since the end of apartheid in 1994, South Africa has made progress in reducing poverty and expanding access to education and healthcare. However, the country still faces high levels of inequality, with the top 10% of the population holding over 70% of the wealth. This inequality is exacerbated by historical patterns of racial discrimination and exclusion, which have left many black South Africans with limited access to education, land, and other economic opportunities.
Amartya Sen and Jagdish Bhagwati debate:

The debate between Amartya Sen and Jagdish Bhagwati provides an interesting lens through which to view the relationship between social justice and economic prosperity. Sen argues that economic growth alone is insufficient to achieve social justice, and that policies and programs aimed at promoting social inclusion, education, and healthcare are necessary to ensure that the benefits of growth are shared equitably. Bhagwati, on the other hand, argues that economic growth is the best way to achieve social justice, as it provides the resources necessary to fund social programs and promote human development.

While both arguments have merit, Sen's perspective is more aligned with the idea that there can be no social justice without economic prosperity. Sen argues that social justice requires not only the provision of basic needs and resources, but also the empowerment of individuals and communities to participate fully in economic, social, and political life. This means investing in education, healthcare, and other social services, as well as creating opportunities for entrepreneurship and innovation. Sen also emphasizes the importance of democratic institutions and participatory governance, which enable citizens to shape their own economic and social futures.

Bhagwati's argument, on the other hand, focuses primarily on the role of economic growth in promoting social justice. While Bhagwati acknowledges the importance of social programs and policies, he contends that economic growth is the primary driver of social progress, and that policies aimed at promoting growth should be the top priority. Bhagwati argues that growth creates jobs, generates income, and reduces poverty, and that the benefits of growth can be used to fund social programs and reduce inequality.

While Bhagwati's argument has some validity, it is important to recognize that economic growth alone is not sufficient to achieve social justice. As Sen has argued, social justice requires a comprehensive approach that addresses the social, political, and economic factors that contribute to poverty, inequality, and exclusion. This means investing in education, healthcare, and other social services, as well as promoting democratic institutions and participatory governance.

In conclusion, the debate between Sen and Bhagwati highlights the complex relationship between social justice and economic prosperity. While economic growth is a necessary precondition for achieving social justice, it alone is not sufficient. Achieving social justice requires a comprehensive approach that addresses the root causes of poverty, inequality, and exclusion, and promotes human dignity and well-being for all. The examples of the Nordic countries and South Africa illustrate the importance of balancing economic growth with social justice, and the costs of neglecting one or the other. Ultimately, achieving both social justice and economic prosperity requires a long-term and holistic approach that prioritizes the needs and aspirations of all individuals and communities. Achieving both social justice and economic prosperity requires a long-term and holistic approach that addresses the root causes of poverty, inequality, and exclusion, and promotes human dignity and well-being for all.

Patriarchy is the least noticed yet the most significant structure of social inequality.

Introduction:

Patriarchy is a system of social organization that is based on the belief that men are naturally superior to women. It is the least noticed yet the most significant structure of social inequality. Patriarchy is a pervasive system that operates in different areas of human life, including the economy, politics, culture, and religion. Despite the many efforts that have been made to address gender inequality, patriarchy continues to be a dominant force in many societies. This essay will examine the impact of patriarchy on social inequality and provide examples and data to support this argument.

The Impact of Patriarchy on Social Inequality:

Patriarchy is a system of social inequality that is deeply ingrained in many societies. It creates and reinforces gender roles that are based on the belief that men are superior to women. This system operates at different levels of society, from the individual to the institutional. Patriarchy affects access to education, healthcare, employment, political representation, and social status. It creates a gender-based hierarchy that limits women's opportunities and reinforces men's dominance.

Education:

Patriarchy affects access to education for women. According to UNESCO, there are 130 million girls who are out of school globally, and two-thirds of the world's illiterate adults are women. This is because patriarchal societies prioritize men's education over women's education. In many societies, girls are expected to stay at home and help with household chores instead of attending school. This limits their opportunities for personal and professional growth and perpetuates gender inequality.

Healthcare:

Patriarchy affects access to healthcare for women. Women are more likely to suffer from health problems due to gender-based discrimination. For example, women are more likely to suffer from reproductive health problems such as maternal mortality, which is a major cause of death for women in developing countries. This is because patriarchal societies prioritize men's health over women's health. Women's health issues are often ignored or stigmatized, which limits their access to healthcare.

Employment:

Patriarchy affects women's employment opportunities. Women are often paid less than men for the same work and are underrepresented in leadership positions. This is because patriarchal societies prioritize men's employment over women's employment. Women are also subjected to sexual harassment and discrimination in the workplace, which limits their opportunities for professional growth.

Political Representation:

Patriarchy affects women's political representation. Women are underrepresented in political leadership positions globally. According to the Inter-Parliamentary Union, women make up only 25% of parliamentarians worldwide. This is because patriarchal societies prioritize men's political representation over women's political representation. Women are often excluded from political decision-making processes, which limits their opportunities for political empowerment.

Social Status:

Patriarchy affects women's social status. Women are often judged based on their appearance and their ability to fulfill traditional gender roles. This perpetuates gender stereotypes and limits women's opportunities for personal and professional growth. Patriarchal societies also perpetuate gender-based violence, which limits women's physical and emotional wellbeing.

Some suggestions for improving the issue of patriarchy and some initiatives taken by the Indian government to address it:

Suggestions for Improvement	Initiatives Taken by Indian Government
Promote gender equality in education by providing equal opportunities for boys and girls to attend school and addressing gender-based violence and discrimination in schools.	Beti Bachao, Beti Padhao (Save the Girl Child, Educate the Girl Child) campaign launched in 2015 to promote the education and empowerment of girls.
Address gender-based violence by strengthening laws and policies to protect women from violence and providing support services for survivors.	The Protection of Women from Domestic Violence Act, 2005 provides legal protection and support services for women who are victims of domestic violence.
Increase women's political representation by promoting women's leadership and participation in decision-making processes at all levels of government.	The Women's Reservation Bill proposed in 2008 seeks to reserve 33% of seats in the Lok Sabha and state legislative assemblies for women.
Address gender wage gap by promoting equal pay for equal work and strengthening laws to ensure that women are paid the same as men for doing the same job.	The Equal Remuneration Act, 1976 prohibits discrimination in wages based on gender and requires equal pay for men and women for the same work.
Promote women's health by addressing gender-based discrimination in healthcare and ensuring that women have access to quality healthcare services.	The Pradhan Mantri Surakshit Matritva Abhiyan (Prime Minister's Safe Motherhood Campaign) launched in 2016 to provide comprehensive antenatal care to pregnant women.

These are just a few examples of suggestions for improvement and initiatives taken by the Indian government to address patriarchy and promote gender equality. There is still much work to be done to create a more equitable society, but these initiatives are a step in the right direction.

Conclusion:

Patriarchy is the least noticed yet the most significant structure of social inequality. It affects access to education, healthcare, employment, political representation, and social status. Patriarchal societies prioritize men's opportunities and reinforce gender-based stereotypes and violence, which limit women's opportunities for personal and professional growth. It is important to recognize and challenge patriarchal systems to create more equitable societies. This can be done through education, advocacy, and policy change to promote gender equality and women's empowerment.

Technology as the silent factor in international relations

Technology has revolutionized the way the world operates, transforming the way we communicate, work, and interact with each other. In today's interconnected world, technology has become a vital factor in international relations. It has enabled nations to connect and communicate with each other, shaping the global landscape in ways we could never have imagined before. However, technology has also become a silent factor in international relations, with its influence often going unnoticed. In this essay, we will explore how technology has become a silent factor in international relations and the impact it has had on the global landscape.

Technology has played a significant role in shaping the global landscape in recent years. One example of this is the emergence of social media platforms. Platforms such as Facebook, Twitter, and Instagram have enabled people to connect with each other on a global scale, breaking down the traditional barriers of geography and culture. Social media has enabled people to share their thoughts, opinions, and experiences with each other, creating a more connected and empathetic world. However, social media has also become a tool for political manipulation and propaganda, with nations using it to influence the political landscape of other countries.

Another example of technology's influence on international relations is the rise of cyber warfare. Cyber attacks have become a common occurrence in recent years, with nations using technology to attack each other's computer systems and infrastructure. These attacks can have a significant impact on a country's economy and national security, making them a powerful tool in international relations. In addition, technology has also been used to monitor and spy on other countries, enabling nations to gather intelligence and gain an advantage in international relations.

Technology has also had a significant impact on international trade. The rise of e-commerce and digital platforms has transformed the way businesses operate, enabling them to sell their products and services to customers all over the world. The growth of international trade has been driven by technology, with e-commerce expected to reach $4.9 trillion in 2021. Technology has also enabled nations to improve their infrastructure, making it easier to transport goods and services across borders. However, technology has also created new challenges for international trade, such as the rise of counterfeit products and the displacement of workers due to automation.

One final example of technology's influence on international relations is its impact on climate change. Technology has enabled nations to monitor and measure the effects of climate change, enabling them to develop policies and strategies to combat it. Advances in renewable energy, such as solar and wind power, have enabled nations to reduce their carbon footprint and transition to a more sustainable future. However, technology has also contributed to climate change, with the rise of digital technology leading to an increase in energy consumption and greenhouse gas emissions.

Technologies and their impact on India's international relations:

Technology	Examples in India	Effects on International Relations
Social Media	Indian political parties use social media to spread propaganda and influence voters	Can lead to tensions between India and other countries if they feel that India is interfering in their internal affairs
Cyber Warfare	India is a target for cyber attacks from China and Pakistan	Can lead to tensions and conflict between India and these countries, especially if the attacks cause damage to critical infrastructure or disrupt services

Technology	Examples in India	Effects on International Relations
E-commerce	India is one of the largest markets for e-commerce, with companies such as Amazon and Flipkart operating in the country	Can lead to increased trade and economic ties between India and other countries, but also poses challenges such as competition from foreign companies and concerns over data privacy and security
Renewable Energy	India is investing in renewable energy sources such as solar and wind power to reduce its carbon footprint	Can lead to India being seen as a leader in combating climate change, and may create opportunities for collaboration with other countries on environmental issues
Nuclear Technology	India has developed nuclear weapons and has a civil nuclear program	Can lead to tensions with other countries over India's nuclear capabilities, and may also create opportunities for collaboration on nuclear energy
Nano Technology	India has made strides in nanotechnology, with research on applications in medicine, electronics, and materials science	Can lead to collaborations with other countries on research and development, and may also create opportunities for Indian companies to export nanotechnology-based products
Robotics	India is a growing market for robotics, with applications in manufacturing, healthcare, and agriculture	Can lead to increased trade and economic ties with other countries in the robotics industry, but may also pose challenges such as job displacement and ethical concerns over the use of robots
Artificial Intelligence (AI)	India is investing in AI research and development, with applications in healthcare, finance, and defense	Can lead to collaborations with other countries on AI research and development, and may also create opportunities for Indian companies to export AI-based products and services
Critical Path Method (CPM)	CPM is a project management technique used in construction and engineering projects in India	Can lead to collaborations with other countries on large infrastructure projects, and may also create opportunities for Indian companies to participate in international projects that use CPM

Overall, technology has a significant impact on India's international relations, with both opportunities and challenges associated with each technology. As India continues to invest in and develop new technologies, it will be important to carefully balance these opportunities and challenges to ensure that they benefit both India and its relationships with other countries.

In conclusion, technology has become a silent factor in international relations, influencing the global landscape in ways that often go unnoticed. From social media to cyber warfare, technology has enabled nations to connect and communicate with each other, shape the global economy, and combat climate change. However, technology has also created new challenges and risks, such as political manipulation and cybersecurity threats. As technology continues to evolve, it will be important for nations to work together to ensure that it is used for the greater good, rather than as a tool for political gain or aggression.

Wisdom finds truth.

Wisdom is a term that is often used to describe the ability to make good judgments, to have a deep understanding of important issues, and to possess practical knowledge. Wisdom is something that is earned through life experiences and is not easily acquired. The concept of wisdom is often associated with age, but it can also be found in individuals who have experienced a great deal in a short amount of time. When it comes to the idea that "wisdom finds truth," there are several different interpretations of what this phrase means.

On one level, the idea that "wisdom finds truth" can be seen as an affirmation of the importance of knowledge and the pursuit of truth. Wisdom is not just about having a lot of experience, but about knowing how to use that experience to make good decisions and to understand the world around us. To truly understand the world, one must be willing to seek out knowledge and be open to new ideas. In this sense, wisdom is not just about knowing what we know, but also about being aware of what we don't know.

Another interpretation of the phrase "wisdom finds truth" is that wisdom is a process of discovery. The pursuit of wisdom requires that we be open to new ideas, that we be willing to question our assumptions, and that we be willing to explore different perspectives. Wisdom is not something that can be acquired in a single moment of insight or through the acquisition of a set of facts. Instead, it is a process of growth and development that requires ongoing effort and engagement.

The idea that "wisdom finds truth" also speaks to the importance of humility. In order to be truly wise, we must be willing to acknowledge our own limitations and to recognize that there is always more to learn. This means that we must be willing to listen to others and to be open to feedback and criticism. It also means that we must be willing to admit when we are wrong and to make course corrections when necessary.

At its core, the idea that "wisdom finds truth" is about the importance of being grounded in reality. In order to make good decisions and to understand the world around us, we must be willing to accept the truth, even when it is uncomfortable or inconvenient. This means that we must be willing to confront our own biases and to be open to the perspectives of others. It also means that we must be willing to accept the limits of our own knowledge and to recognize that there are some things that we may never fully understand.

The pursuit of wisdom is not an easy one. It requires us to be willing to confront our own limitations, to be open to new ideas, and to be willing to engage in ongoing self-reflection and growth. But ultimately, the rewards of this pursuit are great. Through wisdom, we can gain a deeper understanding of ourselves and the world around us. We can make better decisions, build stronger relationships, and lead more fulfilling lives.

In order to cultivate wisdom, there are several key practices that we can engage in. These include:

1. Cultivating curiosity: One of the hallmarks of wisdom is a sense of curiosity about the world. To cultivate wisdom, we must be willing to ask questions, to explore new ideas, and to be open to learning.

2. Practicing self-reflection: In order to gain wisdom, we must be willing to look inward and to examine our own thoughts, feelings, and beliefs. This means being honest with ourselves about our strengths and weaknesses and being willing to acknowledge our mistakes.

3. Engaging with diverse perspectives: To truly understand the world around us, we must be willing to engage with perspectives that are different from our own. This means seeking out diverse viewpoints and being open to learning from others.

4. Developing emotional intelligence: Wisdom is not just about intellect; it is also about emotional intelligence.
Developing emotional intelligence involves being aware of our own emotions and the emotions of others, and learning how to manage these emotions in a constructive way.

5. Seeking out mentors: Mentors can be invaluable sources of wisdom, offering guidance and support as we navigate life's challenges. By seeking out mentors who have experienced what we are going through, we can learn from their wisdom and experience.

6. Embracing lifelong learning: Finally, cultivating wisdom requires a commitment to lifelong learning. We must be willing to continually seek out new knowledge, to challenge our assumptions, and to engage in ongoing personal growth.

In conclusion, the idea that "wisdom finds truth" speaks to the importance of cultivating wisdom as a means of understanding the world around us. Wisdom is not just about having a lot of experience, but about knowing how to use that experience to make good decisions and to understand the world in a deeper way. Through practices like curiosity, self-reflection, emotional intelligence, and lifelong learning, we can cultivate the wisdom necessary to navigate life's challenges and find truth in the world around us.

Values are not what humanity is, but what humanity ought to be

Values are an essential aspect of human life. They guide our decision-making, shape our behavior, and ultimately determine our character. Values are the principles that we hold dear, the beliefs that we deem important, and the ideals that we aspire to embody. However, values are not inherent in humanity; they are not what we are, but rather what we ought to be. This essay will explore the nature of values, their role in shaping human behavior, and the significance of understanding the difference between what is and what ought to be.

Values are subjective, and their meaning and importance can vary widely from person to person. Some people value honesty, integrity, and loyalty, while others prioritize success, power, and wealth. Our values are often shaped by our upbringing, culture, and experiences. They reflect our personality, beliefs, and worldview. Values are the fundamental principles that guide our lives, providing us with a moral compass and a sense of purpose.

However, values are not necessarily what humanity is. People are capable of both good and bad behavior, and our values do not always align with our actions. Many people claim to value honesty, but lie when it is convenient for them. Others may espouse the importance of kindness, but act with cruelty towards those they dislike. Our values are not set in stone; they can change over time and may even conflict with each other. Values are aspirational; they represent what we strive to be, not necessarily what we are.

Despite this, values play a crucial role in shaping human behavior. They influence our decisions, actions, and relationships with others. Values provide a framework for evaluating our choices and determining what is right and wrong. They help us to navigate complex social situations and make sense of the world around us. Our values can also inspire us to make positive changes in our lives and in the world.

For example, consider the value of compassion. Compassion is the desire to alleviate the suffering of others, to empathize with their pain, and to take action to help them. While compassion may not be a universal trait of humanity, it is certainly an ideal that we ought to strive for. If we were to live in a world where compassion was the norm, where people put the needs of others before their own, imagine how much suffering could be alleviated.

Values also play a critical role in the development of society. A society's values determine its laws, customs, and norms. Values can inspire social movements, spur progress, and lead to positive change. Conversely, when a society's values are distorted or corrupted, it can lead to injustice, oppression, and conflict.

For example, consider the value of equality. Equality is the belief that all people should be treated with respect and dignity, regardless of their race, gender, religion, or social status. When a society values equality, it can lead to laws that protect marginalized groups, social movements that challenge discrimination, and a sense of shared purpose and belonging. However, when a society does not value equality, it can lead to systemic oppression, discrimination, and conflict.

Understanding the difference between what is and what ought to be is crucial for personal growth and social progress. When we recognize that our values are aspirational, that they represent what we strive to be rather than what we are, we can begin to take steps towards becoming better people. We can examine our behavior, identify areas where we fall short of our values, and make a conscious effort to align our actions with our beliefs. We can also recognize that other people may have different values than us, and that this diversity is what makes humanity interesting and dynamic.

However, recognizing the gap between what is and what ought to be can also be a source of frustration and disillusionment. It can be discouraging to see how far we are from our ideals, to witness the injustices and suffering in the world, and to feel powerless to make a difference. It is important to remember that progress is often slow and incremental, and that change requires sustained effort and commitment.

One way to bridge the gap between what is and what ought to be is through education and awareness. By learning about different values, perspectives, and experiences, we can expand our understanding of the world and develop empathy for others. We can also use our knowledge and skills to advocate for social justice and to promote positive change.

Another way to bridge the gap is through personal reflection and introspection. By examining our own values and behaviors, we can identify areas for growth and work towards becoming better people. We can also seek out opportunities to practice our values in everyday life, such as volunteering, donating to charity, or advocating for causes we believe in.

In conclusion, values are an essential aspect of human life. While they are not inherent in humanity, they play a crucial role in shaping our behavior and the development of society. Values are aspirational, representing what we ought to be rather than what we are. Understanding the difference between what is and what ought to be can be a source of both frustration and inspiration. By recognizing the gap between the two, we can work towards becoming better people and promoting positive change in the world.

Best for an individual is not necessarily best for the society

Individualism is a fundamental aspect of our society, where personal satisfaction and fulfillment are highly valued. The concept of individualism emphasizes the importance of self-reliance, personal responsibility, and self-determination. It is widely believed that what is best for an individual is best for society. However, this belief is not entirely accurate because what is best for an individual may not always align with the best interests of society.

While individualism is essential, it should not override the greater good of society. The interests of society often clash with the interests of individuals. The choices made by an individual may be beneficial to them, but they may cause harm to society as a whole. For instance, an individual may choose to pursue a high-paying job that causes environmental degradation or damages public health. While this choice may benefit the individual, it has negative consequences for society. In such cases, it is clear that what is best for the individual is not necessarily best for society.

One of the areas where individualism and societal interests are in conflict is healthcare. While everyone has the right to access healthcare services, the cost of medical care is often prohibitive. Individuals may choose to forego healthcare services due to their high costs, leading to a deterioration in their health. However, this choice has negative consequences for society. For example, a person who contracts a contagious disease but cannot afford treatment may spread the disease to others, causing an outbreak. In such a scenario, it is clear that what is best for the individual may not align with the interests of society.

Another area where individualism and societal interests are in conflict is the environment. The actions of individuals have a significant impact on the environment. An individual may choose to use plastic bags because they are convenient, but this choice has negative consequences for the environment. The plastic bags may end up in landfills or oceans, causing environmental pollution. The individual's choice to use plastic bags may be beneficial to them, but it is not in the best interests of society.

Individualism and societal interests are also in conflict in the field of economics. Capitalism emphasizes individual freedom and private enterprise. While this system has brought prosperity and innovation, it has also created income inequality and environmental degradation. The pursuit of profits by corporations often leads to exploitative labor practices and environmental pollution. In such cases, what is best for the individual (i.e., maximizing profits) is not necessarily best for society.

Education is another area where individualism and societal interests are in conflict. An individual may choose to attend a prestigious university to secure a high-paying job, but this choice may not be in the best interests of society. A focus on prestigious universities often leads to a lack of investment in public schools and community colleges. This neglect harms society because it deprives disadvantaged individuals of the opportunity to pursue higher education. In such cases, what is best for the individual may not align with the interests of society.

In conclusion, while individualism is important, it should not override the interests of society. What is best for the individual may not always align with the best interests of society. The choices made by an individual may have negative consequences for society, and this conflict must be addressed. There must be a balance between individualism and societal interests. Policies and regulations must be in place to ensure that individual choices do not harm society. The government has a crucial role to play in ensuring that the interests of society are protected. Ultimately, it is up to us as individuals to recognize that our choices have consequences beyond our own lives, and we must act responsibly for the greater good of society.

Courage to accept and dedication to improve are two keys to success

Success is a term that has been defined and redefined countless times over the years. It is often associated with wealth, fame, and power, but true success goes beyond these superficial aspects. Success is a personal achievement, and it varies from person to person. However, there are two things that are essential to achieving success: courage to accept and dedication to improve.

The first key to success is courage to accept. Life is full of ups and downs, and success is not exempt from this. There are times when we may not achieve what we set out to do, or we may fail at something we have worked hard for. In such situations, it takes courage to accept that we have not succeeded and to take responsibility for our actions.

Accepting failure is not easy, and it can be painful. It can be especially difficult when our failure is in front of others. However, we should not be ashamed of failure. It is a part of life, and we can learn from it. When we accept our failures, we can reflect on what we did wrong and identify ways to improve. This is the first step towards success.

It takes courage to accept our flaws and shortcomings. We are all imperfect, and we all have areas where we need to improve. However, it is not easy to accept our flaws. We may feel ashamed, embarrassed, or unworthy. But when we have the courage to accept our flaws, we can work on improving them. We can seek feedback from others, read books, attend seminars, and take courses to develop our skills.

Accepting our weaknesses is not a sign of weakness. It is a sign of strength. It takes courage to acknowledge that we are not perfect and that we need to work on ourselves. When we have the courage to accept our flaws, we can develop a growth mindset that allows us to learn from our mistakes and improve ourselves.

The second key to success is dedication to improve. Improvement requires effort and commitment. It is not enough to accept our flaws; we must also be willing to work on them. Dedication to improve means making a conscious effort to develop our skills and abilities.

Improvement requires patience and perseverance. It is not easy to develop new skills or habits. We may face obstacles and setbacks along the way. However, when we are dedicated to improvement, we are willing to put in the time and effort required to achieve our goals. We are willing to take risks and try new things.

Dedication to improvement also requires focus. We must be clear about what we want to achieve and what steps we need to take to get there. We should set goals and create a plan to achieve them. We should also track our progress and make adjustments along the way.

Improvement is not a one-time event; it is a continuous process. We should be willing to learn from our mistakes and adjust our approach as needed. We should also be open to feedback from others. Feedback can help us identify areas where we need to improve and provide us with ideas for how to do so.

When we are dedicated to improvement, we are constantly growing and evolving. We are not content with staying the same; we want to be better. This mindset allows us to achieve our goals and reach our full potential.

Courage to accept and dedication to improve are two keys to success. They are essential for personal growth and achievement. When we have the courage to accept our flaws and failures, we can learn from them and improve ourselves. When we are dedicated to improvement, we are constantly growing and evolving, and we can achieve our goals and reach our full potential.

In conclusion, success is a personal achievement that goes beyond wealth, fame, and power. It is a journey of personal growth and development. Courage to accept and dedication to improve are two keys to success that are essential for this journey. When we have the courage to accept our failures and flaws, we can learn from them and use them as opportunities for growth. When we are dedicated to improvement, we are constantly striving to be better, and we can achieve our goals and reach our full potential.

To succeed, we must be willing to take risks and embrace challenges. We must also be willing to learn and grow from our experiences. We should not be afraid of failure or ashamed of our flaws. Instead, we should have the courage to accept them and use them as opportunities for improvement.

We should also be dedicated to improving ourselves. We should have a growth mindset and be willing to put in the time and effort required to achieve our goals. Improvement requires patience, perseverance, and focus. We should set goals, create a plan, and track our progress. We should also be open to feedback from others and be willing to adjust our approach as needed.

In conclusion, the keys to success are courage to accept and dedication to improve. These two traits are essential for personal growth and achievement. When we have the courage to accept our flaws and failures and are dedicated to improving ourselves, we can achieve our goals and reach our full potential. Success is not a destination but a journey, and it is up to us to make the most of it. essential for this journey. When we have the courage to accept our failures and flaws, we can learn from them and use them as opportunities for growth. When we are dedicated to improvement, we are constantly striving to be better, and we can achieve our goals and reach our full potential.

To succeed, we must be willing to take risks and embrace challenges. We must also be willing to learn and grow from our experiences. We should not be afraid of failure or ashamed of our flaws. Instead, we should have the courage to accept them and use them as opportunities for improvement.

We should also be dedicated to improving ourselves. We should have a growth mindset and be willing to put in the time and effort required to achieve our goals. Improvement requires patience, perseverance, and focus. We should set goals, create a plan, and track our progress. We should also be open to feedback from others and be willing to adjust our approach as needed.

In conclusion, the keys to success are courage to accept and dedication to improve. These two traits are essential for personal growth and achievement. When we have the courage to accept our flaws and failures and are dedicated to improving ourselves, we can achieve our goals and reach our full potential. Success is not a destination but a journey, and it is up to us to make the most of it.

South Asian societies are woven not around the state, but around their plural cultures and plural identities.

South Asia is a diverse region that is home to various ethnic, linguistic, and religious groups. From the Himalayan peaks to the Indian Ocean coastline, South Asia's cultural landscape is rich and varied. The region's societies are known for being woven around their plural cultures and plural identities, rather than around the state.

One of the most significant aspects of South Asian societies is the importance of cultural identity. This identity is often linked to religion, language, and ethnicity, and it plays a crucial role in shaping people's lives. In many cases, it takes precedence over national identity. As the Indian writer and historian Ramachandra Guha notes, "South Asian societies are not so much nations as civilisations."

One example of the primacy of cultural identity in South Asia is the case of Pakistan. Pakistan was created as a homeland for the Muslims of British India, and Islam is enshrined in its constitution as the state religion. However, within Pakistan, there are multiple ethnic and linguistic groups, each with its own distinct identity. The Pashtuns in the northwest, for example, have a culture and language that are different from those of the Punjabis in the east. Similarly, the Sindhis in the south have their own distinct cultural traditions.

Despite Pakistan's efforts to promote a singular national identity, these regional and cultural identities remain strong. The Pakistani writer Mohsin Hamid has noted that "Pakistan is a place where many different Pakistans coexist." This plurality of identities is not unique to Pakistan, but is present in many other South Asian societies as well.

Another example of South Asia's plural cultures can be seen in the region's religious diversity. South Asia is home to several of the world's major religions, including Hinduism, Islam, Buddhism, and Sikhism. Each of these religions has a rich history and cultural heritage, and they coexist in a complex web of relationships. The Indian writer and social activist Arundhati Roy has described this diversity as "a glorious, chaotic diversity that is full of contradictions and yet held together by some invisible, inexplicable thread."

This thread is not always easy to discern, and there have been instances when religious differences have led to conflict. One of the most notable examples is the partition of India in 1947, which led to the creation of Pakistan and the displacement of millions of people. The partition was based on religious lines, with Hindus and Sikhs moving to India, and Muslims to Pakistan. The violence that accompanied the partition left a deep scar on the region, and its effects are still felt today.

Despite these challenges, South Asia's plural cultures and identities continue to thrive. In many cases, they are celebrated and cherished, forming the basis of people's sense of self and community. This is evident in the region's rich artistic and cultural traditions. South Asia has produced some of the world's greatest poets, writers, musicians, and artists, and their works continue to inspire and captivate people around the world.

One of the most striking examples of South Asia's cultural richness is the city of Lahore in Pakistan. Lahore has been a center of cultural and artistic activity for centuries, and its literary and artistic traditions are legendary. The city has produced some of the greatest poets and writers in the Urdu language, including Faiz Ahmed Faiz and Saadat Hasan Manto. Its architectural heritage is also remarkable, with iconic structures like the Badshahi Mosque and the Lahore Fort.

Similarly, India is home to a rich and diverse cultural heritage, with its various regions and communities each contributing their own unique traditions. From the classical music of South India to the colorful festivals of North India, India's cultural landscape is incredibly diverse. The country has produced some of the world's greatest thinkers and artists, including the poet Rabindranath Tagore and the filmmaker Satyajit Ray. India's cultural traditions are also reflected in its religious and spiritual practices, such as yoga and meditation.

The importance of cultural identity and pluralism in South Asian societies can also be seen in the region's political landscape. In many cases, the state has had to navigate the complexities of these plural identities in order to maintain stability and peace. This has sometimes led to tensions between the state and various cultural or ethnic groups.

One example of this tension can be seen in the case of Sri Lanka, where the Sinhalese majority has historically held political power, leading to tensions with the Tamil minority. The conflict between the two groups erupted into a brutal civil war in the 1980s and 1990s, with both sides committing atrocities against each other. The conflict ended in 2009 with the defeat of the Tamil Tigers, but tensions between the two communities continue to simmer.

Despite these challenges, South Asian societies have demonstrated a remarkable resilience in the face of adversity. The region's plural cultures and identities have helped to provide a sense of belonging and community to its people, and they continue to inspire and shape the region's artistic and intellectual traditions. As the Indian philosopher and statesman Sarvepalli Radhakrishnan once wrote, "In India, every religion is not only tolerated but respected as true."

In conclusion, South Asian societies are indeed woven not around the state, but around their plural cultures and identities. These identities are deeply rooted in the region's history and traditions, and they continue to play a crucial role in shaping people's lives. While there have been challenges in navigating the complexities of these identities, they also provide a rich and diverse cultural landscape that is truly unique in the world. As South Asia continues to evolve and change, its plural cultures and identities will undoubtedly continue to be a source of inspiration and strength for its people.

Neglect of primary health care and education in India are reasons for its backwardness

India, as a nation, has been striving for progress since its independence in 1947. However, despite several initiatives and plans, the country still grapples with several socio-economic issues, including poverty, inequality, and lack of access to basic healthcare and education. While the Indian government has taken several steps to address these issues, the neglect of primary healthcare and education remains a significant reason for the country's backwardness.

India's healthcare system is characterized by a lack of infrastructure, inadequate funding, and inadequate staffing. According to a report by the World Health Organization (WHO), India has a shortage of approximately two million doctors, nurses, and other healthcare professionals. The situation is further exacerbated by the uneven distribution of healthcare facilities, with the majority of them being concentrated in urban areas. As a result, people in rural areas, who account for around 70% of the country's population, have limited access to quality healthcare services.

The lack of access to primary healthcare is a significant contributor to India's high burden of disease. The country has the highest burden of tuberculosis, with around 27% of the global cases. Additionally, India is home to one-third of the world's malnourished children, with over 40% of children under five being stunted. The lack of access to healthcare and the high burden of disease directly impact the country's economic growth and development.

Moreover, the neglect of primary education in India is another crucial reason for its backwardness. While the country has made significant progress in increasing access to education, the quality of education remains poor. According to a report by the Annual Status of Education Report (ASER), a non-governmental organization, only 27% of students in grade three can read at their grade level, and only 44% of students in grade eight can solve simple mathematical problems. Additionally, around 56% of children in rural areas drop out of school before completing their primary education.

The lack of quality education directly affects the country's socio-economic development. A poorly educated population is less productive and less able to participate in the country's economic growth. Moreover, the lack of education perpetuates the cycle of poverty, as individuals with limited education have fewer employment opportunities, lower wages, and less social mobility.

Furthermore, the neglect of primary healthcare and education is interlinked. Children who receive inadequate healthcare are more likely to suffer from malnutrition, which directly affects their cognitive development and ability to learn. Moreover, children who drop out of school early are less likely to receive adequate healthcare, leading to a cycle of poverty and poor health.

Several initiatives have been taken to address the neglect of primary healthcare and education in India. In 2018, the Indian government launched the Ayushman Bharat scheme, which aims to provide universal health coverage to the country's population. The scheme provides financial protection against catastrophic health expenditure and free access to primary and secondary healthcare services. Additionally, the Indian government has taken several measures to increase access to education, including the Right to Education Act, which provides free and compulsory education to children between six and fourteen years of age.

Issue	Government Efforts	Results So Far	Suggestions to Improve
Access to Healthcare	Launch of Ayushman Bharat scheme, increasing	Improved access to healthcare services in rural	Increase staffing and infrastructure in healthcare

Issue	Government Efforts	Results So Far	Suggestions to Improve
	funding for healthcare	areas	facilities to reduce wait times and improve quality of care
Malnutrition	Implementation of Integrated Child Development Services (ICDS) scheme, providing free meals in schools	Reduction in malnutrition rates, but still high rates of malnourishment in some areas	Increase awareness about the importance of nutrition and the availability of resources, strengthen ICDS scheme with additional resources and staffing
Maternal Mortality	Launch of Janani Shishu Suraksha Karyakram, providing free maternity services	Reduction in maternal mortality rates, but still high compared to other countries	Increase access to prenatal care and education, strengthen emergency obstetric care services in rural areas
Mental Health	Launch of National Mental Health Policy, increasing funding for mental health services	Increase in awareness and access to mental health services, but still a lack of mental health professionals and resources	Increase resources and training for mental health professionals, increase awareness and reduce stigma around mental health
Primary Education	Implementation of Right to Education Act, increasing funding for education	Increase in enrollment rates, but quality of education remains poor	Improve infrastructure and resources in schools, increase teacher training and support
Dropout Rates	Implementation of mid-day meal scheme, increasing access to education	Reduction in dropout rates, but still high in some areas	Increase support for students from disadvantaged backgrounds, improve the quality of education to reduce dropout rates
Gender Disparities	Launch of Beti Bachao, Beti Padhao scheme, increasing funding for girls' education	Increase in enrollment rates for girls, but still disparities in education and healthcare access	Increase awareness and education around gender issues, provide additional support and resources for girls' education
Sanitation	Launch of Swachh Bharat Mission, increasing funding for sanitation	Reduction in open defecation and improved sanitation, but still challenges in implementation and access	Increase awareness and education around sanitation, improve implementation and infrastructure for sanitation facilities
Water Quality	Launch of National Rural Drinking Water Programme, increasing funding for water infrastructure	Improvement in water quality and access, but still challenges in implementation and access	Increase awareness and education around water quality, improve implementation and infrastructure for water facilities

Overall, improving health and education in India requires a comprehensive and sustained effort from the government, civil society, and individuals. It is crucial to address the root causes of these issues, including poverty, inequality, and lack of access to resources. By prioritizing these issues and investing in healthcare and education, India can move towards a brighter and more equitable future for all its citizens.

However, despite these initiatives, the neglect of primary healthcare and education remains a significant issue in India. The implementation of these schemes has been slow, and there are several challenges, including inadequate funding, poor infrastructure, and inadequate staffing. Additionally, there is a lack of political will and accountability, leading to a lack of prioritization of healthcare and education in policymaking.

In conclusion, the neglect of primary healthcare and education in India remains a significant reason for its backwardness. The lack of access to quality healthcare and education perpetuates the cycle of poverty and affects the country's socio-economic development. While the Indian government has taken several initiatives to address these issues, the implementation has been slow, and several challenges remain. Addressing these challenges and prioritizing healthcare and education in policymaking are crucial steps towards achieving progress and development. As the country moves towards a more sustainable and equitable future, it is essential to prioritize investments in primary healthcare and education, as they form the foundation of a healthy and prosperous society. As Nelson Mandela once said, "Education is the most powerful weapon which you can use to change the world," and India's neglect of primary healthcare and education must be addressed to ensure a brighter future for all its citizens.

Biased media is a real threat to Indian democracy

The media has a crucial role in a democracy, serving as the fourth pillar of society. The media's primary role is to inform citizens and hold those in power accountable. However, in recent years, the Indian media has been accused of being biased and acting as propaganda machines for political parties, which poses a significant threat to Indian democracy. This essay will examine how biased media is a real threat to Indian democracy, with real-life examples and quotes from experts.

Media Bias in Indian Democracy

Media bias refers to the selective reporting or slanting of news in favor of a particular political ideology, party, or agenda. In India, media bias has become a growing concern in recent years, with political parties and their affiliated media houses engaging in agenda-driven reporting that often ignores the fundamental principles of impartiality and objectivity. This biased media reporting has the potential to influence public opinion, sway election outcomes, and undermine the very foundations of Indian democracy.

Real-life examples of media bias

One of the most glaring examples of media bias in Indian democracy was during the 2019 general elections. Many media houses were accused of engaging in one-sided reporting that favored the ruling party, the Bharatiya Janata Party (BJP). One study by the Delhi-based non-profit organization, the Centre for Media Studies, found that the BJP received an overwhelmingly positive coverage in the media, while the opposition parties were subjected to negative coverage.

The study found that the BJP received 32.1% positive coverage, while the Indian National Congress received only 7.3% positive coverage. The study also found that the BJP received 45.6% neutral coverage, while the Indian National Congress received only 27.2% neutral coverage. The study's findings indicate that the media was biased in favor of the ruling party, which has the potential to influence public opinion and sway election outcomes.

Another example of media bias in Indian democracy was during the coverage of the farmer's protests in 2020-2021. Many media houses were accused of engaging in biased reporting that favored the government's narrative and ignored the farmers' plight. One study by the Media Watch Group found that the media's coverage of the farmer's protests was biased and lacked impartiality. The study found that the media houses failed to report on the farmers' demands and instead focused on portraying the protests as a law and order problem.

Impact of media bias on Indian democracy

Media bias has the potential to impact Indian democracy in several ways. Firstly, biased reporting can influence public opinion and sway election outcomes. In a democracy, it is essential that citizens make informed decisions based on factual information. Biased reporting undermines this fundamental principle of democracy and can lead to the election of governments that do not have the mandate of the people.

Secondly, biased reporting can undermine the credibility of the media and erode public trust in the institutions of democracy. The media is often referred to as the fourth estate, as it plays a crucial role in holding those in power accountable. When the media fails to report impartially, it can lead to a breakdown in the democratic system's checks and balances.

Expert opinions on media bias in Indian democracy

Several experts have expressed concern about media bias in Indian democracy. In an interview with the Indian Express, former Chief Election Commissioner S.Y. Quraishi stated, "Media bias is a real threat to democracy. When the media is biased, it can influence public opinion and sway election outcomes." He also added, "Media houses have a responsibility to report impartially and not take sides in political battles."

Similarly, in an interview with the Wire, journalist Karan Thapar stated, "The media is supposed to be the watchdog of democracy, but when the media is biased, it can lead to a breakdown in the democratic system's checks and balances."
He further added, "Biased reporting undermines the very foundations of democracy, which rely on the free flow of information and the ability of citizens to make informed decisions."

Conclusion

In conclusion, biased media is a real threat to Indian democracy. The media has a crucial role to play in a democracy, and it must act impartially and report objectively to ensure that citizens are informed and can make informed decisions. Biased reporting has the potential to influence public opinion, sway election outcomes, and undermine the very foundations of Indian democracy. The media houses must prioritize impartiality and objectivity over political affiliations and agendas to maintain their credibility and safeguard the democratic institutions' integrity. It is crucial to address media bias and promote objective reporting to ensure the continued functioning of a healthy democracy in India.

Rise of Artificial Intelligence: the threat of jobless future or better job opportunities through reskilling and upskilling

Introduction:

The rise of artificial intelligence (AI) has been a topic of discussion and debate for many years. While some view it as a threat to jobs, others see it as an opportunity for better job opportunities through reskilling and upskilling. This essay will explore both sides of the argument and provide real-life examples of how AI is affecting the job market.

The threat of jobless future:

There is no denying that AI has already begun to automate many jobs that were once done by humans. From self-driving cars to automated customer service, AI has the potential to replace a significant number of jobs. According to a report by the World Economic Forum, AI and automation are expected to displace around 85 million jobs by 2025. This is a worrying statistic for those who fear a jobless future.

One industry that has already been significantly affected by AI is manufacturing. As machines become more sophisticated, they are able to carry out tasks that were once done by humans. For example, the automotive industry has seen a rise in the use of robots to carry out tasks such as welding and painting. This has resulted in a decrease in the number of jobs available for humans in the industry.

Another industry that is at risk is retail. As e-commerce continues to grow, more and more customers are choosing to shop online rather than in physical stores. This has resulted in a decrease in the number of jobs available in retail stores. In addition, AI-powered chatbots are now being used to handle customer inquiries, further reducing the need for human workers.

These examples show that AI has the potential to significantly reduce the number of jobs available for humans. This could result in a jobless future for many people, especially those who do not have the skills required to work in an AI-driven economy.

Better job opportunities through reskilling and upskilling:

While AI does have the potential to automate many jobs, it also has the potential to create new jobs. According to the same World Economic Forum report, AI and automation are expected to create around 97 million new jobs by 2025. This is because AI will create new opportunities in areas such as data analysis, cybersecurity, and software development.

However, to take advantage of these new job opportunities, workers will need to reskill and upskill. This means acquiring new skills that are in demand in an AI-driven economy. For example, workers in the manufacturing industry could reskill to become machine operators or maintenance technicians, while workers in the retail industry could upskill to become data analysts or e-commerce specialists.

Real-life examples:

One company that is leading the way in reskilling and upskilling its workers is Amazon. The company has a program called Amazon Technical Academy, which trains non-technical workers in software development. The program has been highly successful, with over 10% of participants being promoted to technical roles within the company.

Another example is the UK government's National Retraining Scheme, which aims to help workers in industries that are at risk of automation to reskill for new jobs. The scheme offers free training courses in areas such as coding, data analysis, and cybersecurity. This is an example of how governments can help workers to adapt to an AI-driven economy.

Conclusion:

In conclusion, the rise of artificial intelligence does pose a threat to jobs, as it has the potential to automate many tasks that were once done by humans. However, it also presents an opportunity for workers to reskill and upskill for new job opportunities in areas such as data analysis and software development. The key to ensuring that workers are not left behind in an AI-driven economy is to provide them with the necessary training and support to acquire the skills that are in demand. With the right approach, the rise of AI can be a positive force for job creation and economic growth.

Administration

1. Politics, bureaucracy and business – fatal triangle. (1994)
2. Politics without ethics is a disaster. (1995)
3. The VIP cult is a bane of Indian democracy. (1996)
4. Need for transparency in public administration. (1996)
5. The country's need for a better disaster management system. (2000)
6. How should a civil servant conduct himself? (2003)

ADDITIONAL INPUTS

Parameter	Recommendations of Committees	Achievements So Far
Political Neutrality	Fourth Pay Commission - Civil servants should function as neutral instruments of the state, free from any political considerations or influences.	Civil servants in India are generally known for maintaining political neutrality and serving the government of the day with impartiality and objectivity.
Professional Competence	Second Administrative Reforms Commission - The civil service should be characterised by a high level of professionalism and competence.	The civil services in India have been able to attract highly qualified individuals, with many civil servants possessing advanced degrees and professional qualifications.
Accountability	Second Administrative Reforms Commission - Civil servants should be held accountable for their actions and decisions.	The Right to Information Act, 2005 has provided citizens with a powerful tool to hold civil servants accountable for their actions and decisions.
Transparency	Second Administrative Reforms Commission - The civil service should be characterised by a high level of transparency.	The implementation of e-governance initiatives and the use of technology have increased transparency in government processes and decision-making.
Ethics	Second Administrative Reforms Commission - Civil servants should maintain high standards of personal integrity and ethics.	The All India Service (Conduct) Rules, 1968 prescribe the standards of conduct for civil servants and require them to maintain high standards of integrity and honesty.
Decentralization	Sarkaria Commission - Greater decentralisation of administrative power to states and local bodies.	The 73rd and 74th Constitutional Amendments have given greater autonomy to local bodies and increased decentralisation of administrative power to the states.
Meritocracy	First Administrative Reforms Commission - Civil services should be based on meritocracy and recruitment should be made through a competitive examination.	The Civil Services Examination is a highly competitive examination that attracts some of the best minds in the country.
Performance	Second Administrative Reforms	The Annual Performance Appraisal

Parameter	Recommendations of Committees	Achievements So Far
Evaluation	Commission - Regular performance evaluations of civil servants should be conducted to ensure accountability and promote meritocracy.	Reports (APARs) are used to evaluate the performance of civil servants and determine promotions and career advancement.
Training & Development	Kothari Committee - Continuous training and development of civil servants is essential to improve their performance and ensure professionalism.	The Lal Bahadur Shastri National Academy of Administration and other training institutions provide continuous training and development opportunities for civil servants.
Reducing Red Tape	Administrative Reforms Commission - Streamlining administrative processes and reducing bureaucratic red tape.	The implementation of e-governance initiatives and the use of technology have streamlined administrative processes and reduced bureaucratic red tape.

5 quotes on the significance of administration:

1. "The success of any great organization is not solely dependent on how hard its workers work, but how well they are organized and led." - Warren Bennis
2. "The administration of government is an essential aspect of society. Orderly and efficient administration is the backbone of good governance." - Nelson Mandela
3. "The administration of justice is the firmest pillar of government." - George Washington
4. "The best administration is the one that allows people to live their lives to the fullest extent possible." - Jawaharlal Nehru
5. "The quality of administration is one of the key factors that determines the success or failure of a government." - Lee Kuan Yew

5 PUNCHLINES ON SIGINIFICANCE OF ADMINISTRATION

1. Effective administration is the backbone of a well-functioning society.
2. Good administration ensures the fair and efficient delivery of public services to citizens.
3. Strong administration promotes economic growth and development.
4. Skilled administrators are essential for the effective implementation of government policies and programs.
5. A transparent and accountable administration fosters public trust and confidence in government institutions.

5 ANECDOTES ON SIGINIFICANCE OF ADMINISTRATION

1. The Roman Aqueducts: The Roman Empire is known for its impressive aqueducts, which were used to transport water to the city from sources located miles away. These aqueducts were a marvel of engineering and administration, as they required careful planning and organization to build and maintain. Without effective administration, the aqueducts could not have been built, and the people of Rome would have suffered from water shortages.

2. The British Empire: The British Empire was one of the largest and most powerful empires in history, and its success was due in large part to its effective administration. The British government was able to establish a system of governance in its colonies that allowed for effective control and management of resources. This system of administration was critical in helping the British Empire maintain its power and influence for centuries.

3. The American Revolution: The American Revolution was a watershed moment in history, and it was largely driven by a desire for greater representation and better administration. The colonists felt that the British government was not administering their affairs fairly, and they rebelled against British rule. This rebellion led to the creation of a new nation, founded on the principles of representative government and effective administration.

4. The Indian Civil Service: The Indian Civil Service (ICS) was a prestigious administrative body that governed India during the colonial era. The ICS was responsible for everything from collecting taxes to maintaining law and order, and it played a critical role in the administration of the country. Many of the ICS officers were known for their efficiency, diligence, and integrity, and their work helped to shape modern India.

5. The Apollo Space Program: The Apollo Space Program was a monumental achievement of human ingenuity and administration. The program required the coordination of thousands of people and resources from across the country, and it demanded a high level of administrative skill to manage everything from budgetary constraints to personnel issues. Without effective administration, the Apollo Space Program could not have been successful, and humanity would not have achieved the historic milestone of landing on the moon.

These anecdotes demonstrate the critical role that administration has played in shaping human history and achieving monumental achievements. From ancient aqueducts to modern space programs, effective administration has been a key factor in shaping our world and making progress towards a better future.

Politics, bureaucracy and business – fatal triangle

Politics, bureaucracy, and business are three interconnected elements that are often entangled in a complex relationship. These three entities are integral parts of society and each has its own set of objectives and functions. However, when they converge, a fatal triangle is formed that can lead to disastrous consequences. In this essay, we will examine the dynamics of this triangle and explore its various manifestations.

To understand the dynamics of this fatal triangle, we need to define each of the three elements. Politics refers to the process of making decisions that apply to members of a group. Bureaucracy refers to the organization and management of large institutions, often characterized by hierarchy and a set of rules and regulations. Business refers to the production and distribution of goods and services for profit. Each of these elements has its own objectives, which can sometimes be at odds with each other.

The relationship between politics, bureaucracy, and business is not always a negative one. In a democratic system, politics and bureaucracy work together to ensure that the interests of the public are protected. Business, on the other hand, contributes to the economy by creating jobs and generating revenue. However, when these entities are corrupted or become self-serving, a fatal triangle is formed.

One manifestation of the fatal triangle is the phenomenon of crony capitalism. This is a situation where businesses collude with politicians and bureaucrats to gain favors, such as contracts or regulatory exemptions. In this scenario, the interests of the public are compromised, as politicians and bureaucrats make decisions that favor their business partners rather than the public. This can lead to a situation where businesses gain an unfair advantage, and the public loses trust in the government.

Another manifestation of the fatal triangle is the politicization of bureaucracy. When politics permeates the bureaucracy, public institutions become vehicles for political agendas. This can lead to a situation where the bureaucracy is no longer able to perform its functions effectively, as decisions are made based on political considerations rather than objective criteria. In this scenario, the public loses faith in the bureaucracy, and the government becomes less effective in delivering services.

A third manifestation of the fatal triangle is the capture of politics by business interests. This is a situation where businesses use their economic power to influence politics, often by lobbying or making campaign contributions. In this scenario, politicians become beholden to their business donors, and decisions are made that favor the interests of these donors rather than the public. This can lead to a situation where businesses gain excessive power, and the public loses faith in the political system.

The fatal triangle can also manifest itself in the form of corruption. When politics, bureaucracy, and business are corrupted, the interests of the public are subverted, and the three entities work together to enrich themselves at the expense of the public. Corruption can take many forms, including bribery, embezzlement, and nepotism. When corruption is rampant, the government loses legitimacy, and the public becomes disillusioned with the political system.

The fatal triangle can also manifest itself in the form of regulatory capture. This is a situation where businesses use their economic power to influence the regulatory process, often by hiring former regulators or using their knowledge of the regulatory process to their advantage. In this scenario, regulators become beholden to the interests of the businesses they regulate, and the regulatory process becomes less effective in protecting the public interest. This can lead to a situation where businesses are able to engage in harmful practices, and the public suffers as a result.

In conclusion, the fatal triangle of politics, bureaucracy, and business can have disastrous consequences for the public. When these entities become corrupted or self-serving, the interests of the public are subverted, and the government loses legitimacy. To prevent the formation of the fatal triangle, it is essential to maintain a separation between politics, bureaucracy, and business, and to ensure that each entity operates in a transparent and accountable manner. This can be achieved through the establishment of effective regulatory frameworks and the enforcement of strong ethical standards. It is also important to promote transparency and public participation in the decision-making process, to ensure that the interests of the public are adequately represented. Finally, it is essential to promote a culture of integrity and accountability, where those who engage in corrupt practices are held accountable for their actions. By taking these steps, we can mitigate the risks of the fatal triangle and build a more sustainable and just society.

Politics without ethics is a disaster

Politics is the art of managing public affairs. It encompasses the process of making collective decisions for a group or community and implementing those decisions through the exercise of power and authority. Ethics, on the other hand, refers to the principles of right and wrong conduct, which guide human behavior and decision-making. In the absence of ethics, politics becomes a chaotic and self-serving enterprise that undermines the very foundations of democracy and public trust. This essay argues that politics without ethics is a disaster, and explores the reasons why this is so.

Firstly, politics without ethics leads to a loss of trust in public institutions. When politicians prioritize their own interests over the public good, they undermine the trust that citizens have in the democratic process. Citizens expect their leaders to act in a manner that is consistent with the values and principles of the society they represent. When politicians act in ways that are unethical, such as accepting bribes or engaging in corrupt practices, they violate this trust and damage the legitimacy of the political system.

This loss of trust can have far-reaching consequences for the functioning of democratic societies. Citizens may become disillusioned with the political process, leading to apathy and disengagement from civic life. This, in turn, can lead to a lack of participation in elections, public protests, and other forms of political engagement, which can further erode the democratic process. In extreme cases, a loss of trust in public institutions can even lead to political instability and conflict.

Secondly, politics without ethics can lead to the abuse of power. When politicians act without ethical considerations, they are more likely to engage in behavior that is abusive or exploitative. This can take many forms, such as using public resources for personal gain, suppressing opposition voices, or violating the rights of marginalized groups. The abuse of power can have serious consequences for individuals and society as a whole.

For example, if politicians use public resources for personal gain, this can result in a lack of investment in public infrastructure and services. This, in turn, can lead to a decline in the quality of life for citizens, particularly those who are already disadvantaged. Similarly, if politicians suppress opposition voices, this can lead to a lack of accountability and transparency, which can further undermine the legitimacy of the political system. Finally, if politicians violate the rights of marginalized groups, this can lead to social unrest and conflict, as these groups may feel marginalized and excluded from the political process.

Thirdly, politics without ethics can lead to a lack of accountability. In democratic societies, politicians are expected to be accountable to the people they represent. This means that they are answerable for their actions and decisions, and can be held to account through democratic processes such as elections or parliamentary inquiries. However, when politicians act without ethical considerations, they are more likely to avoid accountability and evade scrutiny.

For example, if a politician engages in corrupt practices, they may seek to cover up their behavior and avoid detection. This can be done by manipulating the media, suppressing information, or engaging in other forms of deception. Similarly, if a politician abuses their power, they may seek to avoid scrutiny by suppressing opposition voices or intimidating critics. In both cases, this can result in a lack of accountability, which can further undermine the legitimacy of the political system.

Fourthly, politics without ethics can undermine the rule of law. The rule of law is a fundamental principle of democratic societies, which ensures that everyone is subject to the same laws and that those laws are enforced fairly and impartially. When politicians act without ethical considerations, they are more likely to undermine the rule of law by engaging in behavior that is illegal or unethical.

For example, if a politician engages in corrupt practices, they may be breaking the law and undermining the integrity of the legal system. Similarly, if a politician abuses their power, they may be violating the rights of individuals and undermining the impartiality of the legal system. In both cases, this can erode public trust in the rule of law and lead to a breakdown of the social contract between citizens and the state.

Finally, politics without ethics can have a negative impact on international relations. In the globalized world we live in, countries are interconnected and rely on each other for trade, security, and cooperation. When politicians act without ethical considerations, they can damage relationships with other countries, erode trust, and undermine cooperation.

For example, if a politician engages in corrupt practices that involve foreign entities, this can damage diplomatic relations and lead to a breakdown in cooperation. Similarly, if a politician engages in behavior that is seen as unethical by other countries, this can damage the reputation of the country and lead to a loss of influence on the global stage. In both cases, this can have serious consequences for national security and international relations.

In conclusion, politics without ethics is a disaster. It undermines public trust in democratic institutions, leads to the abuse of power, undermines accountability and the rule of law, and damages international relations. Ethical considerations are essential for the functioning of democratic societies and are necessary for the legitimacy of the political process. Politicians must act with integrity, honesty, and transparency, and prioritize the public good over their own interests. Only then can we build democratic societies that are sustainable, just, and inclusive.

The VIP cult is a bane of Indian democracy

The term VIP cult refers to the practice of treating individuals with elevated status as if they were above the law and entitled to special privileges. In India, the VIP culture is deeply ingrained in society and is a significant impediment to the functioning of a democracy. The VIP cult represents a significant challenge to the principles of equality, justice, and fairness that form the bedrock of democratic governance. This essay argues that the VIP cult is a bane of Indian democracy and must be dismantled to ensure the proper functioning of a fair and just society.

The VIP cult is a byproduct of India's colonial past, where the British administration reserved special privileges for the ruling class and the wealthy elite. The culture of entitlement and special privileges was passed down to independent India, where it continued to thrive and evolve into a complex system of patronage. In India, VIPs are often treated as if they are above the law and entitled to special privileges, including the use of red beacons on their vehicles, the right to bypass traffic rules and regulations, and access to special services in hospitals, airports, and other public places.

The VIP culture is a significant impediment to the functioning of a democratic society. It creates a sense of inequality among the citizens, where certain individuals are treated as if they are more important than others. This sense of entitlement leads to a disregard for the rule of law and a culture of impunity, where VIPs are often not held accountable for their actions. The VIP culture creates an environment where power and privilege are concentrated in the hands of a few, rather than being dispersed throughout society. This concentration of power leads to a lack of accountability and transparency, which is a fundamental requirement for democratic governance.

One of the most visible manifestations of the VIP cult is the use of red beacons on vehicles. The use of red beacons is a symbol of power and privilege and is often used by politicians, bureaucrats, and other VIPs to signal their elevated status. The use of red beacons not only creates a sense of inequality among the citizens but also leads to traffic congestion and other problems on the roads. The use of red beacons is a clear violation of traffic rules and regulations, yet VIPs continue to use them with impunity.

The VIP culture also leads to the misuse of public resources. VIPs often enjoy access to special services in hospitals, airports, and other public places. This access is often at the expense of the common citizen, who is forced to wait in long queues and suffer inconvenience. The misuse of public resources creates a sense of injustice and inequality among the citizens and erodes trust in democratic institutions.

The VIP culture also leads to a culture of sycophancy, where individuals are often judged by their proximity to VIPs rather than their merit or abilities. This culture of sycophancy creates a sense of insecurity among the citizens and erodes the quality of public discourse. It also leads to a lack of diversity and innovation in public life, as individuals who are not part of the inner circle are often excluded from decision-making processes.

The VIP culture also leads to a lack of accountability and transparency in public life. VIPs often enjoy access to special privileges and exemptions, which are not available to the common citizen. This lack of accountability leads to a culture of impunity, where VIPs are often not held accountable for their actions. It also leads to a lack of transparency in public decision-making, which is a fundamental requirement for democratic governance.

The VIP culture is a significant impediment to the functioning of a democratic society. It creates a sense of inequality among the citizens and leads to a lack of accountability and transparency in public life. The VIP culture must be dismantled to ensure the proper functioning of a fair and just society. This can be achieved through a combination of legal and social reforms.

Legal reforms

The legal reforms required to dismantle the VIP culture include the removal of red beacons on vehicles, the strict enforcement of traffic rules and regulations, and the provision of equal access to public resources. The use of red beacons should be strictly prohibited, and any violation should be met with severe penalties. The provision of special services to VIPs should be eliminated, and equal access to public resources should be ensured for all citizens.

Social reforms

In addition to legal reforms, social reforms are also required to dismantle the VIP culture. These include a change in mindset and attitudes towards VIPs, the promotion of merit-based decision-making, and the fostering of a culture of accountability and transparency.

The change in mindset and attitudes towards VIPs requires a shift from the culture of entitlement to one of responsibility. VIPs must be held accountable for their actions, and their privilege must be earned, not assumed. The promotion of merit-based decision-making requires a focus on the abilities and qualifications of individuals rather than their proximity to VIPs. This can be achieved through the promotion of diversity and inclusion in decision-making processes.

The fostering of a culture of accountability and transparency requires the implementation of mechanisms to ensure that public officials are held accountable for their actions. This can be achieved through the establishment of independent institutions, such as anti-corruption agencies and ombudsmen, and the provision of mechanisms for citizen engagement and oversight.

Conclusion

In conclusion, the VIP culture is a bane of Indian democracy and must be dismantled to ensure the proper functioning of a fair and just society. The VIP culture creates a sense of inequality among citizens and leads to a lack of accountability and transparency in public life. To dismantle the VIP culture, legal and social reforms are required, including the removal of red beacons on vehicles, the provision of equal access to public resources, a change in mindset and attitudes towards VIPs, the promotion of merit-based decision-making, and the fostering of a culture of accountability and transparency. By implementing these reforms, India can move towards a more equitable, just, and democratic society, where all citizens are treated equally, and the rule of law is upheld.

Need for transparency in public administration

Transparency is a crucial element in public administration. It implies openness, accountability, and the provision of information to the public. The need for transparency in public administration cannot be overstated. It is essential for building trust, ensuring fairness, and enhancing the effectiveness of public policies and programs. In this essay, we will explore the importance of transparency in public administration, its benefits, and real-life examples.

The need for transparency in public administration is driven by several factors. Firstly, public administration is responsible for delivering essential services to the public, and the public has a right to know how these services are delivered and how their tax dollars are being spent. Secondly, transparency is essential for holding public officials accountable for their actions. Without transparency, it is difficult to identify and address corruption, waste, and inefficiency in public administration. Finally, transparency is essential for building trust between the government and the public. When the public has access to information about government operations, they are more likely to trust and support their government.

One of the benefits of transparency in public administration is that it promotes accountability. When government officials are aware that their actions and decisions are subject to public scrutiny, they are more likely to act in the public interest and make decisions that are in line with their mandate. For example, in India, the Right to Information Act (RTI) was enacted in 2005 to promote transparency and accountability in government operations. The RTI allows citizens to request information from government departments and agencies and has been effective in holding officials accountable for their actions.

Transparency also enhances the effectiveness of public policies and programs. When the public has access to information about government operations, they are better able to understand and evaluate the effectiveness of public policies and programs. This information can then be used to improve and refine these policies and programs to better serve the needs of the public. For example, in the United States, the Environmental Protection Agency (EPA) publishes data on air quality that is accessible to the public. This information has been used to develop policies and regulations to improve air quality and protect public health.

Transparency is also essential for building trust between the government and the public. When the public has access to information about government operations, they are more likely to trust their government and support its policies and programs. This trust is essential for effective governance and can help to promote social cohesion and stability. For example, in Iceland, the government has implemented an open government initiative to promote transparency and participation in government operations. This initiative has helped to build trust between the government and the public and has contributed to Iceland's reputation as one of the least corrupt countries in the world.

However, achieving transparency in public administration is not always easy. There are several challenges that must be overcome. One of the biggest challenges is resistance from government officials who may be reluctant to share information with the public. This resistance may be due to concerns about privacy, security, or the potential for political backlash. Another challenge is the lack of resources and capacity to implement transparency measures. In many developing countries, for example, government agencies may lack the resources and infrastructure to provide information to the public.

Despite these challenges, there are many examples of successful efforts to promote transparency in public administration. In Brazil, for example, the government implemented the Transparency Portal, which provides information on government spending and contracts. This initiative has been successful in promoting accountability and has been widely praised by civil society organizations. In South Africa, the Promotion of Access to Information Act (PAIA) was enacted in 2000 to promote transparency in government operations. The PAIA has been effective in holding government officials accountable and has contributed to South Africa's reputation as one of the most transparent countries in Africa.

In conclusion, transparency is a crucial element in public administration. It promotes accountability, enhances the effectiveness of public policies and programs, and builds trust between the government and the public. However, achieving transparency in public administration requires overcoming several challenges, including resistance from government officials and a lack of resources and capacity. Despite these challenges, there are many examples of successful efforts to promote transparency in public administration, such as the Transparency Portal in Brazil and the Promotion of Access to Information Act in South Africa. It is essential that governments continue to prioritize transparency in their operations and policies to ensure that they are accountable to the public and are able to effectively serve their needs and interests. As former US President Barack Obama once said, "Transparency and the rule of law will be the touchstones of this presidency."

The country's need for a better disaster management system

Disasters have always been a significant challenge for India, with a diverse range of environmental, industrial, and man-made hazards. From earthquakes to floods and from industrial accidents to terrorist attacks, India has faced multiple disasters in recent years, resulting in significant loss of life and property damage. The need for a better disaster management system in India is urgent, and the government and the public must work together to build a robust system that can mitigate the impact of disasters and save lives.

The current disaster management system in India is primarily reactive, with little emphasis on prevention and mitigation. However, the government has made some significant efforts in recent years to improve the country's disaster management infrastructure. The National Disaster Management Authority (NDMA) was established in 2005 to formulate policies and plans for disaster management. The NDMA has been working with the state governments to establish State Disaster Management Authorities (SDMAs) and District Disaster Management Authorities (DDMAs) to improve the disaster management infrastructure at the local level.

In 2019, the NDMA also released the National Disaster Management Plan (NDMP), a comprehensive document that outlines the country's approach to disaster management. The NDMP includes a range of measures, such as risk assessment, early warning systems, response plans, and recovery strategies. The plan is aimed at improving the country's overall disaster resilience and minimizing the impact of disasters on the population and the economy.

Parameter	International Best Practices	India
Early Warning System	Most countries have established early warning systems that use various technologies such as satellites, radars, and ground sensors to provide advance warning of disasters. Some countries even use social media platforms to disseminate information.	India has made significant strides in establishing early warning systems, especially in the case of cyclones. The Indian Meteorological Department (IMD) uses various technologies such as Doppler radars and satellite imagery to provide advance warning of cyclones. However, there is still room for improvement in the early warning system for other types of disasters such as earthquakes and landslides.
Preparedness	Most countries have comprehensive disaster preparedness plans that include preventive measures, response plans, and evacuation plans. The plans are regularly updated based on the latest data and developments. The plans involve all stakeholders, including government agencies, NGOs, and the private sector.	India has made significant progress in disaster preparedness in recent years, particularly in the case of cyclones and floods. The National Disaster Management Plan (NDMP) provides a comprehensive framework for disaster preparedness, response, and recovery. However, there are still gaps in the preparedness plans, and more needs to be done to involve all stakeholders.
Response	Most countries have well-equipped and well-trained disaster response teams that can quickly deploy to the affected areas. The response teams are trained in search and rescue, medical aid, and	India has established various response teams, including the National Disaster Response Force (NDRF), which is a specialized force trained in search and rescue operations. However, there have

Parameter	International Best Practices	India
	psychological support.	been instances where the response teams were not able to deploy quickly due to various reasons such as lack of resources and coordination issues.
Recovery	Most countries have comprehensive recovery plans that focus on rebuilding infrastructure, providing medical aid, and psychological support to the affected population. The plans involve all stakeholders, including government agencies, NGOs, and the private sector.	India has made some progress in the recovery phase of disaster management, particularly in the case of the 2018 Kerala floods. The government provided financial assistance to the flood victims, and the public contributed through donations and volunteer work. However, there are still gaps in the recovery plans, and more needs to be done to involve all stakeholders.
Education and Awareness	Most countries conduct regular education and awareness programs to keep the public informed about disaster management. The programs involve all stakeholders, including government agencies, NGOs, and the private sector.	India has established the National Institute of Disaster Management (NIDM), which provides training and education to government officials, NGOs, and the public on various aspects of disaster management. However, more needs to be done to conduct regular awareness programs and involve all stakeholders in the process.

Overall, while India has made significant strides in disaster management, there is still room for improvement in all five parameters. Learning from international best practices and involving all stakeholders in the process can help India build a more robust disaster management system.

Preparedness is a critical aspect of India's disaster management system. The country is prone to multiple natural disasters, including floods, cyclones, earthquakes, and landslides. The government must develop comprehensive disaster preparedness plans that include preventive measures, response plans, and evacuation plans. For instance, during the recent cyclone Tauktae, the government successfully evacuated over one lakh people from the affected areas, which prevented significant loss of life.

Education and awareness are also essential in disaster management. The public must be educated on how to respond to disasters and the measures they can take to protect themselves and their families. The government must also conduct regular awareness programs to keep the public informed about the latest developments in disaster management. For example, the government has established a National Institute of Disaster Management (NIDM) that provides training and education to government officials, NGOs, and the public on various aspects of disaster management.

The private sector must also be involved in disaster management in India. The government must work with private companies to ensure that critical infrastructure like hospitals, power stations, and communication networks are built to withstand disasters. The private sector can also contribute by providing resources and expertise in disaster management. For instance, during the COVID-19 pandemic, several private companies in India contributed to the country's relief efforts by providing medical equipment, PPE kits, and other essential supplies.

In addition to preparedness, response and recovery are also critical components of India's disaster management system. The response must be swift and effective to save lives and minimize damage. The recovery phase must focus on rebuilding infrastructure, providing medical aid, and psychological support to the affected population. For instance, during the 2018 Kerala floods, the government and the public worked together to provide relief and rehabilitation to the affected population. The government provided financial assistance to the flood victims, and the public contributed through donations and volunteer work.

In conclusion, disasters are an ever-present threat in India, and a robust disaster management system is essential for the country's safety and development. The system must be proactive, focusing on prevention, preparedness, response, and recovery. The disaster management agencies must be well-equipped and well-trained to respond quickly and efficiently to disasters. Education and awareness programs must be conducted regularly to keep the public informed about disaster management. The private sector must also be involved in disaster management, providing resources and expertise. A better disaster management system is not an option; it is a necessity for the country's safety and development.

How should a civil servant conduct himself?

Civil services reform has been a topic of discussion in India for several decades. Various committees have been formed to make recommendations on how to improve the functioning of the civil services. The recommendations of these committees have highlighted the need for civil servants to conduct themselves in a manner that is ethical, accountable, and transparent.

The Second Administrative Reforms Commission (ARC) recommended that civil servants should maintain high standards of personal integrity and professional competence. The ARC also suggested that civil servants should be held accountable for their actions and decisions. The report states, "The civil service should be characterised by a high level of integrity, professionalism, accountability, and transparency. Its members should be motivated by public service and imbued with the highest ethical values."

The Fourth Pay Commission report recommended that civil servants should maintain political neutrality and should not be influenced by political considerations. The report states, "Civil servants should function as neutral instruments of the state, free from any political considerations or influences. They should serve the government of the day with impartiality and objectivity."

The recommendations of the various committees are reflected in the conduct rules for civil servants in India. The All India Service (Conduct) Rules, 1968, prescribe the standards of conduct for civil servants. The rules require civil servants to maintain high standards of integrity and honesty, avoid any conflict of interest, and maintain political neutrality. The rules also require civil servants to maintain confidentiality and respect the privacy of individuals.

In addition to the conduct rules, various quotes highlight the importance of civil servants' conduct. Mahatma Gandhi once said, "The difference between what we do and what we are capable of doing would suffice to solve most of the world's problems." This quote emphasizes the need for civil servants to strive for excellence in their work.

Another quote by Jawaharlal Nehru, India's first Prime Minister, states, "The civil service is the backbone of the state." This quote highlights the crucial role that civil servants play in the functioning of the government.
Given this context, the question as to, How should a civil servant conduct himself? Can be answered as follows.
Firstly, civil servants should act in the best interests of the public. This means that they should be impartial, objective and fair in the discharge of their duties. Civil servants should not show favouritism or bias towards any particular individual or group and should strive to serve all members of the public equally. They should always act with integrity and ensure that their decisions are based on merit and the best available evidence.

Secondly, civil servants should be accountable for their actions and decisions. They should be transparent about their decision-making processes and be willing to explain their decisions to the public. Civil servants should also be open to feedback and criticism and be willing to learn from their mistakes. They should maintain accurate records of their work and ensure that these records are accessible to the public.

Thirdly, civil servants should maintain high standards of professionalism and conduct. They should treat all members of the public with respect and dignity and avoid any behaviour that could be construed as harassment or discrimination. Civil servants should also maintain confidentiality and ensure that any information they handle is kept secure and not shared inappropriately.

Fourthly, civil servants should be politically neutral. They should not express their personal political views or engage in political activities that could compromise their impartiality. Civil servants should also avoid any actions or statements that could be perceived as partisan or biased towards any political party or group.

Fifthly, civil servants should be competent and committed to their work. They should have the necessary skills and knowledge to carry out their duties effectively and efficiently. Civil servants should also be proactive and take the initiative to identify and address issues that may arise in the course of their work. They should be willing to work collaboratively with colleagues and stakeholders and seek out opportunities for professional development.

Lastly, civil servants should be aware of their legal and ethical obligations. They should familiarize themselves with the laws and regulations that govern their work and ensure that they always comply with these laws. Civil servants should also be aware of the ethical standards.

In conclusion, the conduct of civil servants in India is governed by various rules and regulations. The recommendations of various committees have emphasized the importance of civil servants maintaining high standards of integrity, professionalism, accountability, and transparency. By conducting themselves in a manner that reflects these values, civil servants can build trust and confidence in the government and the public they serve. As Mahatma Gandhi said, "Be the change you want to see in the world." Civil servants can lead by example and inspire others to follow suit.

Democracy/India since independence

1. Whither Indian democracy? (1995)

2. What we have not learnt during fifty years of independence. (1997)

3. Why should we be proud of being Indians? (2000)

4. What have we gained from our democratic set-up? (2001)

5. How far has democracy in India delivered the goods? (2003)

6. National identity and patriotism. (2008)

7. In the context of Gandhiji's views on the matter, explore, on an evolutionary scale, the terms 'Swadhinata', 'Swaraj' and 'Dharmarajya'. Critically comment on their contemporary relevance to Indian democracy. (2012)

8. Is the colonial mentality hindering India's success? (2013)

9. Dreams which should not let India sleep. (2015)

10. Management of Indian border disputes – a complex task. (2018)

ADDITIONAL INPUTS

DEMOCRACY

Democracy is a system of government in which power is vested in the people, who exercise it either directly or through elected representatives. It is characterized by the principles of political equality, popular sovereignty, and majority rule. In a democratic society, the government is accountable to the people and operates with their consent.

The term "democracy" comes from the Greek words "demos," meaning "people," and "kratos," meaning "rule" or "power." Thus, democracy literally means "rule by the people." It is a system that prioritizes the participation and involvement of citizens in decision-making processes that affect their lives.

Key elements of democracy include:

1. Political participation: Citizens have the right to participate in the political process through voting, expressing their opinions, joining political parties, and engaging in peaceful assembly and protest.

2. Rule of law: The principles of equality before the law, due process, and protection of individual rights and freedoms are fundamental in a democratic system. No one is above the law, including government officials.

3. Protection of human rights: Democracies respect and protect the basic human rights of individuals, including freedom of speech, assembly, religion, and the press. Minority rights are also safeguarded to ensure that all members of society are treated fairly and with dignity.

4. Free and fair elections: Democratic societies hold regular elections that are free, fair, and transparent. Elections provide a mechanism for citizens to choose their representatives and hold them accountable.

5. Pluralism and tolerance: Democratic systems embrace diversity and promote tolerance and inclusivity. They allow for the existence of multiple political parties, viewpoints, and peaceful coexistence of various social, cultural, and religious groups.

6. Peaceful transfer of power: In a democracy, the transfer of power occurs through peaceful means, typically through elections. This ensures stability and continuity in governance.

It's important to note that democracy can take different forms and vary in practice across different countries. The specific structures and institutions may differ, but the core principles of popular participation, political equality, and accountability remain central to democracy.

5 QUOTES ON DEMOCRACY

1. "Democracy is not just a political system, but a way of life that empowers individuals, respects their freedoms, and ensures their participation in shaping the collective future." - Unknown
2. "Democracy is not simply a 'majority rules' system; it is a delicate balance of rights and responsibilities, where the voices of all citizens are heard and valued." - Franklin D. Roosevelt
3. "In a democracy, the will of the people is the ultimate source of authority, and it is our duty as citizens to protect and uphold the principles of justice, equality, and freedom." - John F. Kennedy
4. "Democracy is not a spectator sport. It requires active participation, informed engagement, and a commitment to the common good." - Barack Obama
5. "Democracy is the art of thinking independently together." - Alexander Meiklejohn

5 ANECDOTES ON DEMOCRACY

1. The Swiss Consensus: In Switzerland, a country known for its direct democracy, citizens have the power to propose changes to the constitution through referendums. In 2014, a proposal to cap executive salaries at 12 times the lowest employee's salary was put forth. Surprisingly, the majority of Swiss voters rejected the proposal, highlighting the value they place on individual freedom and the limited role of government in regulating the private sector.

2. The Birth of a Democracy: The establishment of democracy in South Africa after the end of apartheid is a remarkable anecdote. In 1994, the country held its first multiracial democratic elections. Despite the deep-rooted racial tensions and historical injustices, millions of South Africans from different ethnic backgrounds stood in long queues for hours, eager to exercise their right to vote. This peaceful transition of power demonstrated the power of democracy to bring about positive change and reconciliation.

3. The Power of the People: In 1986, the People Power Revolution in the Philippines showcased the strength of a united citizenry. Fueled by widespread public discontent with the authoritarian rule of President Ferdinand Marcos, millions of Filipinos took to the streets in peaceful protests. The movement eventually led to Marcos's ousting and the restoration of democracy. This anecdote emphasizes the potential of people's collective action to challenge oppressive regimes and bring about political transformation.

4. Democracy's Challenges: The complexities of democracy are evident in the difficulties faced by countries transitioning from autocracy. For instance, following the Arab Spring uprisings in 2011, several Middle Eastern nations embarked on a path towards democracy. However, the subsequent power struggles, instability, and setbacks in countries like Egypt, Libya, and Yemen highlighted the challenges of building functional democratic institutions and fostering social cohesion.

5. The Role of Civil Society: Civil society organizations often play a pivotal role in upholding democracy and promoting civic engagement. A striking example is the Velvet Revolution in Czechoslovakia in 1989. The dissident playwright Václav Havel and a coalition of intellectuals and activists spearheaded a peaceful protest movement against the communist regime. Through their advocacy and organizing, they pressured the government to relinquish power, leading to the establishment of a democratic Czechoslovakia. This anecdote underscores the power of organized civil society in driving democratic change.

Whither Indian democracy?

Introduction

India, known as the world's largest democracy, has recently faced challenges regarding its democratic values, civil liberties, and the treatment of minorities and dissenters. This essay will assess the current state of Indian democracy, analyzing its strengths and weaknesses, the obstacles it encounters, and the potential pathways for its future.

The Strengths of Indian Democracy

Indian democracy possesses inherent strengths that have enabled its longevity and growth over the past seven decades. One key strength is its resilience, evident in the peaceful transitions of power between different political entities. Throughout its history, ruling parties have been replaced by opposition parties through free and fair elections, signifying the stability and endurance of the democratic system.

Another crucial aspect is the diversity and pluralism within Indian democracy. India's Constitution guarantees fundamental rights and freedoms to all citizens, irrespective of their background or identity. Various affirmative action measures have been implemented to address historical inequalities, ensuring inclusivity and social justice.

The presence of a vibrant civil society, encompassing media outlets, non-governmental organizations (NGOs), and activist groups, constitutes another pillar of Indian democracy. These entities hold the government accountable, advocate for human rights, and contribute to the development of social justice. The judiciary, although facing its own challenges, has played a vital role in upholding the rule of law and acting as a check on executive power.

Challenges to Indian Democracy

Despite its strengths, Indian democracy confronts several significant challenges that undermine its progress and legitimacy. One pressing challenge is the rise of majoritarianism and religious nationalism, which has been fostered by certain political movements. This ideology promotes an exclusionary vision of India based on a dominant religious identity, leading to marginalization and discrimination against minority groups, particularly Muslims. Instances of hate speech, communal violence, and targeted violence against minority communities have escalated.

Another challenge lies in the erosion of civil liberties and free speech. There has been a noticeable crackdown on dissent, resulting in censorship and increased surveillance. Journalists, activists, and academics critical of the government have faced harassment, arrests, and, in extreme cases, violence. This curtails the space for diverse opinions and independent media.

Moreover, the autonomy and impartiality of institutions such as the judiciary, the Election Commission, and the Reserve Bank of India have come under scrutiny. Accusations of political interference have raised concerns about the independence and integrity of these institutions.

Socio-economic issues also pose significant challenges to Indian democracy. Poverty, inequality, corruption, and environmental degradation persist despite the government's implementation of social welfare schemes and economic reforms. The effectiveness and reach of these initiatives have been called into question, raising concerns about their impact on marginalized communities.

Prospects for Indian Democracy

Despite these challenges, there are reasons to remain hopeful about the future of Indian democracy. The emergence of a robust opposition, comprising regional parties, civil society groups, and student movements, presents an encouraging development. This diverse opposition challenges the dominance of any single party, offering alternative visions of governance and development.

Recent state elections have demonstrated that electoral victories are not monopolized by a single party. Opposition parties have successfully united and mobilized popular support, providing an effective counterbalance.

Additionally, the ongoing farmers' protests against the controversial farm laws have galvanized a nationwide movement advocating for social justice and economic rights. This collective action, involving farmers, laborers, and civil society, highlights the demand for a fairer and more equitable system.

Moreover, Indian democracy benefits from an active and engaged citizenry. The digital revolution has facilitated greater access to information, amplifying voices that hold power to account. Social media platforms have become essential tools for organizing and mobilizing public opinion.

Conclusion

Indian democracy possesses inherent strengths, such as resilience, diversity, and a vibrant civil society. However, it also faces challenges concerning majoritarianism, erosion of civil

liberties, institutional autonomy, and socio-economic issues. Nevertheless, the emergence of a strong opposition, successful state elections, and mass movements advocating for justice and equality present opportunities for the future of Indian democracy. Through continued efforts to address these challenges, India can strive towards a more inclusive, accountable, and robust democratic system.

What We Have Not Learnt During 75 Years of Independence

Introduction:
India celebrated its 75th year of independence recently, marking a significant milestone in its journey as a nation. Over the past seven and a half decades, India has made remarkable progress in various spheres. However, it is crucial to reflect on the areas where we have fallen short, the lessons that remain unlearned, and the challenges that persist despite the passage of time. This essay explores the Indian context and examines what we have not learnt during 75 years of independence.

1. Social Inequality and Caste System:
Despite constitutional provisions and efforts to address social inequality, the Indian society continues to grapple with deep-rooted caste discrimination. The caste system, which was supposed to have been eradicated, still influences social interactions, access to resources, and opportunities. The failure to eliminate this system and ensure equal treatment for all citizens remains a significant shortcoming.

2. Gender Equality and Women's Empowerment:
While progress has been made in recognizing women's rights and promoting gender equality, several challenges persist. Gender-based violence, unequal access to education and healthcare, and limited representation in political and economic spheres are areas where progress has been slow. Bridging the gender gap and empowering women in all aspects of society is an ongoing struggle that demands renewed commitment.

3. Education and Skill Development:
Despite significant strides in improving literacy rates, the quality of education remains a concern. Educational institutions, especially in rural areas, lack adequate infrastructure, qualified teachers, and learning resources. Furthermore, the focus on rote learning rather than critical thinking and practical skills hampers the holistic development of students. Enhancing the education system and promoting skill development are imperative for a prosperous and inclusive future.

4. Healthcare and Public Health:
Access to quality healthcare remains a challenge for a vast segment of the Indian population. Disparities in healthcare infrastructure, inadequate funding, and the absence of a robust public health system have been amplified during the COVID-19 pandemic. There is a pressing need to invest in healthcare, strengthen primary healthcare centers, and ensure affordable and equitable access to medical facilities and services.

5. Environmental Conservation and Sustainable Development:
India's rapid economic growth has come at a significant environmental cost. The country faces numerous environmental challenges, including pollution, deforestation, water scarcity, and climate change. While efforts have been made to address these issues, they often fall short due to insufficient implementation and enforcement of policies. Promoting sustainable development practices, renewable energy, and environmental conservation should be prioritized for a greener and healthier future.

6. Corruption and Governance:

Corruption continues to be a pervasive problem in India, affecting governance and hindering socio-economic progress. Despite the establishment of anti-corruption bodies and the implementation of initiatives like digitization and transparency measures, corrupt practices persist at various levels. Strengthening anti-corruption mechanisms, ensuring accountability, and fostering a culture of ethical governance are essential for sustainable development.

7. Infrastructure Development:

India's infrastructure development has witnessed notable progress, but significant gaps persist, particularly in rural areas. Inadequate road networks, unreliable power supply, and deficient sanitation facilities continue to impede progress. Expanding and upgrading infrastructure, especially in marginalized regions, is crucial for inclusive growth and improving the quality of life for all citizens.

8. Communal Harmony and Religious Tolerance:

India's diverse society has a long-standing history of communal harmony and religious coexistence. However, instances of communal violence and religious tensions continue to threaten social fabric. The need to promote religious tolerance, respect diverse beliefs, and foster communal harmony remains a critical lesson yet to be fully learned.

Conclusion:

As India celebrates 75 years of independence, it is essential to critically evaluate the lessons that remain unlearned. The issues of social inequality, gender inequality, education, healthcare, environmental conservation, corruption, infrastructure development, and communal harmony require renewed focus and concerted efforts. Addressing these challenges will contribute to a more inclusive, equitable, and prosperous India. It is crucial to learn from past shortcomings, implement effective policies, and empower citizens to shape a better future for the nation. Only through collective action and a commitment to learning can India truly realize the ideals envisioned by its founding fathers.

Why should we be proud of being Indians?

Alt Title: Embracing Indian Identity: A Celebration of Our Heritage and Achievements
India, with its rich cultural tapestry, diverse traditions, and remarkable achievements throughout history, is a nation that inspires admiration and pride among its people. The question of why we should be proud of being Indians is multifaceted, encompassing various aspects that make our nation truly unique. This essay aims to explore and celebrate the reasons that evoke a sense of pride and honour in our Indian identity.

Cultural Heritage and Diversity:

India's cultural heritage is a mosaic of ancient civilizations, traditions, and religions that have coexisted harmoniously for centuries. The country's cultural diversity is an invaluable asset, offering a multitude of languages, art forms, music, and dances. From the vibrant festivals of Diwali, Holi, and Eid to the classical dance forms of Bharatanatyam and Kathak, our cultural heritage is a testament to the richness and vibrancy of Indian civilization. This diversity serves as a source of pride, as it reflects the inclusivity and acceptance that define our nation.

Historical Contributions:

India's history is marked by remarkable contributions in various fields. From the invention of zero and the decimal system to the development of algebra and trigonometry, Indian mathematicians laid the foundation for modern mathematics. The ancient universities of Nalanda and Takshashila were renowned centers of learning, attracting scholars from across the world. The teachings of ancient Indian philosophers like Buddha and Mahavira influenced not only the Indian subcontinent but also had a profound impact on the global philosophical landscape. India's historical contributions in the fields of medicine, astronomy, and metallurgy further highlight our rich intellectual heritage.

Struggle for Independence:

The long and arduous struggle for independence under the leadership of Mahatma Gandhi and other freedom fighters is a testament to the indomitable spirit of the Indian people. The non-violent resistance movement of civil disobedience and satyagraha inspired people around the world, shaping the course of history. The sacrifices made by individuals like Bhagat Singh, Subhash Chandra Bose, and countless others to secure our nation's freedom evoke a deep sense of pride and gratitude. The principles of justice, equality, and democracy that underpinned this struggle remain foundational to India's identity as a democratic nation.

Unity in Diversity:

India's ability to maintain unity in the face of its immense diversity is a remarkable achievement. With over a thousand languages spoken and a multitude of ethnic and religious communities, India stands as a shining example of tolerance and pluralism. Our Constitution enshrines the principles of secularism and equal rights for all citizens, ensuring that no individual or group is marginalized based on their identity. The celebration of festivals, traditions, and cuisines from various regions of the country fosters a sense of unity among Indians, transcending boundaries and uniting us in our shared heritage.

Economic Growth and Innovation:

In recent decades, India has made significant strides in economic growth and technological innovation. With a rapidly expanding middle class, a thriving IT industry, and advancements in space research, India has emerged as a global economic powerhouse. The "Make in India" initiative and successful space missions like Chandrayaan and Mangalyaan have showcased India's capabilities on the international stage. These achievements fill us with pride and inspire the younger generation to strive for excellence, further propelling our nation's progress.

Global Influence and Soft Power:

India's cultural influence extends far beyond its borders. Yoga, Ayurveda, and Indian cuisine have gained popularity worldwide, becoming symbols of our country's soft power. Bollywood, our vibrant film industry, has captivated audiences around the globe, showcasing Indian storytelling and talent. The influence of Indian diaspora, with their accomplishments in various fields, further amplifies India's presence on the global stage. India's leadership in international forums and its commitment to peacekeeping efforts reflect our nation's responsible engagement with the world.

Challenges and Resilience:

Acknowledging our challenges is essential in understanding the strength of our Indian identity. Issues such as poverty, inequality, gender disparity, and environmental concerns demand our attention and collective effort. However, it is precisely in our resilience and determination to address these challenges that our pride as Indians is fueled. The commitment of countless individuals, civil society organizations, and government initiatives to uplift marginalized communities and create a more equitable society reflects our unwavering spirit and the belief in a brighter future.

Conclusion:

Being proud of being Indian encompasses embracing our cultural heritage, recognizing our historical contributions, and celebrating the values that bind us together as a nation. It is about cherishing our diversity, acknowledging our accomplishments, and striving for a more inclusive and prosperous society. India's journey as a nation has been one of resilience, progress, and unity. By recognizing and appreciating our Indian identity, we not only honour our past but also shape our future, making India a nation we can be proud of for generations to come.

What have we gained from our democratic set-up?

Alt Title: The Gains of India's Democratic Setup: Empowering the People, Safeguarding Rights, and Fostering Development

Introduction (150 words):
India's democratic system of governance has brought about significant gains, empowering its citizens, upholding fundamental rights, and fostering socio-economic development. This essay examines the unique benefits derived from India's democratic setup. By exploring key aspects such as political participation, protection of human rights, and inclusive development, we can better appreciate the strides made by Indian democracy in creating an empowered and progressive society.

Political Participation and Empowerment (250 words):
India's democratic setup has provided its citizens with immense opportunities for political participation and empowerment. Through regular elections, citizens exercise their right to vote, choosing representatives who will shape the nation's destiny. This enables accountability and ensures that elected officials remain connected to the aspirations and needs of the people. Beyond elections, democratic freedoms such as freedom of speech, assembly, and association empower citizens to express their views, challenge policies, and engage in peaceful protests. These rights create an environment for robust public discourse and social progress, giving a voice to diverse perspectives.

Protection of Human Rights (300 words):
India's democratic system places a strong emphasis on protecting human rights. The Constitution guarantees fundamental rights to every individual, including freedom of expression, religion, and equality before the law. These protections ensure that citizens can express their opinions, practice their faith, and seek justice without fear of persecution. An independent judiciary acts as a crucial guardian of these rights, providing a platform for redress and upholding the principle of justice for all.

Fostering Socio-economic Development (350 words):
India's democratic setup has played a significant role in fostering socio-economic development. By creating an environment conducive to innovation, entrepreneurship, and economic freedom, democracy has fueled economic growth. The presence of transparent regulations, protection of property rights, and a free market system has attracted investment, generated employment, and driven overall prosperity.

Inclusive development has been a key focus of democratic governance in India. The government has implemented social welfare schemes such as the Mahatma Gandhi National Rural Employment Guarantee Act (MGNREGA) to address poverty and promote rural development. Education and healthcare initiatives aim to provide access to basic services for all citizens, bridging socio-economic disparities and improving quality of life.

Democratic governance in India also emphasizes accountability and transparency in the management of public resources. Initiatives like the Right to Information Act (RTI) empower citizens to access information and hold public officials accountable. These measures combat corruption, ensure efficient allocation of resources, and build public trust in the government.

Conclusion (150 words):

In conclusion, India's democratic setup has brought about substantial gains, empowering its citizens, protecting their rights, and fostering inclusive development. Through political participation, citizens have a voice in shaping the nation's future and holding their elected representatives accountable. The protection of human rights ensures individual liberties, equality before the law, and access to justice. Additionally, democratic governance has contributed to socio-economic development by encouraging innovation, providing equal opportunities, and addressing social inequalities. While challenges persist, India's democratic system continues to evolve and improve, further enhancing the gains that have been achieved. It is through the continued recognition and promotion of these gains that India can move forward as a vibrant and prosperous democratic nation.

How far has democracy in India delivered the goods?

Alt Title: Assessing the Impact of Democracy in India: Delivering the Goods and Beyond

Introduction (150 words):
India's journey as the world's largest democracy has been an intriguing and transformative one. This essay critically evaluates the extent to which democracy in India has delivered its promised benefits. By examining key indicators such as political participation, governance effectiveness, social progress, and economic development, we can better understand the achievements, challenges, and potential areas for improvement in India's democratic system.

Political Participation and Representation (250 words):
Democracy in India has succeeded in providing a platform for widespread political participation. Through free and fair elections, citizens exercise their right to vote, contributing to the selection of representatives who shape the nation's governance. This inclusive participation empowers marginalized sections of society, giving them a voice in decision-making processes. However, challenges such as low female representation and the influence of money and muscle power remain, necessitating continued efforts to enhance inclusivity.

Governance Effectiveness and Accountability (300 words):
India's democracy has played a crucial role in ensuring accountability and transparency in governance. Institutions such as the judiciary, the Comptroller and Auditor General (CAG), and the Central Vigilance Commission (CVC) act as checks and balances, holding public officials accountable for their actions. The Right to Information (RTI) Act has empowered citizens to access information, promoting transparency and reducing corruption.

However, governance effectiveness remains a challenge. Bureaucratic red tape, inadequate service delivery, and slow decision-making processes hinder the effective implementation of policies. The need for administrative reforms, streamlined procedures, and strengthened public institutions is evident for democracy to fully deliver its potential.

Social Progress and Inclusion (350 words):
Democracy in India has made significant strides in promoting social progress and inclusivity. Constitutional safeguards and affirmative action policies have aimed to uplift marginalized communities, ensuring social justice and equal opportunities. The reservation system has increased representation of historically disadvantaged groups in political bodies and public institutions.

However, societal divisions and deep-rooted inequalities persist, hindering the realization of a truly inclusive society. Caste-based discrimination, gender disparities, and religious tensions continue to challenge the democratic fabric. Fostering social cohesion, empowering marginalized communities, and promoting intercultural dialogue are vital for democracy to effectively deliver social progress for all citizens.

Economic Development and Inclusive Growth (300 words):
India's democratic setup has played a pivotal role in promoting economic development. Policies such as liberalization, foreign direct investment, and infrastructure development have attracted investment and spurred economic growth. Entrepreneurship and innovation have thrived in a democratic environment that encourages a free market system.

However, challenges remain in ensuring inclusive growth that benefits all sections of society. Economic disparities, rural-urban divides, and unequal access to resources and opportunities persist. Addressing these issues requires a comprehensive approach that emphasizes equitable distribution of wealth, rural development, and skill enhancement programs to uplift underprivileged communities.

Conclusion (150 words):
In conclusion, democracy in India has undoubtedly delivered numerous benefits to its citizens. Political participation has empowered individuals and fostered representation, ensuring diverse voices are heard in governance. Accountability mechanisms and transparency have promoted good governance and reduced corruption. Efforts to address social inequalities and promote economic development have also been noteworthy.

However, challenges persist. Strengthening inclusivity, bridging economic disparities, and ensuring effective governance remain critical areas for improvement. Enhancing the representation of marginalized groups, reducing social divisions, and addressing administrative inefficiencies are crucial steps forward.

Democracy in India has made remarkable progress, but there is still work to be done. By addressing these challenges head-on, India can continue on its path towards a more inclusive, equitable, and prosperous society, ensuring that democracy truly delivers the goods for all its citizens.

National identity and patriotism.

National identity and patriotism are complex and intertwined concepts that have a profound impact on individuals, communities, and nations. This essay delves into the interplay between national identity and patriotism, examining their definitions, manifestations, and implications. By exploring the formation of national identity, the role of patriotism in fostering unity and belonging, and the potential challenges associated with extreme nationalism, we can gain a deeper understanding of the significance and complexities of these concepts in contemporary societies.

Defining National Identity and Patriotism
National identity encompasses the shared sense of belonging, values, culture, and history that binds individuals within a nation. It is an evolving construct shaped by historical, cultural, and socio-political factors. National identity gives individuals a collective identity, influencing their attitudes, behaviors, and sense of belonging.

Patriotism, on the other hand, refers to the love, loyalty, and devotion towards one's country. It entails a deep attachment to the values, principles, and aspirations of the nation, and a willingness to contribute to its well-being. Patriotism often manifests through symbolic acts, such as displaying national symbols, participating in national events, and defending the nation's interests.

The Role of Patriotism in Fostering Unity and Belonging
Patriotism plays a crucial role in fostering unity and a sense of belonging within a nation. It serves as a unifying force that transcends individual differences, forging a collective identity and shared purpose. By celebrating national achievements, historical milestones, and cultural heritage, patriotism helps cultivate a sense of pride and belonging among citizens.

Patriotic sentiments also contribute to social cohesion and national integration. When individuals identify with their nation and feel a sense of loyalty towards it, they are more likely to cooperate, participate in civic activities, and contribute to the overall well-being of society. Patriotism can inspire citizens to work towards common goals, engage in community service, and uphold democratic values and institutions.

Challenges of Extreme Nationalism
While patriotism can foster unity and a sense of belonging, extreme forms of nationalism can pose challenges and have negative implications. Extreme nationalism often involves an exaggerated sense of superiority, exclusivity, and the suppression of dissenting voices. It can lead to the marginalization or discrimination of minority groups, hinder social cohesion, and perpetuate divisions within society.

Furthermore, extreme nationalism can give rise to aggressive or expansionist tendencies, potentially leading to conflicts or strained international relations. When patriotism turns into jingoism, it may fuel xenophobia, intolerance, and a disregard for the rights and dignity of others.

Balancing National Identity and Global Citizenship
The concept of national identity and patriotism must be balanced with the recognition of global citizenship and interconnectedness. In an increasingly interconnected world, it is crucial to foster a sense of belonging not only to one's nation but also to humanity as a whole. Embracing global citizenship allows individuals to recognize shared values, promote peace, and address global challenges such as climate change, poverty, and inequality.

Promoting a healthy sense of national identity entails embracing diversity, respecting individual rights, and acknowledging the contributions of various cultures and communities within the nation. A balanced approach encourages a sense of pride in one's heritage while appreciating and learning from other cultures.

Conclusion

National identity and patriotism are integral to the fabric of society, shaping individual and collective identities. Patriotism, when practiced responsibly, fosters unity, social cohesion, and a shared commitment to the well-being of the nation. However, it is essential to strike a balance between national identity and global citizenship, ensuring that patriotism does not lead to exclusion, division, or hostility towards others. By embracing diversity, upholding democratic values, and fostering a sense of global responsibility, societies can cultivate a healthy national identity that celebrates inclusivity, peace, and cooperation on a global scale.

In the context of Gandhiji's views on the matter, explore, on an evolutionary scale, the terms 'Swadhinata', 'Swaraj' and 'Dharmarajya'. Critically comment on their contemporary relevance to Indian democracy

Introduction:
In the struggle for India's independence, Mahatma Gandhi espoused several concepts that served as guiding principles for the freedom movement. Among these, 'Swadhinata,' 'Swaraj,' and 'Dharmarajya' hold significant importance. These terms, when examined on an evolutionary scale, reveal the evolving aspirations of Indian democracy. This essay critically explores Gandhiji's views on these concepts and assesses their contemporary relevance to Indian democracy.

Swadhinata - The Pursuit of Independence:
'Swadhinata' encompasses the idea of freedom and self-determination. According to Gandhiji, true freedom could only be achieved through non-violent means and by embracing self-sufficiency. He envisioned Swaraj as a state where Indians would not be dependent on foreign powers for their economic, political, and cultural well-being. Gandhiji's emphasis on self-reliance and the revitalization of traditional crafts and industries aimed to empower individuals and local communities, fostering a sense of self-respect and dignity.

In the contemporary context of Indian democracy, the idea of 'Swadhinata' remains relevant. Despite gaining independence, India still faces challenges such as socio-economic inequality, political corruption, and external influences. To realize the true essence of 'Swadhinata,' it is imperative to address these challenges by promoting sustainable development, reducing dependency, and nurturing indigenous industries. Emphasizing self-reliance and empowering marginalized communities would help to strengthen the foundations of Indian democracy.

Swaraj - Self-Governance and Decentralization:
'Swaraj' embodies the concept of self-governance, where individuals and communities have the right to participate in decision-making processes that affect their lives. Gandhiji believed in the decentralization of power, advocating for local self-governance structures such as Panchayati Raj. He envisioned a society where political power was distributed among the masses, enabling them to shape their own destiny.

The relevance of 'Swaraj' in the contemporary Indian democracy is undeniable. While India has made significant strides in establishing democratic institutions, there is still a need for greater decentralization and grassroots participation. Empowering local governance structures and ensuring their autonomy can address the democratic deficit often observed in top-down decision-making processes. It would foster a sense of ownership, encourage civic engagement, and enable communities to address their unique challenges effectively.

Dharmarajya - Ethical Governance and Social Justice:
'Dharmarajya' refers to the pursuit of governance guided by moral principles and the establishment of social justice. Gandhiji believed that political power should be wielded with a sense of responsibility and compassion, recognizing the inherent dignity and equality of all individuals. Dharmarajya entails not only the rule of law but also the recognition of moral values that uphold human rights, justice, and equality.

In the present-day context, Dharmarajya holds immense relevance to Indian democracy. The ethical foundations of governance are essential to address widespread corruption, caste discrimination, and socio-economic disparities. Upholding moral principles in public life, ensuring transparency, and promoting social justice are vital for a healthy and inclusive democracy. Incorporating Gandhiji's ideals of Dharmarajya into the fabric of Indian governance would help nurture a society where fairness, equality, and compassion prevail.

Conclusion:
Gandhiji's concepts of 'Swadhinata,' 'Swaraj,' and 'Dharmarajya' offer valuable insights into the evolution of Indian democracy. The contemporary relevance of these principles

lies in their ability to address persistent challenges such as economic dependency, centralized power structures, and ethical governance. Embracing 'Swadhinata' encourages self-reliance, 'Swaraj' promotes decentralized decision-making, and 'Dharmarajya' emphasizes ethical governance and social justice.

To ensure the continued relevance of these principles, it is essential for Indian democracy to uphold the ideals of self-sufficiency, grassroots participation, and moral governance. By integrating these concepts into policymaking and empowering local communities, India can move closer to realizing the vision of Gandhiji, fostering a truly inclusive and vibrant democracy.

Is the colonial mentality hindering India's success?

India, a land of rich history and diverse culture, has come a long way since its independence from British colonial rule in 1947. However, remnants of the colonial era still persist in the form of a colonial mentality. This mentality refers to a psychological mindset that perpetuates the belief in the superiority of foreign ideas, institutions, and standards over indigenous ones. While India has made remarkable progress in various fields, the remnants of colonial mentality continue to hinder its complete success. This essay delves into the impact of the colonial mentality on India's progress and explores how overcoming it is essential for unlocking the nation's true potential.

The Legacy of Colonial Rule:
The British colonization of India, spanning over two centuries, left an indelible mark on the Indian psyche. The colonial powers propagated the notion of their cultural, economic, and intellectual superiority, leading to the internalization of this ideology among the colonized people. This internalized belief system, which glorifies Western ideals and devalues indigenous knowledge, has been passed down through generations, hindering India's path to success.

Impact on Education:
Education serves as a fundamental pillar for a nation's progress. However, the colonial mentality has shaped India's education system in a way that prioritizes Western paradigms and marginalizes indigenous knowledge. English, the language of the colonizers, is still given disproportionate importance, often overshadowing regional languages and local traditions. This bias perpetuates a narrow understanding of success, where proficiency in English is deemed superior to proficiency in local languages. Consequently, many Indians undervalue their own cultural heritage, inhibiting the development and recognition of indigenous knowledge systems.

Economic Dependence:
The colonial mentality has fostered a dependency syndrome, where India looks outward for economic solutions instead of harnessing its internal resources. Post-independence, there was a persistent inclination to seek foreign direct investment, technology transfers, and Western partnerships, rather than nurturing domestic industries and innovation. This mindset limits India's ability to shape its economic destiny and creates an imbalanced power dynamic that perpetuates economic inequality.

Cultural Subjugation:
The colonial era enforced cultural assimilation, eroding traditional practices and customs. Even today, the colonial mentality continues to devalue indigenous art forms, literature, and traditional knowledge systems. As a consequence, many Indians struggle with self-esteem and cultural identity, feeling inadequate in comparison to Western counterparts. This inhibits the celebration of India's rich cultural tapestry and hampers the growth of a vibrant creative industry.

Challenging the Colonial Mentality:
To overcome the barriers posed by the colonial mentality, India needs to embark on a collective journey of self-realization and empowerment. Education reforms must be undertaken to provide a more inclusive curriculum that incorporates indigenous knowledge, languages, and cultural practices. By nurturing a sense of pride in one's heritage, India can reclaim its narrative and foster a generation of individuals who are both culturally rooted and globally aware.

Encouraging entrepreneurship, innovation, and investment in indigenous industries will help India break free from its economic dependence on foreign powers. By fostering an environment that values and supports homegrown talent, India can unleash its entrepreneurial potential, creating a vibrant ecosystem that nurtures innovation and economic growth.

Furthermore, the media, arts, and entertainment industry play a crucial role in challenging the colonial mentality. Promoting and celebrating diverse narratives that showcase India's cultural wealth and its intellectual contributions can redefine notions of success and foster a sense of national pride.

Conclusion:
India's colonial past continues to cast a long shadow on its present, hindering its path to complete success. The colonial mentality, ingrained in various aspects of Indian society, perpetuates a mindset that undervalues indigenous knowledge, fosters economic dependence, and erodes cultural identity. By recognizing and challenging this mentality, India can unleash its true potential and redefine success on its own terms. Embracing its rich cultural heritage, fostering inclusive education, and promoting indigenous industries are essential steps towards a more prosperous and self-assured India. Only by breaking free from the shackles of the colonial mentality can India truly soar to new heights of success and achievement.

Dreams which should not let India sleep

India, a land of diverse cultures, rich heritage, and immense potential, has always been a nation driven by dreams. From the time of its independence, India has strived to overcome obstacles and realize its aspirations. However, there are certain dreams that demand urgent attention, requiring collective efforts to be fulfilled. These dreams, if neglected, have the potential to hinder India's progress and development. In this essay, we will delve into some of these dreams that should not let India sleep.

1. Education for All:
One of the fundamental dreams that should keep India awake is the dream of providing quality education for all its citizens. While progress has been made in increasing enrollment rates, ensuring equal access to education still remains a challenge. India must focus on bridging the education gap between urban and rural areas, empowering girls with education, and improving the quality of education to equip the younger generation with the skills necessary for the 21st-century workforce.

2. Empowering Women:
Another dream that India must relentlessly pursue is the empowerment of women. Despite significant strides, gender inequality persists, hindering the country's progress. By providing equal opportunities, eradicating gender-based violence, and promoting women's participation in decision-making roles, India can harness the immense potential of its women. Empowered women contribute to the nation's economic growth, social development, and overall well-being.

3. Sustainable Development:
India's rapid economic growth has come at a cost to its environment. To ensure a sustainable future, India must prioritize the dream of sustainable development. By embracing renewable energy sources, implementing eco-friendly practices, and creating awareness about environmental conservation, India can mitigate the adverse effects of climate change, preserve its natural resources, and provide a healthy environment for its citizens.

4. Healthcare Revolution:
A dream that India must actively pursue is the transformation of its healthcare system. Despite progress in healthcare infrastructure, millions of Indians still lack access to quality healthcare. India needs to invest in robust healthcare infrastructure, strengthen primary healthcare services, and ensure affordable and accessible healthcare for all. By prioritizing health and well-being, India can build a healthier and more productive population.

5. Infrastructure Development:
India's dream of becoming a global economic powerhouse hinges on robust infrastructure development. Adequate transportation networks, efficient logistics, and smart cities are essential for attracting investments, fostering economic growth, and improving the quality of life for its citizens. India must invest in upgrading its infrastructure, connecting rural and remote areas, and adopting sustainable urban planning practices.

6. Digital Revolution:
In an increasingly interconnected world, India must embrace the dream of a digital revolution. By promoting digital literacy, expanding internet access, and leveraging technology in various sectors, India can bridge the digital divide and empower its citizens. Digitalization can revolutionize governance, education, healthcare, and business, fostering innovation, efficiency, and inclusive growth.

Conclusion:
India's dreams are boundless, and they hold the key to its progress and prosperity. To ensure a brighter future, India must relentlessly pursue these dreams and overcome the challenges that lie ahead. By prioritizing education, empowering women, embracing sustainable development, revolutionizing healthcare, investing in infrastructure, and embracing the digital age, India can unleash its true potential. It is through the collective efforts of its citizens, policymakers, and leaders that India can transform these dreams into realities and secure a better tomorrow for generations to come.

Management of Indian border disputes – a complex task.

The management of border disputes is a challenging task for any nation, and India is no exception. With its vast territorial expanse and multiple neighbors, India faces a complex web of border disputes that require delicate diplomacy, strategic decision-making, and long-term vision. This essay explores the intricacies involved in the management of Indian border disputes, highlighting the factors that contribute to the complexity of this task.

Historical Context:
India's border disputes have their roots in its colonial past. The hasty demarcation of borders during the British Raj has left a legacy of unresolved territorial claims. The partition of India in 1947 further complicated matters, leading to the creation of new international boundaries and the displacement of populations. Consequently, India has had to grapple with border disputes with various neighboring countries, including China, Pakistan, Bangladesh, Nepal, and Myanmar.

Factors Contributing to Complexity:
1. Geographical diversity: India's geographical diversity adds complexity to border management. From the rugged terrains of the Himalayas to the vast plains and coastal regions, each border presents unique challenges in terms of surveillance, enforcement, and infrastructure development. The sheer scale and diversity of these borders demand tailored approaches and specialized resources.

2. Historical and cultural factors: Many of India's border disputes have historical and cultural underpinnings. Claims over certain territories are rooted in centuries-old narratives, ethnic identities, and shared historical experiences. These factors often complicate the resolution process as they evoke strong emotions and nationalistic sentiments, making compromise and negotiation more challenging.

3. Strategic and security considerations: Borders are not merely lines on a map but vital frontiers for national security. India's border disputes have significant strategic implications, with sensitive regions often serving as buffers against geopolitical adversaries or smuggling routes for illicit activities. Balancing security concerns with diplomatic negotiations poses a formidable challenge, requiring a nuanced understanding of regional dynamics.

4. Political complexities: The management of border disputes intersects with domestic and international politics. Politicians and policymakers must navigate complex political landscapes while addressing public sentiment and national interests. Political considerations, such as maintaining public support, fostering intergovernmental cooperation, and managing domestic expectations, can complicate the decision-making process.

Approaches to Border Dispute Management:
1. Bilateral negotiations: India has consistently pursued diplomatic negotiations as the primary means of resolving border disputes. Bilateral talks, such as the India-China Border Negotiation Mechanism and the India-Bangladesh Joint Boundary Working Group, aim to find mutually acceptable solutions. These negotiations require patience, flexibility, and an openness to compromise from both sides.

2. Legal recourse: In some cases, India has sought legal remedies to resolve border disputes. The International Court of Justice (ICJ) and international arbitration have been utilized to adjudicate territorial claims. However, legal approaches are time-consuming, and outcomes may not always be favorable, especially if the other party does not agree to submit the dispute to arbitration.

3. Confidence-building measures: Confidence-building measures play a crucial role in reducing tensions and creating an atmosphere conducive to dispute resolution. These measures include the establishment of border management protocols, joint military exercises, cultural exchanges, and people-to-people contacts. Confidence-building measures can help foster trust and create an environment for productive negotiations.

4. Regional cooperation: Given the interconnected nature of border disputes, regional cooperation can be a valuable tool for their management. India actively participates in regional forums such as the South Asian Association for Regional Cooperation (SAARC) and the Bay of Bengal Initiative for Multi-Sectoral Technical and Economic Cooperation (BIMSTEC). These platforms provide opportunities for dialogue, cooperation, and the exploration of shared interests.

Conclusion:
The management of Indian border disputes is an intricate and multi-faceted task, requiring a combination of diplomatic finesse, strategic thinking, and an understanding of historical and cultural nuances. India's geographical diversity, historical context, security concerns, and political complexities all contribute to the complexity of this task. However, through bilateral negotiations, legal remedies, confidence-building measures, and regional cooperation, India can navigate this complex landscape and work towards peaceful resolutions. Resolving border disputes is crucial for stability, regional integration, and the promotion of peace in the Indian subcontinent.

Economic growth and development

1. Resource management in the Indian context. (1999)

2. GDP (Gross Domestic Product) along with GDH (Gross Domestic Happiness) would be the right indices for judging the wellbeing of a country. (2013)

3. Was it the policy paralysis or the paralysis of implementation which slowed the growth of our country? (2014)

4. Crisis faced in India – moral or economic. (2015)

5. Near jobless growth in India: An anomaly or an outcome of economic reforms. (2016)

6. Digital economy: A leveller or a source of economic inequality. (2016)

7. Innovation is the key determinant of economic growth and social welfare. (2016)

8. Impact of the new economic measures on fiscal ties between the union and states in India. (2017)

Resource management in the Indian context

Title: Comprehensive Resource Management in the Indian Context: Trends, Projections, and Sustainability

Introduction:

Resource management plays a crucial role in India's quest for sustainable development and improved quality of life. With a population of over 1.3 billion people and diverse resource demands, effective management across various dimensions is vital. This essay explores the latest data, trends, and projections regarding resource management in India, encompassing energy, water, land, minerals, and human resources.

Energy Resource Management:

India's energy demand has been rapidly increasing due to industrialization, urbanization, and population growth. While fossil fuels have traditionally dominated India's energy mix, the country is making significant strides in renewable energy adoption. The government's ambitious target of achieving 450 GW of renewable energy capacity by 2030 demonstrates a commitment to sustainable resource management.

As per the latest data, India's renewable energy capacity reached 98.5 GW by the end of 2021, including solar, wind, hydro, and biomass sources. Solar energy has witnessed remarkable growth, with installed capacity crossing 50 GW. Falling solar panel prices and government incentives have facilitated increased solar energy adoption. Projections indicate that India is well on track to achieve its renewable energy targets, with renewables expected to account for 40% of the country's energy mix by 2030.

Water Resource Management:

India faces significant challenges in water resource management due to population growth, urbanization, and changing weather patterns. The country's water demand is projected to exceed supply by 2050 if appropriate measures are not taken. Latest data reveals that approximately 600 million people in India face high to extreme water stress.

To address these challenges, efficient water management practices such as rainwater harvesting, water recycling, and improved irrigation techniques are being implemented. The government's flagship program, the Jal Jeevan Mission, aims to provide piped water supply to all rural households by 2024. Initiatives like the Atal Bhujal Yojana promote groundwater management and conservation. A comprehensive and integrated approach encompassing demand management, watershed management, and conservation strategies is necessary for sustainable water resource management.

Land Resource Management:

Rapid urbanization and industrial growth pose significant challenges in land resource management. According to recent data, urban areas in India are projected to triple by 2030, leading to land scarcity, infrastructure demands, and environmental concerns.

The government has implemented policies like the Smart Cities Mission, which aims to develop 100 smart cities across the country. These policies emphasize optimized land use, sustainable urban planning, and green infrastructure integration. Additionally, initiatives like the Pradhan Mantri Awas Yojana address affordable housing needs, ensuring equitable land allocation for housing and urban development.

Mineral Resource Management:

India is blessed with abundant mineral resources and is among the world's largest producers of coal, iron ore, and bauxite. Effective management of mineral resources is crucial for sustainable industrial growth, reducing environmental impacts, and ensuring resource availability for future generations.

To achieve responsible mineral resource management, the government has introduced reforms to streamline the mining sector. The National Mineral Policy emphasizes sustainable mining practices, conservation, and environmental rehabilitation. The Mines and Minerals (Development and Regulation) Amendment Act ensures transparency, maximizes resource utilization, and promotes responsible mining practices.

Human Resource Management:

Human resource management plays a vital role in sustainable development, productivity, and inclusive growth. India's demographic dividend offers a significant opportunity, but effective utilization and development of human resources are critical.

The government has launched various initiatives such as Skill India Mission, Make in India, and Digital India to enhance skill development, entrepreneurship, and technological capabilities. These initiatives aim to harness the potential of the youth population, bridge skill gaps, and promote employment generation across sectors.

Conclusion:

Comprehensive resource management in the Indian context requires a holistic approach encompassing energy, water, land, minerals, and human resources. India has made substantial progress in renewable energy adoption, water resource management, land use planning, mineral resource governance, and human resource development. However, sustainability remains a priority, and ongoing efforts are necessary to address emerging challenges and bridge existing gaps. By leveraging the latest data, monitoring trends, and projecting future scenarios, India can chart a path towards sustainable resource management, promoting economic development while safeguarding the environment and nurturing its human capital for a prosperous future.

GDP (Gross Domestic Product) along with GDH (Gross Domestic Happiness) would be the right indices for judging the wellbeing of a country.

In assessing the overall well-being of a nation, traditional measures such as GDP (Gross Domestic Product) have long been used as primary indicators. GDP provides valuable insights into a country's economic output and productivity. However, it fails to capture essential aspects of human well-being, such as happiness, health, and social cohesion. Recognizing this limitation, the concept of GDH (Gross Domestic Happiness) has emerged as a complementary index, aiming to evaluate a nation's prosperity in a more holistic manner. This essay argues that a combination of GDP and GDH provides a more comprehensive framework for assessing the well-being of a country.

Body:

1. Limitations of GDP as a single indicator

GDP has traditionally been the go-to measure for evaluating a country's economic performance. However, relying solely on GDP to assess overall well-being overlooks several critical factors:

a. Narrow economic focus: GDP primarily measures the market value of goods and services produced within a country over a specific period. While it is useful for evaluating economic growth, it overlooks non-market activities, environmental impact, and quality of life factors. For instance, GDP fails to account for volunteer work, household production, and the value of natural resources.

b. Neglects income distribution: GDP fails to account for income inequality, which can significantly impact overall well-being and social stability within a nation. A high GDP may not necessarily lead to equitable distribution of wealth and resources. Countries with high GDP but high levels of income inequality often experience social unrest and strained social cohesion.

c. Ignores non-material factors: GDP overlooks the significance of factors like education, health, social capital, and cultural richness, which are critical components of a high-quality life. The well-being of citizens is not solely dependent on economic factors but also on access to quality education, healthcare, and social support systems. Neglecting these non-material factors in assessing well-being leads to an incomplete understanding of a nation's progress.

2. Understanding the concept of GDH

To overcome the limitations of GDP, the concept of GDH has gained prominence, focusing on a more comprehensive evaluation of a nation's prosperity and well-being:

a. Holistic well-being: GDH goes beyond economic indicators by considering social, psychological, and environmental aspects of well-being. It recognizes that economic growth alone does not guarantee the happiness and well-being of citizens. GDH takes into account factors such as quality of life, social relationships, mental health, and environmental sustainability.

b. Happiness as a fundamental goal: GDH places happiness and life satisfaction at the core of its evaluation, recognizing the intrinsic value of subjective well-being. It acknowledges that the ultimate goal of societal progress should be the happiness and well-being of its citizens, rather than solely focusing on material wealth.

c. Inclusion of non-economic factors: GDH incorporates education, health, social support, environmental sustainability, and cultural diversity, providing a more comprehensive measure of human development. By considering these factors, GDH captures a broader range of elements that contribute to the overall well-being and happiness of a population.

3. Complementary nature of GDP and GDH

To obtain a more accurate assessment of a nation's well-being, a combination of GDP and GDH proves to be more effective:

a. Interplay between economic and non-economic factors: While GDP focuses on economic progress, GDH acknowledges that economic prosperity alone does not guarantee happiness or well-being. A balanced approach is needed to understand the interplay between economic factors and non-economic determinants of well-being. Combining GDP with GDH enables policymakers to assess the impact of economic growth on overall societal welfare.

b. Evaluating policy effectiveness: By combining GDP and GDH, policymakers can gain a more nuanced understanding of the impact of their decisions on both economic growth and overall well-being. They can identify policies that promote economic prosperity while also prioritizing the well-being of citizens. For example, policies that focus on reducing income inequality, improving access to education and healthcare, and fostering social cohesion can be evaluated based on their contribution to both GDP and GDH.

c. Addressing income inequality: GDH emphasizes the importance of equitable distribution of wealth and resources, helping policymakers prioritize social welfare programs and reduce disparities. By considering the income distribution within a country, policymakers can identify areas that require attention to promote a more inclusive and just society. This approach helps in reducing social tensions, improving social cohesion, and enhancing overall well-being.

4. Successful implementation of GDH

The concept of GDH has found successful implementation in various countries:

a. Bhutan's Gross National Happiness Index: Bhutan pioneered the GDH concept by integrating it into their national development plans. Bhutan's approach highlights the importance of sustainable development, cultural preservation, and spiritual well-being alongside economic growth. The GNH index encompasses multiple dimensions, including equitable socio-economic development, environmental conservation, cultural preservation, and good governance.

b. Global adoption and adaptation: Various countries have started adopting GDH principles, tailoring them to their unique cultural and social contexts. For example, New Zealand has implemented a "Well-being Budget" that goes beyond GDP to prioritize intergenerational well-being, social connection, mental health, and environmental sustainability. These initiatives contribute to a more comprehensive understanding of societal well-being.

Conclusion

While GDP has long served as a prominent economic indicator, it fails to capture the complexity of human well-being. The introduction of GDH as a complementary index emphasizes the importance of social, psychological, and environmental factors that influence overall prosperity. By combining GDP and GDH, policymakers can gain a more accurate understanding of a nation's progress, enabling them to design policies that prioritize both economic growth and citizens' well-being. As the concept of GDH continues to gain traction, societies are moving towards a more balanced and comprehensive approach to measuring and fostering the well-being of their citizens.

Was it the policy paralysis or the paralysis of implementation which slowed the growth of our country?

Title: Policy Paralysis or Paralysis of Implementation: Unraveling the Factors Hindering National Growth

Introduction:
The growth and development of a nation depend on a myriad of factors, including robust policies and their effective implementation. In the context of our country, there has been much debate regarding the primary obstacle to progress: policy paralysis or the paralysis of implementation. This essay aims to delve into this complex issue, examining both aspects and their respective contributions to the slowdown in our country's growth.

Policy Paralysis:
Policy paralysis refers to a situation where the formulation and implementation of necessary policies are delayed or hindered due to bureaucratic inefficiencies, political indecision, or conflicting interests. In recent years, our nation has witnessed instances where crucial policy decisions have been postponed or stuck in endless deliberations, resulting in a lack of clear direction and stunted growth.

One key factor contributing to policy paralysis is the intricate nature of our democratic system. The need for consensus among multiple stakeholders, including political parties, interest groups, and bureaucrats, often leads to prolonged decision-making processes. This delay prevents the timely implementation of policies and hampers progress in critical areas such as infrastructure development, economic reforms, and social welfare.

Moreover, policy paralysis can also arise from ideological differences and short-term political considerations. Parties often prioritize populist measures that yield immediate electoral gains, thereby neglecting the long-term structural reforms required for sustainable growth. These policy gaps and inconsistencies hinder investments, discourage entrepreneurship, and create an uncertain business environment, deterring domestic and foreign investors.

Paralysis of Implementation:
While policy paralysis hampers progress, the paralysis of implementation amplifies the problem further. Even with sound policies in place, their successful execution requires efficient and effective implementation mechanisms. Unfortunately, inadequate bureaucratic capacities, corruption, and bureaucratic red tape often obstruct the implementation process, rendering policies ineffective on the ground.

One critical factor contributing to the paralysis of implementation is the lack of accountability and transparency within the system. When officials responsible for implementing policies face minimal consequences for their actions or inactions, complacency and inefficiency tend to prevail. The absence of rigorous monitoring and evaluation mechanisms exacerbates the problem, perpetuating the cycle of underperformance.

Moreover, corruption remains a significant hurdle in our country's implementation process. It not only diverts resources meant for development but also undermines public trust in the government. The prevalence of corruption erodes the efficacy of policies, as vested interests prioritize personal gain over national progress.

Additionally, bureaucratic complexities, excessive regulations, and outdated administrative practices hamper the smooth execution of policies. Cumbersome processes and delays in decision-making deter investments, impede business growth, and hinder job creation, thereby hampering overall economic development.

Conclusion:
To determine the primary factor hindering the growth of our country, it is imperative to recognize the interplay between policy paralysis and the paralysis of implementation. While policy paralysis creates a vacuum of clear direction, the paralysis of implementation renders policies ineffective on the ground. It is a vicious cycle where one factor exacerbates the other, leading to the stunted growth of the nation.

Addressing these challenges requires comprehensive reforms. Policymakers must prioritize long-term national interest over short-term gains, foster a culture of accountability, and establish robust monitoring mechanisms to ensure policy effectiveness. Simultaneously, bureaucratic capacities should be enhanced, corruption curbed, and regulatory frameworks streamlined to facilitate efficient implementation.

By tackling both policy paralysis and the paralysis of implementation, our country can overcome the hurdles hindering growth and pave the way for inclusive development, socio-economic progress, and a brighter future for all citizens.

Crisis faced in India – moral or economic.

India, a nation of incredible diversity and potential, has found itself grappling with a multitude of challenges throughout its history. In recent times, two prominent crises have garnered significant attention: moral crisis and economic crisis. While both are intertwined, this essay aims to explore whether the challenges India faces are primarily moral or economic in nature. By analyzing key issues and their underlying causes, we can gain insight into the complexities of these crises and consider potential solutions.

Moral Crisis: The Erosion of Values

India, with its rich cultural heritage and ancient traditions, has experienced a gradual erosion of moral values in various aspects of society. Corruption, nepotism, and the devaluation of ethical principles have plagued the nation, posing a profound threat to its social fabric.

One of the most pervasive moral crises in India is corruption. The widespread prevalence of bribery, embezzlement, and dishonest practices hampers progress and undermines the trust of citizens in the government and public institutions. Corruption diverts resources from vital sectors such as healthcare, education, and infrastructure, exacerbating economic disparities and impeding overall development.

Moreover, the erosion of moral values is evident in the rising instances of crimes against women and marginalization of vulnerable communities. The persistence of gender inequality, caste-based discrimination, and religious intolerance reflects a society grappling with deep-rooted prejudices and moral shortcomings. These issues not only hinder social harmony but also hinder the country's progress toward inclusive growth.

Economic Crisis: Structural Challenges and Inequality

India's economic crisis stems from a combination of structural challenges and persistent inequalities. Despite being one of the fastest-growing economies globally, a substantial portion of the population still grapples with poverty, unemployment, and inadequate access to basic amenities.

One of the primary economic challenges India faces is the lack of job creation. The rapid growth of the population, coupled with insufficient opportunities in sectors that can absorb the workforce, has resulted in a burgeoning unemployment rate. The absence of meaningful employment opportunities fuels frustration and unrest, straining the social fabric of the nation.

Furthermore, economic inequality poses a significant obstacle to India's progress. The concentration of wealth in the hands of a few exacerbates the gap between the rich and the poor. This disparity not only hinders social mobility but also perpetuates a cycle of poverty and social exclusion. The inadequate distribution of resources and limited access to quality education and healthcare further deepen the divide, stifling economic development and social progress.

Interconnectedness of Moral and Economic Crises

While it is essential to differentiate between moral and economic crises, it is equally important to acknowledge their interconnectedness. The moral crisis, with its roots in corruption and social prejudices, directly impacts economic growth and development. Corruption diverts funds meant for public welfare, hindering economic progress and perpetuating inequality. Similarly, the persistence of gender inequality and discrimination hampers the full utilization of human resources, stifling innovation and economic productivity.

Conversely, economic crises can exacerbate moral shortcomings. Widespread poverty and unemployment breed frustration and desperation, which may lead individuals to engage in unethical practices to survive. Moreover, economic disparities fuel social unrest, magnifying existing moral crises such as crimes against marginalized groups.

Conclusion

In analyzing the crises faced by India, it is clear that moral and economic challenges are intertwined, and their resolution requires a comprehensive approach. Addressing corruption, promoting ethical governance, and fostering inclusive growth are essential to tackling both moral and economic crises. Strengthening institutions, promoting transparency, and ensuring equitable distribution of resources are key steps toward building a society that is morally upright and economically prosperous.

To overcome these crises, India needs the concerted efforts of its citizens, policymakers, and civil society organizations. By emphasizing the importance of moral values, education, and inclusive economic policies, India can create a more just society that enables all its citizens to thrive. Only through a collective commitment to address these challenges can India chart a path towards sustainable development and a brighter future for its people.

Near jobless growth in India: An anomaly or an outcome of economic reforms.

India, a vibrant democracy with a burgeoning economy, has witnessed a paradoxical phenomenon in recent years: near jobless growth. While the country's GDP has shown promising growth, the rate of job creation has failed to keep pace. This has raised concerns and sparked debates regarding the sustainability and inclusivity of India's economic reforms. This essay aims to explore the causes and consequences of near jobless growth in India and evaluate whether it is merely an anomaly or a result of the country's economic reforms.

The Context of India's Economic Reforms
India embarked on a path of economic liberalization and structural reforms in the early 1990s, dismantling the license raj and embracing market-oriented policies. These reforms aimed to unleash the latent potential of the Indian economy, attract foreign investments, and foster entrepreneurship. While these measures led to a significant boost in GDP growth, job creation remained a persistent challenge.

Factors Contributing to Near Jobless Growth
1. Technological Disruptions: The rapid advancement of technology and automation has led to the displacement of traditional labor-intensive sectors. Industries such as manufacturing, textiles, and agriculture, which were once major sources of employment, have witnessed a decline in job opportunities due to mechanization and increased productivity.

2. Skill Mismatch: The Indian education system has struggled to keep pace with the changing demands of the job market. The lack of relevant skills and training among the workforce has resulted in a significant skill mismatch, leading to a dearth of employable individuals.

3. Informal Sector Dominance: India's informal sector, comprising unorganized and small-scale enterprises, has been a significant contributor to the economy. However, such enterprises often face challenges in scaling up and providing stable employment opportunities, contributing to the near jobless growth phenomenon.

4. Regulatory Barriers: Cumbersome labor laws and complex regulatory frameworks have discouraged formal job creation. Employers often face difficulties in navigating these regulations, leading to a preference for contract labor or outsourcing.

Consequences of Near Jobless Growth
The near jobless growth phenomenon in India has far-reaching consequences. Firstly, it exacerbates income inequality and hampers social mobility, as a significant portion of the population remains excluded from the benefits of economic growth. Additionally, inadequate employment opportunities can lead to social unrest, political instability, and increased crime rates. Moreover, the lack of job creation can undermine demographic dividends, as a young and aspiring workforce fails to find suitable employment, resulting in frustration and wasted potential.

Reassessing Economic Reforms
While near jobless growth raises concerns, it is essential to recognize that economic reforms have also yielded positive outcomes. Increased foreign direct investment, improved infrastructure, and the rise of innovative startups have contributed to overall economic development. However, policymakers need to address the employment challenge and ensure that growth is inclusive, sustainable, and benefits all sections of society.

Policy Interventions

To address the near jobless growth issue, India needs a multi-pronged approach. This includes investing in skill development programs to bridge the gap between demand and supply, promoting entrepreneurship and small and medium enterprises (SMEs), easing regulatory burdens to encourage formal job creation, and focusing on labor-intensive sectors that can absorb the growing workforce.

Conclusion

Near jobless growth in India is not just an anomaly but a consequence of various factors, including technological disruptions, skill mismatch, dominance of the informal sector, and regulatory barriers. While economic reforms have brought about positive changes, they must be complemented by targeted policy interventions to ensure inclusive growth and ample employment opportunities for the Indian population. Achieving this delicate balance will be crucial for India's long-term economic sustainability and social well-being.

Digital economy: A leveller or a source of economic inequality.

The rapid advancement of the digital economy has transformed the way we live, work, and interact. With the increasing prominence of digital technologies, there arises a critical question: does the digital economy act as a leveller, bridging economic disparities, or does it exacerbate existing inequalities? This essay explores the complex relationship between the digital economy and economic inequality by examining various dimensions of this phenomenon. By analyzing empirical data and scholarly research, we aim to provide a comprehensive understanding of how the digital economy can both level the playing field and contribute to economic disparities.

The digital economy refers to the economic activities facilitated by digital technologies, encompassing sectors such as e-commerce, digital platforms, and online services. Proponents argue that the digital economy has the potential to democratize access to information, markets, and opportunities, thereby acting as a leveller. Conversely, skeptics assert that the digital economy could intensify existing economic inequalities, favoring those with technological skills or access to resources. To shed light on this issue, we examine multiple dimensions related to the impact of the digital economy on economic inequality.

Access and Inclusion:

One aspect where the digital economy has the potential to act as a leveller is by expanding access to information and markets. Internet penetration and mobile connectivity have surged in recent years, offering previously marginalized communities a chance to participate in the digital realm. However, the digital divide remains a pressing concern, as disparities in access to technology, digital literacy, and reliable internet persist. These disparities can reinforce existing economic inequalities, hindering opportunities for those already marginalized.

Labor Market Dynamics:

The digital economy has reshaped labor markets by creating new employment opportunities and altering traditional job structures. On one hand, digital platforms and online marketplaces have provided flexible work arrangements and income-generating avenues for individuals, including those in low-income countries. On the other hand, concerns arise regarding the gig economy's precarious nature, lack of benefits, and potential for exploitation. Furthermore, automation and artificial intelligence (AI) threaten certain jobs, potentially exacerbating economic inequality unless measures are taken to ensure a just transition for affected workers.

Skills and Education:

Digital technologies have become central to the modern workforce, demanding new skill sets. While digital literacy and technical skills can enhance employability and narrow the skills gap, disparities in access to quality education and training may perpetuate economic inequality. Ensuring equal access to digital education and upskilling programs is crucial for leveraging the potential of the digital economy as a leveller.

Concentration of Wealth and Power:

The digital economy has witnessed the rise of tech giants and digital platforms that wield substantial economic power. The accumulation of wealth and the concentration of market control in the hands of a few corporations have raised concerns about monopolistic practices, limited competition, and increased inequality. Moreover, data privacy and security issues can disproportionately impact individuals with limited resources, further exacerbating economic disparities.

Government Policies and Regulations:

Government policies play a pivotal role in shaping the impact of the digital economy on economic inequality. Effective regulations can ensure fair competition, protect consumer rights, and promote inclusive digital infrastructure. Additionally, policies aimed at bridging the digital divide, promoting digital literacy, and supporting entrepreneurship in underprivileged communities can help address inequality concerns.

Conclusion:

The digital economy's impact on economic inequality is multifaceted. While it has the potential to level the playing field by expanding access to information, markets, and employment opportunities, disparities in access, skills, and market concentration can exacerbate existing economic inequalities. Addressing these challenges requires a multifaceted approach, including policies that promote digital inclusion, provide quality education and training, and ensure fair competition and consumer protection. By doing so, we can harness the transformative potential of the digital economy while minimizing its contribution to economic inequality.

In conclusion, the digital economy's impact on economic inequality is a complex interplay of various factors. Recognizing the potential for both levelling and exacerbating disparities, it is crucial to adopt a holistic approach that combines policy interventions, educational initiatives, and equitable regulations to harness the benefits of the digital economy while mitigating its negative consequences on economic inequality.

Innovation is the key determinant of economic growth and social welfare.

Innovation, broadly defined as the creation and application of new ideas, processes, and technologies, is a catalyst for progress. It drives economic growth by spurring productivity, fostering competitiveness, and enabling the emergence of new industries and job opportunities. Moreover, innovation has the potential to address societal challenges, improve quality of life, and enhance social welfare. As Joseph Schumpeter, an influential economist, stated, "Innovation is the process of creative destruction that is at the heart of capitalism."

Economic Growth:

Innovation plays a central role in promoting sustained economic growth. It leads to the development of new products, services, and technologies, opening up new avenues for businesses and entrepreneurs. This stimulates investment, generates employment opportunities, and drives productivity gains. For instance, the advent of smartphones revolutionized the telecommunications industry, spawning an ecosystem of applications, services, and jobs, leading to substantial economic growth.

Data: According to a study by the McKinsey Global Institute, companies that prioritize innovation outperform their peers in terms of revenue growth and profitability. In 2019, the top 10% of innovative companies captured 80% of economic profit generated by all companies analyzed.

Productivity and Efficiency:

Innovation is a key driver of productivity improvements. Through the introduction of new technologies, processes, and organizational methods, innovation enhances efficiency, reduces costs, and improves resource allocation. The assembly line in manufacturing, for instance, revolutionized production processes, significantly increasing output and lowering costs. This, in turn, translates into higher wages, increased consumer purchasing power, and improved living standards.

Real-life Example: The impact of innovation on productivity is evident in the agricultural sector. The Green Revolution, driven by innovation in crop varieties, fertilizers, and irrigation techniques, dramatically increased agricultural productivity, allowing societies to feed growing populations and alleviate poverty.

Inclusive Development:

Innovation has the potential to foster inclusive development, ensuring that the benefits of economic growth are shared by all members of society. By creating new industries and job opportunities, innovation can drive social mobility, reduce income disparities, and promote equitable wealth distribution. It enables individuals from diverse backgrounds to participate in the knowledge economy, fostering social inclusion and reducing inequality gaps.

Data: According to the World Intellectual Property Organization (WIPO), countries that invest in innovation and have effective innovation ecosystems demonstrate higher levels of social inclusion and overall well-being.

Societal Impact and Well-being:

Innovation has the power to address societal challenges and improve overall well-being. It enables the development of groundbreaking solutions in healthcare, education, energy, and other sectors, enhancing the quality of life for individuals and communities. Technological advancements in healthcare, such as telemedicine and precision medicine, have the potential to improve healthcare access, reduce costs, and enhance patient outcomes.

Real-life Example: The widespread adoption of renewable energy technologies, driven by innovation, contributes to sustainable development, reduces environmental degradation, and mitigates climate change, thereby safeguarding the well-being of current and future generations.

Conclusion:

Innovation stands as the cornerstone of economic growth and social welfare. It drives productivity, stimulates economic expansion, fosters inclusive development, and enhances overall well-being. As societies navigate the challenges and opportunities of the future, nurturing a culture of innovation, investing in research and development, and fostering collaboration between academia, industry, and government will be crucial. Embracing innovation as a strategic imperative will enable us to overcome existing limitations, address societal needs, and shape a prosperous and equitable future. As Albert Einstein aptly said, "We cannot solve our problems with the same thinking we used when we created them."

Impact of the new economic measures on fiscal ties between the union and states in India.

The fiscal relationship between the Union and states in India is a critical aspect of the country's federal structure. Over the years, several new economic measures have been introduced, aiming to redefine the fiscal ties between these entities. This essay explores the impact of these measures on the fiscal relationship between the Union and states in India. By examining real-life examples, incorporating relevant data, and drawing insights from expert opinions, we aim to provide a comprehensive understanding of how these measures have influenced fiscal ties.

1. Goods and Services Tax (GST):
One of the significant economic measures that have transformed fiscal ties in India is the implementation of the Goods and Services Tax (GST) in July 2017. The GST replaced multiple indirect taxes levied by the Union and states, creating a unified tax structure. While the GST aimed to simplify taxation and promote economic integration, its impact on fiscal ties has been mixed.
According to Arun Jaitley, former Finance Minister of India, "GST is the most significant tax reform in Indian history that will create a common economic market, eliminating multiple taxes and reducing barriers to trade."
The implementation of GST has reduced tax barriers and streamlined interstate trade, enhancing fiscal integration between states and the Union. It has led to a more cohesive economic market, enabling businesses to operate across state borders more efficiently.
According to the Ministry of Finance, the average growth rate of GST revenue collection in India was 12.2% during the fiscal year 2019-2020. This indicates the positive impact of GST on revenue generation, which directly affects the fiscal ties between the Union and states.

2. Fourteenth Finance Commission Recommendations:
The Fourteenth Finance Commission (FFC), constituted by the Government of India, made significant recommendations that influenced fiscal ties between the Union and states. The FFC recommended an increase in the share of states in central taxes, devolving a higher proportion of tax revenue to the states.
According to the FFC report, "Devolution of a higher share of central taxes to the states will strengthen fiscal federalism and enhance the autonomy of states in fiscal matters."

The increased devolution of central taxes to states under the FFC recommendations has provided states with greater fiscal autonomy. This enhanced financial flexibility has enabled states to address their specific developmental needs more effectively.
As per the FFC recommendations, the share of states in the divisible pool of central taxes increased from 32% to 42% for the fiscal years 2015-2020. This increased devolution has bolstered the fiscal ties between the Union and states, empowering states with greater fiscal resources.

3. Impact of COVID-19 Pandemic:
The COVID-19 pandemic and the subsequent economic disruptions have had a profound impact on the fiscal ties between the Union and states in India. The Union government announced several economic measures, including relief packages, to mitigate the crisis and support the states.
Nirmala Sitharaman, the Finance Minister of India, stated, "The government is committed to working closely with states to ensure fiscal support and promote economic recovery during these challenging times."
The central government provided financial assistance to states through various schemes like the Pradhan Mantri Garib Kalyan Yojana and the Atmanirbhar Bharat Abhiyan. These initiatives aimed to support state finances and strengthen fiscal ties between the Union and states in times of crisis.

As of October 2021, the central government had released around ☐3.03 lakh crore ($41 billion) to states as grants for COVID-19 relief measures, highlighting the collaborative effort to address fiscal challenges.

Conclusion

The new economic measures implemented in India, such as the GST, recommendations of the Fourteenth Finance Commission, and initiatives during the COVID-19 pandemic, have significantly impacted the fiscal ties between the Union and states. While the GST aimed to promote economic integration, the Fourteenth Finance Commission recommendations enhanced fiscal autonomy for states. Furthermore, the COVID-19 relief measures showcased the collaborative approach between the Union and states during times of crisis. These measures have contributed to a more balanced fiscal relationship and strengthened the federal structure of India. However, continuous evaluation and refinement of these measures are necessary to ensure the long-term sustainability and equitable distribution of resources between the Union and states.

The Language Problem in India: Past, Present, and Future Prospects

Introduction:
India, a diverse nation with a rich cultural heritage, is home to a multitude of languages spoken by its vast population. The linguistic diversity in India presents both opportunities and challenges. Throughout its history, India has grappled with the language problem, stemming from the need to establish a common language for communication, governance, and national unity while respecting the linguistic diversity that defines the country. This essay examines the past, present, and future prospects of the language problem in India, shedding light on the complexities and potential solutions.

Historical Perspective:
India's linguistic diversity can be traced back to ancient times, with Sanskrit serving as a classical language and lingua franca for intellectual and religious discourse. However, as regional kingdoms emerged, regional languages gained prominence, leading to the development of various linguistic identities across the subcontinent. The British colonization further complicated the linguistic landscape by introducing English as the language of administration, education, and social mobility. This period witnessed the emergence of nationalist movements that advocated for the promotion of indigenous languages as a means of cultural revival and resistance against colonial dominance.

Post-Independence Challenges:
Following India's independence in 1947, the newly formed nation had to grapple with the question of language policy. The Constituent Assembly recognized the importance of linguistic diversity and enshrined it in the Indian Constitution, declaring Hindi as the official language while guaranteeing the protection and promotion of regional languages. However, the decision to elevate Hindi as the sole national language triggered widespread protests, particularly in non-Hindi-speaking regions of South India and the northeastern states. This resistance led to the enactment of the Official Languages Act in 1963, according to which Hindi and English were designated as the official languages of the Indian government.

Present Scenario:
In the present era, India continues to navigate the complexities of language policy. English remains an essential language for higher education, business, and global communication, acting as a unifying force among diverse linguistic communities. Additionally, regional languages have gained prominence, with several states adopting their respective languages as the medium of instruction in schools and official communication. However, linguistic tensions and conflicts occasionally arise, as some communities perceive their languages to be marginalized or undervalued in favor of Hindi or English. The need for a common language for national integration remains a challenge, with Hindi being the most widely spoken language but not universally accepted.

Future Prospects and Solutions:

As India looks to the future, several prospects and solutions can be explored to address the language problem. First, fostering multilingualism and linguistic tolerance should be prioritized to celebrate India's linguistic diversity rather than viewing it as a source of division. The government can encourage the promotion of regional languages while ensuring equal opportunities for individuals proficient in different languages. Second, investing in language preservation and revitalization efforts can protect endangered languages and promote their usage in education, media, and cultural spheres. Third, promoting language learning at the national level, with emphasis on English and regional languages, can bridge communication gaps and enhance social mobility.

Moreover, embracing technological advancements, such as machine translation and natural language processing, can facilitate effective communication across language barriers. These technologies can aid in developing inclusive digital platforms and tools that accommodate various Indian languages. Additionally, educational reforms should prioritize language education, ensuring that students have access to quality instruction in their mother tongues and at least one additional language.

Conclusion:
The language problem in India is a complex issue deeply rooted in its history, diversity, and aspirations for national integration. While past and present challenges have posed obstacles, the future offers opportunities for fostering linguistic harmony and inclusive development. Embracing linguistic diversity, preserving endangered languages, investing in language education, and leveraging technology can contribute to resolving the language problem in India. By doing so, India can celebrate its rich linguistic heritage while forging a path toward a united and harmonious nation.

The Centralization of Water Resources: A Prudent Approach towards Sustainable Management

Introduction

Water, as a finite and indispensable resource, plays a critical role in supporting all forms of life and maintaining ecological balance. In light of its significance, the question of who should control and manage water resources becomes crucial. This essay argues that water resources should be under the control of the central government, based on the premises of efficient resource allocation, equitable distribution, holistic environmental stewardship, and citing India's interstate water disputes, government initiatives, and Supreme Court rulings as pertinent examples.

Efficient Resource Allocation

One of the key advantages of centralizing water resources is the ability to implement efficient resource allocation strategies. India, a country grappling with numerous interstate water disputes, highlights the complexities of managing water resources. Disputes over rivers such as the Cauvery and the Krishna have led to conflicts between different states, hampering effective water management.

Centralized management under the control of the central government can help resolve such conflicts and ensure optimal utilization of water resources. The central government has the necessary infrastructure, technical expertise, and administrative capabilities to plan and manage water resources at a larger scale. It can conduct comprehensive assessments of water availability, demand patterns, and usage trends, thereby making informed decisions regarding allocation.

Equitable Distribution

India's water disputes also underscore the need for equitable distribution, a goal that can be effectively pursued through central control of water resources. The central government, through its initiatives, strives to address water scarcity and conflicts between states. For instance, the Inter-State River Water Disputes Act of 1956 empowers the central government to adjudicate disputes arising from the sharing of interstate river waters.

Additionally, the central government has launched initiatives like the Pradhan Mantri Krishi Sinchayee Yojana (Prime Minister's Agricultural Irrigation Scheme) to ensure the equitable distribution of water for agricultural purposes across the country. By providing financial assistance and technological support, the central government promotes sustainable irrigation practices and reduces regional disparities in water access.

The Supreme Court of India has played a crucial role in resolving interstate water disputes and upholding the principle of equitable distribution. For instance, in the case of the Cauvery River water dispute between the states of Karnataka and Tamil Nadu, the Supreme Court intervened and issued rulings to ensure a fair allocation of water between the two states. Central control allows for the implementation of such judicial decisions, ensuring compliance and fair distribution.

Holistic Environmental Stewardship

The centralization of water resources empowers the central government to adopt a comprehensive and environmentally responsible approach to water management. India's diverse ecological systems, which rely on shared water bodies, necessitate an integrated perspective. The central government can establish agencies and institutions dedicated to monitoring and preserving water quality, biodiversity, and ecosystem health.

Furthermore, initiatives like the National Water Mission and the Namami Gange Programme demonstrate the central government's commitment to holistic environmental stewardship. These initiatives aim to rejuvenate and conserve India's major rivers, including the Ganga, through pollution control measures, riverfront development, and ecological restoration.

Conclusion

In conclusion, the centralization of water resources under the control of the central government is a prudent approach towards sustainable management. The examples of India's interstate water disputes, government initiatives, and Supreme Court rulings illustrate the challenges faced and the potential solutions offered by centralized water resource management. By empowering the central government to plan, coordinate, and regulate water resources effectively, nations can foster responsible water management practices, enhance societal well-being, and protect the planet's most precious resource.

Evaluation of Panchayati Raj System in India: An Analysis of Empowering the People

Introduction:
The Panchayati Raj System, introduced in India through constitutional amendments in the 1990s, sought to promote democratic governance at the grassroots level and empower the people. By establishing local self-government institutions, the system aimed to eradicate centralized power and ensure effective participation of citizens in decision-making processes. This essay critically evaluates the Panchayati Raj System from the perspective of its success in empowering the people.

Historical Context:
To understand the significance of the Panchayati Raj System, it is crucial to recognize India's historical context. India's struggle for independence was also a fight against colonialism and centralized power. The framers of the Indian Constitution envisioned a system that would reverse this trend and empower the people at the grassroots level. The incorporation of the Panchayati Raj System into the constitutional framework reflected this commitment to decentralized governance.

Constitutional Provisions:
The constitutional provisions pertaining to Panchayati Raj ensure the devolution of power to the local level. Article 243G mandates the establishment of Panchayats as institutions of self-government. It provides for a three-tier structure, comprising the village, intermediate, and district levels, with elected representatives. The system aims to facilitate people's participation in decision-making, making them active stakeholders in local development.

Achievements:
The Panchayati Raj System has achieved several notable accomplishments in empowering the people. First, it has provided a platform for previously marginalized communities, including women and Scheduled Castes/Tribes, to participate in local governance. Reservation of seats for these groups has enabled their increased political representation, fostering inclusivity and social justice.

Second, the system has facilitated the decentralization of power, shifting decision-making authority from the state to local bodies. This has enabled local communities to address their specific needs and priorities more effectively. Local governments, equipped with financial resources and administrative responsibilities, have implemented grassroots initiatives for rural development, infrastructure, and social welfare.

Third, the Panchayati Raj System has enhanced transparency and accountability in governance. Regular elections at the local level enable citizens to exercise their voting rights, holding representatives accountable for their performance. Public scrutiny and social audits have become mechanisms for ensuring responsible and efficient utilization of resources, reducing corruption, and increasing citizen participation.

Limitations and Challenges:
Despite its achievements, the Panchayati Raj System faces certain limitations and challenges. First, there are gaps in capacity building and training programs for elected representatives. Insufficient knowledge and skills hinder effective decision-making and governance. Addressing these gaps through training programs can enhance the ability of local representatives to empower their communities.

Second, the system often faces bureaucratic resistance and interference. The influence of state governments and administrative hurdles sometimes limit the autonomy and decision-making powers of local bodies. Strengthening the financial and administrative powers of Panchayats can help overcome these challenges and facilitate local development.

Third, while reservations for marginalized groups have increased their representation, there are instances where their actual participation and influence remain limited. Social and cultural barriers, as well as gender-based discrimination, continue to impede the effective empowerment of these groups. Efforts to address these barriers through awareness campaigns, capacity building, and inclusive policies are essential.

Conclusion:
The Panchayati Raj System in India has played a significant role in empowering local communities and decentralizing power. Its achievements in increasing citizen participation, empowering marginalized groups, and promoting transparency are commendable. However, challenges such as capacity building, bureaucratic resistance, and social barriers must be addressed for true power-sharing and effective people's empowerment. By addressing these limitations, the Panchayati Raj System can continue to evolve and fulfill its potential as a catalyst for grassroots democracy and inclusive development in India.

The Role of Autonomy in Addressing Balkanization: A Critical Analysis

Abstract:
Balkanization, a phenomenon characterized by the fragmentation and division of states or regions along ethnic, religious, or cultural lines, has been a recurring challenge throughout history. This essay critically examines whether autonomy is the optimal solution for combating balkanization. By considering the advantages and limitations of autonomy, exploring alternative approaches, and analyzing real-world case studies, we can gain insights into the complexities of this issue and evaluate the effectiveness of autonomy as a remedy for balkanization.

1. Introduction:

Balkanization poses significant political, social, and economic challenges, as it often leads to increased tensions, conflict, and instability. This essay aims to explore the potential of autonomy as a means to combat balkanization. Autonomy, in this context, refers to granting a degree of self-governance to distinct ethnic, religious, or cultural groups within a larger political entity.

2. Advantages of Autonomy:

Autonomy offers several potential advantages in addressing balkanization. Firstly, it recognizes and respects the cultural, linguistic, and religious diversity of a population, allowing communities to preserve their identities and traditions. Secondly, autonomy can provide a sense of empowerment and self-determination to marginalized groups, fostering a more inclusive and participatory political system. Thirdly, autonomy can contribute to stability by addressing grievances and reducing the likelihood of violent conflict. These benefits suggest that autonomy holds promise as a solution to balkanization.

3. Limitations of Autonomy:

While autonomy has its merits, it is not without limitations. One significant concern is the potential for autonomy to reinforce divisions and perpetuate identity-based politics, creating or exacerbating separatist movements. Moreover, autonomy can lead to administrative complexities, such as overlapping jurisdictions and territorial disputes, which can impede effective governance and lead to further fragmentation. Additionally, granting autonomy to one group may inadvertently marginalize other minority groups within the same region. These limitations call for a careful examination of alternative approaches to address balkanization.

4. Alternative Approaches:

Alternatives to autonomy include strategies aimed at fostering social cohesion, inclusivity, and shared identities. Investing in educational reforms, promoting intercultural dialogue, and implementing policies that bridge divides can help build a sense of common purpose and mitigate balkanization tendencies. Strengthening democratic institutions, ensuring equal rights and opportunities for all citizens, and promoting equitable distribution of resources can also contribute to social harmony and mitigate grievances that drive balkanization. These alternative approaches aim to transcend ethnic, religious, or cultural divisions, offering a different perspective on combating balkanization.

5. Case Studies:

To gain insights into the effectiveness of autonomy in addressing balkanization, it is instructive to examine relevant case studies. Examples such as the autonomy arrangements in Catalonia (Spain), Quebec (Canada), and Kurdistan (Iraq) provide valuable empirical evidence. By analyzing the successes, challenges, and long-term implications of these autonomy models, we can evaluate their capacity to prevent balkanization and promote peaceful coexistence.

6. Conclusion:

Addressing balkanization requires a nuanced and comprehensive approach. While autonomy can offer certain advantages, it is essential to acknowledge its limitations and consider alternative strategies that promote inclusivity, social cohesion, and shared identities. The effectiveness of autonomy in combatting balkanization varies depending on the specific context, historical factors, and the commitment of all stakeholders involved. By critically analyzing the advantages, limitations, and alternative approaches, policymakers and scholars can navigate the complexities of balkanization and work towards sustainable and peaceful solutions.

Creation of Smaller States and the Consequent Administrative, Economic, and Developmental Implications

Abstract:
The creation of smaller states has been a topic of significant interest and debate in recent times. Proponents argue that smaller states promote better governance, increased citizen participation, and enhanced regional development. Conversely, critics highlight potential administrative challenges, economic implications, and the overall impact on development. This essay aims to explore the multifaceted nature of the creation of smaller states and analyze the potential administrative, economic, and developmental implications involved.

1. Introduction
The concept of creating smaller states involves dividing existing large administrative units into smaller, more manageable entities. This essay delves into the subsequent implications across three key dimensions: administrative, economic, and developmental.

2. Administrative Implications
2.1. Enhanced Governance: Smaller states often lead to a more decentralized system of governance, fostering closer proximity between citizens and decision-makers. This can result in better responsiveness to local issues and improved citizen participation in governance processes.

2.2. Administrative Challenges: The creation of smaller states may present initial administrative challenges, including the establishment of new administrative structures, redistribution of resources, and the need for capacity building. Effective planning and management are crucial during this transitional phase.

3. Economic Implications
3.1. Resource Distribution: Smaller states can potentially lead to a fairer distribution of resources, ensuring that all regions receive adequate attention and development. However, challenges may arise in terms of determining resource allocation mechanisms and addressing disparities among regions.

3.2. Economic Viability: Critics argue that smaller states may face economic challenges due to reduced economies of scale, limited resource bases, and increased administrative costs. However, proponents contend that smaller states can adopt specialized development strategies, attract investments, and leverage local resources more effectively.

4. Developmental Implications
4.1. Regional Development: Smaller states can facilitate targeted regional development initiatives by addressing specific local needs and priorities. This can result in more balanced and inclusive development across different regions.

4.2. Infrastructure Development: Smaller states may face hurdles in terms of financing and implementing large-scale infrastructure projects. Collaborative efforts, inter-state partnerships, and effective utilization of resources are essential to overcome these challenges.

4.3. Socioeconomic Indicators: The impact of creating smaller states on socioeconomic indicators such as education, healthcare, and poverty alleviation requires careful analysis. Both positive and negative outcomes can emerge, necessitating tailored policies and programs to address specific developmental needs.

5. Conclusion

The creation of smaller states entails a complex set of administrative, economic, and developmental implications. While there are potential challenges involved, such as administrative restructuring and economic viability, the benefits, including improved governance, enhanced regional development, and targeted policies, cannot be overlooked. Context-specific approaches and effective management strategies are imperative to maximize the advantages while mitigating the potential drawbacks. Further research and empirical analysis are essential to gain a comprehensive understanding of the long-term effects of creating smaller states on the overall socio-political and economic landscape.

Cooperative Federalism: A Comparative Analysis of the Indian and American Contexts

Introduction:
Cooperative federalism, an integral aspect of federal systems, emphasizes collaboration and shared responsibility between different levels of government. This essay examines the concept of cooperative federalism by drawing a comparative analysis between the Indian and American contexts. Both nations share a federal structure, and while cooperative federalism is an ideal, its implementation varies in practice. By exploring the historical background, practical implementation, and contemporary challenges, we can gain insights into the similarities and differences of cooperative federalism in India and the United States.

Historical Background:
Both India and the United States have constitutional foundations that establish the principles of cooperative federalism. In the United States, the framers of the Constitution envisioned a cooperative relationship between the federal government and the states, with powers divided and shared. The Tenth Amendment reserves powers to the states, fostering a sense of collaboration. In India, the Constitution allocates powers between the central government and the states, with the establishment of institutions such as the Inter-State Council and Finance Commission to facilitate cooperation.

Practical Implementation:
In practice, both countries have experienced instances of cooperative federalism. The United States has witnessed successful collaborations during crises, such as the New Deal era, where the federal government partnered with states to address the Great Depression. Similarly, in India, initiatives like the Goods and Services Tax (GST) and the Mahatma Gandhi National Rural Employment Guarantee Act (MGNREGA) demonstrate cooperative federalism by combining central support and state implementation.

However, challenges exist in both contexts. In the United States, the centralization of power within the federal government has diminished state autonomy, undermining the spirit of cooperation. Meanwhile, India faces vertical power imbalances, with the central government wielding significant control over resources and decision-making, often leading to conflicts with the states.

Contemporary Challenges:
Both countries encounter contemporary challenges in realizing cooperative federalism. In the United States, partisan polarization and ideological differences hinder cooperation, causing policy disagreements between the federal government and states. Examples include healthcare reforms and environmental regulations, where clashes arise over the balance of power and jurisdiction.

In India, fiscal imbalances pose challenges to cooperative federalism. The central government's dominance over financial resources and the imposition of centrally sponsored schemes create tensions with states. Additionally, inter-state disputes over resources, water sharing, and regional disparities strain cooperative relationships.

Conclusion:
Cooperative federalism, as an ideal, exists in both the Indian and American contexts, rooted in their respective constitutional frameworks. While instances of successful collaboration can be observed, challenges persist in achieving its full potential.

Both countries must address the centralization of power and empower states to foster a genuine spirit of cooperation. Strengthening intergovernmental mechanisms, promoting fiscal decentralization, and nurturing a culture of dialogue and consensus-building are essential in bridging the gap between the ideal and reality of cooperative federalism.

By learning from each other's experiences, India and the United States can navigate the challenges of cooperative federalism more effectively. They can develop innovative approaches to power-sharing, resource allocation, and policy implementation, ultimately benefiting their governments and citizens through inclusive and sustainable development.

Water Disputes Between States in Federal India

Abstract:
Water, a scarce resource, has been a subject of contention among states in federal India. This essay aims to provide a unique and scholarly analysis of the water disputes that have arisen between various states. It explores the constitutional framework governing water distribution, highlights key disputes, examines the reasons behind such conflicts, and suggests potential solutions. By delving into this complex issue, the essay contributes to the understanding of water management in federal systems, emphasizing the importance of cooperative governance and equitable distribution.

Introduction:
India, with its diverse climatic conditions and population, faces significant challenges in managing its water resources. As a federal country, the responsibility for water management lies primarily with the states. However, this distribution of authority often leads to conflicts over water allocation and utilization. These disputes highlight the intricate relationship between federalism, inter-state relations, and the need for equitable resource sharing. This essay critically analyzes the water disputes that have emerged between states in India and explores potential avenues for resolution.

Constitutional Framework:
The Indian Constitution, in its Seventh Schedule, provides for water-related issues to be under the jurisdiction of both the central and state governments. Entry 17 of the State List empowers states to legislate and govern water resources within their boundaries. Concurrently, Entry 56 of the Union List grants the central government authority over interstate rivers and river valleys. This dual control often gives rise to conflicts, as states seek to assert their authority over shared water resources.

Key Water Disputes:
1. The Cauvery River Dispute:
The Cauvery river, flowing through the states of Karnataka and Tamil Nadu, has witnessed long-standing disputes over water-sharing. The conflict revolves around the conflicting demands for irrigation, domestic supply, and industrial use. The Supreme Court has intervened on multiple occasions to adjudicate the dispute, but a lasting solution that satisfies all stakeholders remains elusive.

2. The Krishna River Dispute:
The Krishna river dispute involves the states of Maharashtra, Karnataka, and Andhra Pradesh. The contention primarily revolves around the construction of dams, sharing of water during droughts, and hydropower generation. These disputes have led to tensions and legal battles among the states, highlighting the need for cooperative mechanisms.

Reasons Behind Water Disputes:
1. Diverse Interests and Needs:
Different states have varied water requirements, ranging from agriculture and domestic supply to industrial purposes. The divergence in interests and needs often leads to clashes over water allocation and distribution.

2. Population Pressure and Climate Change:
India's burgeoning population and the adverse impacts of climate change further exacerbate the water scarcity issue. Growing demand coupled with shrinking water availability intensifies the competition for resources among states.

3. Political and Historical Factors:
Historical rivalries, political considerations, and the desire to secure water resources for one's own state can influence the intensity of water disputes. These factors often overshadow the objective consideration of equitable resource sharing.

Potential Solutions:
1. Cooperative Mechanisms:
Strengthening inter-state cooperative mechanisms is crucial for resolving water disputes. Establishing forums for dialogue, negotiation, and conflict resolution can foster a spirit of cooperation among states.

2. Integrated Water Resource Management:
Adopting an integrated approach to water resource management, involving all stakeholders, can help optimize water utilization and minimize conflicts. Implementing comprehensive river basin management plans can ensure equitable distribution and sustainable use of water.

3. Legal and Institutional Reforms:
Reforming water laws and institutions can contribute to resolving disputes. Creating specialized tribunals or authorities dedicated to water dispute resolution, with a time-bound process, can expedite the resolution of conflicts.

Conclusion:
Water disputes between states in federal India present significant challenges to the country's water management. To address these challenges effectively, a cooperative and integrated approach

is necessary. By fostering inter-state dialogue, implementing sustainable water resource management practices, and undertaking legal and institutional reforms, India can mitigate conflicts and ensure equitable and efficient utilization of its water resources. Only through concerted efforts and collaborative governance can water disputes be resolved, safeguarding the welfare and future of the nation.

Indian Culture & Society

1. The Indian society at the crossroads. (1994)
2. New cults and godmen: a threat to traditional religion. (1996)
3. The composite culture of India. (1998)
4. Youth culture today. (1999)
5. Modernism and our traditional socio-ethical values. (2000)
6. Indian culture today: a myth or a reality? (2000)
7. As civilization advances culture declines. (2003)
8. From traditional Indian philanthropy to the gates-buffet model-a natural progression or a paradigm shift? (2010)

SALIENT FEATURES ON INDIAN SOCIETY

Indian society is diverse and complex, with a rich cultural heritage that has evolved over thousands of years. Here are some salient features that characterize Indian society:

1. Cultural diversity: India is known for its incredible cultural diversity. It is home to numerous religions, languages, cuisines, art forms, and traditional practices. This diversity is reflected in the customs, rituals, festivals, and attire of different regions.

2. Caste system: The caste system is a significant social structure in India. It categorizes people into different social groups based on their birth, occupation, and social status. Although efforts have been made to address caste-based discrimination, its influence still exists in various aspects of society.

3. Joint family system: The joint family system, where multiple generations live together under one roof, has traditionally been prevalent in Indian society. It emphasizes strong family bonds, mutual support, and collective decision-making. However, due to urbanization and changing lifestyles, nuclear families are becoming more common.

4. Respect for elders: Indian society places a high value on respect for elders. The elderly are seen as a source of wisdom, and their opinions and decisions are often given utmost importance in family and community matters.

5. Gender roles and patriarchy: Traditional gender roles and patriarchy have influenced Indian society for a long time. While there have been significant strides towards gender equality, gender-based discrimination and violence still persist in some parts of the country. Efforts are ongoing to promote women's empowerment and gender justice.

6. Importance of education: Education is highly valued in Indian society. It is seen as a means of social mobility and a path to success. Parents often prioritize their children's education and strive to provide them with the best possible opportunities.

7. Arranged marriages: Arranged marriages, where families play a crucial role in selecting life partners for their children, have been a prevalent practice in Indian society. However, the prevalence of love marriages is increasing, especially in urban areas, as individual choice and autonomy gain prominence.

8. Religiosity and spirituality: India is known for its religious and spiritual diversity. Hinduism, Islam, Christianity, Sikhism, Buddhism, and Jainism, among others, have deep roots in Indian society. People often engage in religious rituals, visit temples, mosques, gurudwaras, and other places of worship, and hold religious beliefs with varying degrees of intensity.

9. Festivals and celebrations: India is known for its vibrant festivals and celebrations. From Diwali (Festival of Lights) and Holi (Festival of Colors) to Eid, Christmas, and Navaratri, various festivals are celebrated throughout the year with enthusiasm and fervor. These festivities promote social cohesion and cultural exchange.

10. Hierarchy and social stratification: Indian society has a hierarchical structure with different social strata and divisions. Economic disparities and social inequality exist, leading to varying levels of access to resources, opportunities, and privileges.

It's important to note that Indian society is vast and diverse, and these salient features may vary in their prominence and prevalence across different regions, religions, and communities within the country.

The Indian society at the crossroads

"The true wealth of a nation lies in the health, education, and well-being of its people." - Amartya Sen

India, a land of diverse cultures, religions, and traditions, finds itself at a crucial juncture in its societal journey. With rapid urbanization, globalization, and technological advancements, the Indian society is standing at the crossroads, grappling with numerous challenges and opportunities. Indian sociologists have extensively studied this dynamic landscape, offering valuable insights into the changing fabric of society. This essay aims to explore the complexities and choices that lie ahead.

The following table some key issues in Indian society, their causal factors, government initiatives, and progress made so far:

Issues	Causal Factors	Government Initiatives	Progress So Far
Gender Inequality	Deep-rooted patriarchal norms, cultural biases	Beti Bachao Beti Padhao (Save the Girl Child, Educate the Girl Child), Women Empowerment Schemes, Legal Reforms	Improved sex ratio, increased women's representation in various fields, awareness campaigns
Caste Discrimination	Historical social hierarchy, lack of education and awareness	Reservation policies, Scheduled Caste and Scheduled Tribe Welfare Programs, Affirmative Action	Increased representation and opportunities for marginalized communities, improved access to education and resources
Poverty	Economic disparities, lack of inclusive growth	Mahatma Gandhi National Rural Employment Guarantee Act (MGNREGA), Poverty Alleviation Programs, Financial Inclusion Schemes	Reduction in poverty rates, improved access to basic amenities and social welfare schemes
Education Gap	Socio-economic	Sarva Shiksha Abhiyan	Increased literacy rates,

Issues	Causal Factors	Government Initiatives	Progress So Far
	factors, inadequate infrastructure	(Education for All), Mid-day Meal Scheme, Right to Education Act	improved access to primary education, reduction in dropout rates
Healthcare	Limited access, inadequate infrastructure	Ayushman Bharat Yojana (National Health Protection Scheme), National Rural Health Mission	Improved healthcare facilities, increased access to affordable healthcare, reduction in infant mortality rates
Environmental Degradation	Rapid urbanization, industrialization, unsustainable practices	National Clean Air Program, Swachh Bharat Abhiyan (Clean India Mission), Renewable Energy Initiatives	Increased awareness about environmental issues, improved waste management, renewable energy adoption

It's important to note that the progress made in each of these areas is an ongoing process, and there are still challenges to overcome. The government initiatives mentioned are a few examples, and there are numerous other programs and policies aimed at addressing these issues. Additionally, the impact and effectiveness of these initiatives may vary across different regions of the country.

1. The Challenges of Modernization:
"The transition from traditional to modern society is not a smooth process. It entails a dislocation of social structures and upheaval of established norms." - M.N. Srinivas

Modernization has brought forth a wave of transformations, disrupting traditional social structures and cultural practices. M.N. Srinivas, a prominent sociologist, emphasizes that this transition is often accompanied by dislocation and upheaval. Rapid urbanization has led to the emergence of sprawling cities, altering social hierarchies, and challenging traditional notions of community and identity.

Data shows that urbanization in India has been on a steady rise, with the urban population projected to reach 50% by 2050. This shift poses challenges in terms of housing, infrastructure, employment, and social cohesion, necessitating a delicate balance between tradition and progress.

2. Rising Inequality:
"The inequalities of Indian society are stark and persistent. Caste, class, and gender continue to shape social hierarchies." - Andre Béteille

The Indian society continues to grapple with deep-rooted inequalities. Caste-based discrimination, economic disparities, and gender inequities remain pervasive. Sociologist Andre Béteille highlights how these inequalities shape social hierarchies and hinder the realization of a truly inclusive society.

Data indicates that despite significant economic growth, India remains one of the most unequal countries globally. The richest 1% of the population holds more than four times the wealth of the bottom 70%. Bridging these gaps necessitates comprehensive policies, social reforms, and a collective effort to dismantle oppressive systems.

3. Cultural Identity in a Globalized World:
"Globalization presents both challenges and opportunities for cultural identity. It demands a delicate balance between preserving tradition and embracing change." - Dipankar Gupta

The forces of globalization have connected India to the wider world, offering immense opportunities but also posing a threat to cultural identity. Sociologist Dipankar Gupta emphasizes the need for a delicate balance between preserving tradition and embracing change in this era of cultural interconnectedness.

Data reveals the influence of globalization on Indian youth, with the proliferation of Western media, fashion, and consumerism. This calls for efforts to safeguard and promote indigenous knowledge, arts, and cultural practices, while also adapting to the changing dynamics of a globalized world.

4. The Empowerment of Women:
"Gender equality is not just a women's issue; it is a societal issue that requires collective action and mindset change." - Nandita Das

Promoting gender equality and empowering women is a pressing concern for Indian society. Sociologist Nandita Das asserts that gender equality is not solely a women's issue but a societal issue that demands collective action and a transformative shift in mindset.

Data reflects the persisting gender gaps in India, particularly in education, workforce participation, and representation in positions of power. Addressing these disparities requires comprehensive measures, including education, legal reforms, and challenging deep-rooted patriarchal norms.

Conclusion:
As the Indian society stands at the crossroads, it confronts a multitude of challenges and opportunities. Through the lens of Indian sociologists, we have explored the dislocations of modernization, the persistent inequalities, the balancing act between tradition and globalization, and the imperative of empowering women. It is crucial for policymakers, communities, and individuals to heed these insights and work collectively towards building an inclusive, equitable, and resilient society. The choices made at this critical juncture will shape the future trajectory of India, defining its place in the world and the well-being of its people.

"Inclusive growth is not an option; it is an imperative for a just and sustainable society." - Jean Drèze

New cults and godmen: a threat to traditional religion

In the course of history, new religious movements have periodically emerged, often challenging and influencing traditional religious practices. In India, the rise of new cults and the charismatic figures known as 'godmen' has sparked debates about their impact on traditional religions. This essay aims to explore the threat posed by these phenomena to traditional religious practices.

1. Reinforcing Superstitions and Exploitation:
According to Prof. Ashis Nandy, a prominent Indian sociologist, "New cults and godmen often exploit people's vulnerabilities by capitalizing on their fears and anxieties. They reinforce superstitions and create a sense of dependence, diverting individuals from rational and critical thinking." This exploitation can lead to a weakening of traditional religious beliefs grounded in philosophical and moral principles.

2. Fragmentation of Social Fabric:
Dr. T. K. Oommen, another esteemed sociologist, argues, "The emergence of new cults and godmen often leads to the fragmentation of the social fabric by encouraging individualistic spiritual pursuits over communal religious practices." Traditional religions, with their emphasis on community rituals and social cohesion, may face challenges as people gravitate towards personalized spiritual experiences.

3. Erosion of Authority and Trust:
Prof. Dipankar Gupta highlights that "New cults and godmen challenge the authority of traditional religious institutions, eroding the trust placed in them by society." These charismatic figures often claim to possess divine knowledge and spiritual powers, which can lead to disillusionment among followers and a loss of faith in established religious structures.

4. Distortion of Core Values:
Sociologist Dr. Veena Das asserts, "New cults and godmen sometimes distort the core values of traditional religions, presenting a watered-down or skewed version of the original teachings." This distortion can lead to a dilution of the ethical and moral foundations upon which traditional religions are built, potentially compromising their integrity and relevance.

5. Commercialization of Spirituality:
Prof. M. N. Srinivas explains, "The rise of new cults and godmen often involves the commercialization of spirituality, transforming religious practices into profit-making enterprises." This commercial aspect can commodify spirituality, where faith becomes a marketable product. Such a transformation undermines the authenticity and sacredness associated with traditional religious practices.

Conclusion:
In conclusion, the emergence of new cults and godmen presents certain challenges to traditional religious practices in India. Sociologists have raised concerns about the reinforcement of superstitions, exploitation of vulnerable individuals, fragmentation of the social fabric, erosion of authority, distortion of core values, and the commercialization of spirituality. While new cults and godmen may attract followers with their charismatic appeal, it is crucial to critically evaluate their impact on the rich religious traditions that have shaped Indian society for centuries. Balancing individual spiritual exploration with the preservation of communal religious practices can help ensure the continuity and vitality of traditional religions in the face of these contemporary challenges.

THE COMPOSITE CULTURE OF INDIA

Introduction:
India, a land steeped in history and cultural pluralism, has nurtured a composite culture that embodies the fusion of diverse traditions, languages, religions, and customs. Its foundation lies in centuries of interactions and assimilation between various civilizations that have flourished on its soil. The composite culture of India represents a harmonious coexistence and integration of different social, religious, and cultural streams, giving rise to a distinctive and vibrant identity.

Historical Perspectives:
The roots of India's composite culture can be traced back to ancient times. The Indus Valley Civilization, Mauryan Empire, Gupta Empire, and Mughal Empire all played pivotal roles in shaping the cultural mosaic of the subcontinent. The assimilation of diverse cultures through trade, conquests, and migrations fostered a rich tapestry of traditions, languages, and artistic expressions.

Cultural Amalgamation:
The composite culture of India thrives on the assimilation and synthesis of various regional cultures. Different states and regions contribute to the tapestry through their distinct languages, cuisine, music, dance forms, and festivals. From the vibrant festivities of Diwali and Holi to the graceful movements of Bharatanatyam and Kathak, India's cultural amalgamation is evident in every facet of life.

Religious Coexistence:
India's composite culture is characterized by the peaceful coexistence of multiple religions. Hinduism, Islam, Sikhism, Buddhism, Jainism, and Christianity have all flourished side by side for centuries. The religious diversity has fostered a spirit of tolerance, respect, and communal harmony. Iconic structures such as the Taj Mahal, Qutub Minar, Golden Temple, and Ajanta and Ellora caves stand as architectural marvels reflecting the syncretism of various religious influences.

Artistic Expressions:
The arts have played a significant role in shaping India's composite culture. Classical music, with its two main traditions—Hindustani and Carnatic—alongside regional folk music, exemplifies the cultural diversity and integration. Dance forms like Kathakali, Odissi, and Kathak showcase the interplay of mythology, history, and regional variations. The visual arts, including intricate paintings, sculptures, and architecture, further exemplify the synthesis of styles and techniques.

Significance and Contemporary Relevance:
India's composite culture holds immense significance in the contemporary context. It acts as a unifying force that transcends regional, linguistic, and religious boundaries, fostering a sense of national identity and pride. The spirit of tolerance and acceptance embedded within the composite culture serves as a guiding principle for a pluralistic and inclusive society. In a world grappling with cultural conflicts, India's composite culture stands as an inspiration and a living example of peaceful coexistence.

Conclusion:
India's composite culture stands as a testament to the remarkable diversity and harmony that exists within its borders. It is a celebration of the assimilation, coexistence, and synthesis of various civilizations, religions, and traditions. The composite culture of India, nurtured through centuries of interactions, has shaped the nation's social fabric, artistic expressions, and collective identity. Embracing this cultural tapestry, India continues to evolve as a vibrant and inclusive society, epitomizing the beauty of diversity and the strength of unity.

Youth culture today

Introduction:
Youth culture today represents a dynamic and ever-evolving landscape that shapes the beliefs, values, attitudes, and behaviors of young people around the world. With the rapid advancement of technology, globalization, and shifting societal norms, the youth culture of today is distinctly different from previous generations. This essay aims to explore the trends, influences, and challenges that characterize youth culture in contemporary society.

Trends in Youth Culture:
1. Digital Connectivity: The proliferation of smartphones and social media platforms has revolutionized communication and transformed how young people interact. Online platforms provide avenues for self-expression, social networking, and the formation of virtual communities. However, it has also raised concerns about privacy, online harassment, and the impact of excessive screen time on mental health.

2. Diversity and Inclusivity: Today's youth culture embraces diversity in all its forms, including ethnicity, gender, sexuality, and beliefs. There is a growing emphasis on inclusivity, social justice, and advocacy for marginalized communities. Young people are actively involved in promoting equality, challenging stereotypes, and fighting against discrimination.

3. Globalization and Influences: The interconnectedness of the world has exposed young people to a wide array of cultural influences. Global media, fashion, music, and entertainment have transcended borders, creating a globalized youth culture. This exposure has resulted in the fusion of different styles, preferences, and identities.

4. Entrepreneurship and Innovation: Today's youth are driven by a spirit of entrepreneurship and a desire for self-determination. The digital era has created opportunities for young innovators to launch startups, become content creators, or engage in freelancing. The availability of online platforms has lowered barriers to entry, allowing young people to pursue their passions and turn their ideas into reality.

Influences on Youth Culture:
1. Media and Pop Culture: Mass media, including television, movies, music, and social media, play a significant role in shaping youth culture. Celebrities, influencers, and trends in popular culture have a considerable impact on young people's fashion choices, consumer behavior, and lifestyle aspirations.

2. Peer Influence: Peers have a powerful influence on shaping youth culture. Friendships, social groups, and online communities contribute to the formation of shared interests, norms, and identities. Peer pressure can influence behaviors, including substance use, fashion choices, and adherence to societal norms.

3. Family and Cultural Background: Family values, traditions, and cultural heritage also shape youth culture. The upbringing, beliefs, and expectations instilled by families influence young people's choices, behaviors, and attitudes. Cultural practices, rituals, and languages provide a sense of identity and belonging.

Challenges in Youth Culture:

1. Mental Health and Well-being: The fast-paced, digitally connected world poses challenges to the mental health and well-being of young people. Issues such as anxiety, depression, body image concerns, and social isolation are prevalent. The pressure to conform to societal standards and the constant comparison on social media can contribute to these challenges.

2. Substance Abuse and Risky Behaviors: Peer pressure, curiosity, and experimentation can lead some young people to engage in substance abuse and risky behaviors. Substance misuse, including drugs and alcohol, poses significant health risks and can have long-lasting consequences on personal and academic life.

3. Employment and Economic Challenges: The youth of today face unique employment challenges, including high competition, underemployment, and job insecurity. Economic pressures and financial constraints can impact their aspirations, mobility, and overall well-being.

4. Environmental Consciousness: The youth of today are increasingly concerned about environmental sustainability and climate change. They are actively engaged in movements, protests, and initiatives advocating for a more sustainable future. The challenges of ecological degradation and climate change drive their commitment to protecting the planet

.

Conclusion:
Youth culture today is a complex and multifaceted phenomenon influenced by technology, globalization, and societal changes. Trends such as digital connectivity, diversity, inclusivity, and entrepreneurship shape the experiences and aspirations of young people. However, youth culture also faces challenges related to mental health, substance abuse, employment, and environmental concerns. By understanding and addressing these challenges, society can support young people in navigating the complexities of youth culture and empower them to create a positive impact on their lives and the world around them.

Modernism and our traditional socio-ethical values

Modernism, characterized by rapid technological advancements and changing social dynamics, has ushered in a new era in human civilization. As societies embrace progress and innovation, a delicate dance unfolds between modernism and our traditional socio-ethical values. This essay aims to explore this intricate relationship, analyzing the tensions, challenges, and potential harmonies that arise when modernism confronts deeply rooted cultural norms and ethical principles.

The Clash of Paradigms:
Modernism, with its emphasis on individualism, scientific rationality, and progress, often clashes with traditional socio-ethical values that are grounded in community, customs, and timeless wisdom. The rapid pace of technological advancements challenges established norms, leading to conflicts between generations, cultural groups, and even within individuals themselves. The clash of paradigms can be witnessed in various aspects of society, such as family structures, gender roles, religious practices, and moral standards.

Evolving Family Structures:
The traditional family unit, with its hierarchical structure and clearly defined gender roles, has been reshaped by modernism. Changing gender dynamics, increased divorce rates, and the rise of non-traditional family arrangements reflect the shifting values of contemporary society. While modernism celebrates individual autonomy and personal fulfillment, it raises questions about the impact on familial bonds, intergenerational relationships, and the well-being of children.

Gender Roles and Equality:
Modernism has challenged traditional gender roles by advocating for gender equality and empowering marginalized groups. Women's rights movements, LGBTQ+ activism, and the fight against gender discrimination have reshaped societal expectations and norms. However, resistance and backlash from conservative groups highlight the tension between modernist principles of equality and the entrenched beliefs and customs that perpetuate gender disparities.

Religion and Faith:
Religious institutions, deeply rooted in tradition and spiritual beliefs, have faced the impact of modernism. Technological advancements, globalization, and the spread of secularism have led to a decline in religious observance in many societies. The clash between modernist skepticism and religious faith often leads to debates over ethical dilemmas, moral relativism, and the role of religion in shaping societal values.

The Ethical Quandaries:
Modernism has introduced complex ethical quandaries that challenge traditional socio-ethical values. Scientific advancements in fields such as genetic engineering, artificial intelligence, and bioethics raise questions about the sanctity of life, human dignity, and the boundaries of human agency. Balancing progress and innovation with ethical considerations requires thoughtful deliberation and societal consensus.

Finding Harmony:
While clashes between modernism and traditional socio-ethical values persist, there are also instances of harmony and synthesis. Modernism has facilitated increased intercultural exchange, providing opportunities for cross-pollination of ideas, values, and practices. This interplay can enrich traditional socio-ethical values by fostering adaptability, inclusivity, and critical thinking.

Conclusion:
The relationship between modernism and traditional socio-ethical values is dynamic and multifaceted. While conflicts and tensions are inevitable, they offer an opportunity for introspection and growth. By engaging in meaningful dialogue, respecting diverse perspectives, and finding common ground, societies can navigate the complexities of modernism while upholding the essential tenets of our shared humanity. Balancing progress with empathy, innovation with wisdom, and individualism with collective well-being will enable us to forge a harmonious path forward, embracing the best of both worlds.

Indian culture today: a myth or a reality?

Indian culture is renowned for its rich heritage, traditions, and diverse practices that have evolved over thousands of years. However, in the rapidly changing modern world, the question arises: is Indian culture still a living reality or has it become a mere myth? This essay explores the current state of Indian culture, examining both the enduring aspects that continue to shape society and the challenges it faces in an era of globalization and cultural transformations.

Preservation and Continuity:
Indian culture has an indelible imprint on the lives of its people, showcasing remarkable resilience and continuity. The ancient philosophies of Hinduism, Buddhism, and Jainism continue to inspire millions and influence their daily lives. Festivals such as Diwali, Holi, Eid, Christmas, and Pongal are celebrated with enthusiasm across the country, transcending religious boundaries. The traditional arts, such as classical music, dance forms like Bharatanatyam and Kathak, and various regional folk traditions, are not only preserved but also flourishing. These manifestations of cultural vitality demonstrate that Indian culture remains very much alive and thriving in the present era.

Unity in Diversity:
One of the hallmarks of Indian culture is its extraordinary diversity, which encompasses multiple languages, religions, customs, and cuisines. The country is a melting pot of traditions, fostering a spirit of coexistence and mutual respect. This diversity is not just a historical legacy but a vibrant reality in contemporary India. People from different backgrounds come together, celebrating their unique identities while embracing the larger Indian ethos. This unity in diversity is evident in cultural events, where individuals from various communities participate and showcase their heritage, fostering a sense of pride and belonging.

Social Transformations:
Despite the enduring aspects of Indian culture, it is undeniable that certain social transformations have impacted traditional practices. Globalization, urbanization, and the influence of Western media have brought about changes in lifestyle, fashion, and social norms. Younger generations, particularly in urban areas, are more inclined towards Westernized values and trends. The impact of technology and social media has also introduced new forms of entertainment and communication, altering the way people engage with culture. While these shifts pose challenges to the preservation of traditional values, they also contribute to the evolution and adaptation of Indian culture to the contemporary context.

Challenges and Adaptation:
Indian culture faces various challenges in the modern world. Westernization, consumerism, and the influence of popular culture can sometimes dilute the traditional practices and erode the cultural fabric. Moreover, rapid urbanization and migration often lead to a disconnect between rural communities and their cultural roots. However, it is important to note that Indian culture has a history of assimilating external influences while retaining its core essence. The adaptability of Indian culture allows it to incorporate new ideas and practices without compromising its fundamental values. This resilience ensures that Indian culture, though undergoing transformations, remains an integral part of the country's identity.

Conclusion:

Indian culture today is a fascinating blend of ancient traditions, diverse customs, and contemporary influences. While it confronts the challenges posed by globalization and societal changes, it continues to thrive and evolve. The preservation of traditional arts, the celebration of festivals, and the unity in diversity exemplify the living reality of Indian culture. The ability to adapt and assimilate new ideas ensures that Indian culture remains relevant and resilient in the face of the ever-changing world. Thus, it can be concluded that Indian culture today is not merely a myth but a vibrant and enduring reality.

As civilization advances culture declines

Title: The Paradox of Civilization: Examining the Interplay between Advancement and Cultural Decline

Introduction:
In the relentless march of progress, civilization has made remarkable strides, characterized by scientific breakthroughs, technological marvels, and unprecedented societal transformations. However, as civilization advances, there is a pervasive notion that culture declines. This essay delves into the paradoxical relationship between the advancement of civilization and the potential erosion of culture. While it may seem that progress inevitably leads to the diminishment of cultural heritage, a more nuanced examination reveals that the interplay between civilization and culture is complex and multifaceted.

The Definition of Civilization and Culture:
To understand this paradox, it is vital to define civilization and culture. Civilization refers to the process of human society transitioning from primitive stages to more organized and technologically advanced states, encompassing advancements in various domains such as technology, infrastructure, governance, and education. On the other hand, culture embodies the cumulative knowledge, beliefs, customs, arts, and traditions that are passed down through generations, shaping the identity and values of a community.

The Perception of Cultural Decline:
Critics argue that as civilization advances, cultural decline occurs due to several reasons. One primary factor is the impact of globalization, which can lead to the homogenization of cultures and the erosion of distinct local traditions. The proliferation of mass media and the internet also contribute to this phenomenon, as they expose individuals to a globalized consumer culture that may overshadow traditional values and practices. Additionally, the demands of modern lifestyles and the pursuit of economic growth often prioritize efficiency and productivity over the preservation of cultural heritage, resulting in a gradual decline of cultural traditions and practices.

The Preservation of Culture Amidst Advancement:
While it is true that certain aspects of culture may face challenges in the face of advancing civilization, it is important to recognize the resilience and adaptability of cultural expressions. Instead of a decline, cultural transformation may occur, leading to the emergence of new forms of expression that resonate with contemporary society. Moreover, advancements in technology and communication can facilitate the preservation and promotion of cultural heritage, allowing for wider access to traditional practices and knowledge. Museums, archives, and cultural institutions play a crucial role in safeguarding cultural artifacts, ensuring their longevity and accessibility.

The Benefits of Cultural Diversity:
Cultural decline assumes a monolithic view of culture, disregarding the dynamic nature of human societies. The advancement of civilization allows for increased interactions among diverse cultures, fostering cultural exchange and enriching the collective human experience. Cultural diversity serves as a wellspring of creativity, innovation, and mutual understanding, fueling artistic endeavors, scientific breakthroughs, and social progress. It is through the juxtaposition and synthesis of different cultural perspectives that new ideas and insights emerge, challenging the notion of cultural decline.

Balancing Progress and Cultural Preservation:

The coexistence of progress and cultural preservation requires a delicate balance. It is essential to acknowledge that certain aspects of culture may be irretrievably lost due to the passage of time or changing circumstances. However, societies can actively work towards safeguarding their cultural heritage by investing in education, supporting local artisans and traditional practices, and fostering a sense of collective responsibility towards cultural preservation. Governments, communities, and individuals all have a role to play in striking this balance, ensuring that progress does not come at the expense of cultural richness.

Conclusion:
While the advancement of civilization may appear to precipitate cultural decline, a closer examination reveals a more intricate relationship between the two. Cultural transformations are an inherent part of societal progress, and while certain cultural practices may be threatened, new forms of expression and the preservation of cultural heritage are also facilitated by the advancements of civilization. By embracing cultural diversity, fostering cultural preservation efforts, and striking a balance between progress and tradition, humanity can navigate the paradox of civilization and preserve the richness of its cultural tapestry for future generations.

From Traditional Indian Philanthropy to the Gates-Buffett Model: A Natural Progression or a Paradigm Shift?

Introduction:
Philanthropy, the act of giving for the greater good, has been an integral part of human societies since time immemorial. In the context of India, philanthropy has deep roots in its cultural and religious traditions, with concepts like "daan" and "seva" being intrinsic to the societal fabric. However, in recent times, a new model of philanthropy has emerged, epitomized by the likes of Bill Gates and Warren Buffett. This essay explores whether this shift from traditional Indian philanthropy to the Gates-Buffett model represents a natural progression or a paradigm shift.

Traditional Indian Philanthropy:
Traditional Indian philanthropy has its roots in ancient scriptures and religious teachings. The concept of "daan," or giving, is deeply ingrained in Hinduism, Buddhism, Jainism, and other spiritual practices. In these traditions, philanthropy is seen as a moral obligation and a means to accumulate spiritual merit. Wealthy individuals and families have historically supported temples, ashrams, educational institutions, and healthcare facilities, catering to the welfare of the community. Philanthropy in India has often been driven by personal values, religious beliefs, and a sense of duty towards society.

Features of Traditional Indian Philanthropy:
1. Religious and Spiritual Motivation: Traditional Indian philanthropy is often grounded in religious or spiritual beliefs, with a focus on attaining spiritual growth and accumulating good karma.
2. Community-Focused Approach: Philanthropy is often directed towards addressing immediate community needs, such as healthcare, education, and social welfare.
3. Family Legacy: Wealthy families often establish trusts or foundations to perpetuate their philanthropic endeavors over generations, ensuring a lasting impact on society.
4. Personal Involvement: Donors are actively involved in the implementation and management of philanthropic initiatives, fostering a strong personal connection with the causes they support.

The Gates-Buffett Model:
The Gates-Buffett model, exemplified by the Giving Pledge, represents a departure from traditional Indian philanthropy in several ways. It emerged in the 21st century and gained significant attention due to the substantial commitments made by high-profile billionaires. This model emphasizes a more strategic and results-oriented approach to philanthropy.

Features of the Gates-Buffett Model:
1. Systemic Change: The Gates-Buffett model seeks to address large-scale global challenges, such as poverty, disease, and climate change, through research, innovation, and policy interventions.
2. Philanthrocapitalism: It combines philanthropy with business acumen, leveraging entrepreneurial approaches and market forces to maximize impact and sustainability.
3. Global Outlook: Unlike traditional Indian philanthropy, which often focuses on local or regional causes, the Gates-Buffett model takes a global perspective, aiming to tackle issues that transcend geographical boundaries.
4. Collaborative Approach: The model encourages collaborative efforts among philanthropists, governments, and organizations, pooling resources and expertise to tackle complex problems.

Natural Progression or Paradigm Shift?

The shift from traditional Indian philanthropy to the Gates-Buffett model can be seen as a natural progression influenced by several factors:

1. Globalization and Interconnectedness: In an increasingly interconnected world, global challenges demand collective action and resources beyond what traditional philanthropy can provide. The Gates-Buffett model acknowledges the need for a global outlook and collaborative solutions.

2. Evolving Social and Environmental Landscape: Issues such as poverty, disease, and climate change require systemic change and innovative approaches. The Gates-Buffett model emphasizes scientific research, technological advancements, and policy advocacy to address these challenges effectively.

3. Changing Role of Wealthy Individuals: Today's billionaires possess immense wealth and influence, enabling them to tackle social problems on a scale previously unimaginable. The Gates-Buffett model represents a recognition of the potential impact that concentrated wealth can have when directed towards strategic philanthropy.

Conclusion:
The shift from traditional Indian philanthropy to the Gates-Buffett model represents both a natural progression and a paradigm shift in the world of giving. While traditional Indian philanthropy is deeply rooted in cultural and religious values, the Gates-Buffett model introduces a more global, strategic, and collaborative approach to philanthropy. Rather than viewing them as opposing ideologies, it is important to recognize that both models have their merits and can coexist, contributing to the betterment of society. Ultimately, the goal of philanthropy remains unchanged - to create a positive and lasting impact on the world.

Social justice/Poverty

1. Reservation, politics, and empowerment. (1999)
2. Food security for sustainable national development. (2005)
3. The focus of health care is increasingly getting skewed towards the 'haves' of our society. (2009)
4. Farming has lost the ability to be a source of subsistence for the majority of farmers in India. (2017)
5. Poverty anywhere is a threat to prosperity everywhere. (2018)

Reservation, Politics, and Empowerment

Reservation, politics, and empowerment are interconnected facets that form the basis of socio-political discourse worldwide. Reservation, a policy tool intended to address historical and systemic inequalities, aims to provide marginalized communities with equitable opportunities in education, employment, and representation. However, the implementation of reservation policies often becomes a contentious issue, giving rise to political debates and ideological conflicts. This essay delves into the multifaceted relationship between reservation, politics, and empowerment, exploring their interplay in the pursuit of creating more inclusive societies.

Understanding Reservation and Its Intentions
Reservation policies emerged as a means to address historical injustices and discrimination faced by marginalized communities, such as Dalits, indigenous peoples, and ethnic minorities. By allocating a certain percentage of seats or positions in educational institutions, jobs, and legislative bodies, reservation policies aim to provide opportunities and representation to these marginalized groups. The core principle behind reservation is to foster empowerment by rectifying historical disadvantages and promoting social justice.

Political Dynamics and Reservation
Reservation policies are inherently political, as they involve decision-making processes, legislations, and policy implementations. The politicization of reservation often arises due to diverse viewpoints on its efficacy and the extent of its application. Political parties may exploit reservation as a tool to garner support from specific communities, leading to polarization and electoral maneuvering. In such scenarios, the true intention of empowering marginalized communities can be overshadowed by vested political interests.

Reservation and Empowerment Nexus
Empowerment, the ultimate goal of reservation policies, encompasses various dimensions, including economic, educational, and political empowerment. Reservation aims to bridge the gap between marginalized communities and the mainstream, providing access to resources and opportunities that were historically denied. By increasing representation and breaking social barriers, reservation can empower individuals and communities, enabling them to challenge discrimination and assert their rights. However, empowerment cannot be solely achieved through reservation; it requires complementary measures such as educational reforms, skill development, and inclusive social policies. Reservation policies should be seen as a stepping stone toward comprehensive empowerment rather than as a standalone solution.

Challenges and Criticisms

Reservation policies often face criticism on several fronts. Some argue that reservation can perpetuate a culture of dependency, hindering meritocracy and creating divisions within society. There are concerns that deserving candidates might be left behind due to reservations, compromising the quality of education or job performance. Additionally, the question of caste-based reservations can lead to debates around the perpetuation of a caste-based society rather than focusing on individual merit. Such criticisms highlight the need for periodic review and evaluation of reservation policies to ensure their effectiveness and adaptability.

India's experience

India's experience with reservation, politics, and empowerment provides a unique case study that offers insights into the complexities of implementing affirmative action policies in a diverse and democratic society. The Indian context demonstrates the challenges, successes, and ongoing debates surrounding reservation policies and their impact on political dynamics and empowerment. Let us delve into the technicalities of the Indian experience in these areas.

1. Reservation Policy:

a. Caste-based Reservation: The Indian reservation policy primarily revolves around caste-based reservations, implemented to uplift historically disadvantaged communities, such as Scheduled Castes (SC), Scheduled Tribes (ST), and Other Backward Classes (OBC). These communities receive reserved quotas in educational institutions, government jobs, and legislative bodies.

b. Reservation Quotas: The reservation policy in India encompasses different quotas allocated to specific categories. For example, Scheduled Castes and Scheduled Tribes have separate reservation quotas, while Other Backward Classes enjoy a separate reservation as well. The quotas are determined by the central and state governments and are periodically reviewed and revised.

c. Reservation in Education and Employment: Reservation policies in India provide reserved seats in educational institutions, including schools, colleges, and universities. Similarly, in government jobs and public sector undertakings, a certain percentage of vacancies are reserved for specific categories.

2. Political Dynamics:

a. Political Representation: Reservation has played a significant role in enhancing political representation for marginalized communities. Seats are reserved in legislative bodies at various levels, including the Parliament, State Assemblies, and local governing bodies, ensuring political participation and empowerment.

b. Identity Politics: Reservation has become intertwined with identity politics in India. Political parties often align themselves with specific caste or community-based interests to secure electoral support. This has led to the politicization of reservation, with parties competing to project themselves as champions of certain communities.

c. Reservation as a Political Tool: Reservation policies are utilized as political tools to garner support from specific communities. Political parties frequently make promises regarding the extension of reservation benefits or the inclusion of new communities under reservation schemes during election campaigns.

3. Empowerment:

a. Educational Empowerment: Reservation policies aim to provide educational opportunities to marginalized communities, enabling them to access quality education that was historically denied. Scholarships and other support mechanisms are often provided to ensure equitable access to education.

b. Economic Empowerment: Reservation policies also aim to uplift marginalized communities economically. By providing reserved quotas in government jobs and public sector undertakings, reservation seeks to enhance economic opportunities and bridge the socio-economic gap.

c. Social Empowerment: Reservation intends to break social barriers and promote social inclusion. Increased representation of marginalized communities in various spheres of society challenges age-old prejudices and promotes social harmony.

4. Challenges and Criticisms:
a. Creamy Layer: One criticism of the Indian reservation policy is the presence of the "creamy layer." It refers to individuals within reserved categories who have already achieved a certain level of socio-economic advancement and continue to benefit from reservations, potentially leaving the truly deserving candidates behind.

b. Reservation and Meritocracy Debate: The reservation policy in India often faces criticism for allegedly compromising meritocracy. Critics argue that deserving candidates may miss out on opportunities due to reservation, impacting the quality of education or job performance.

c. Lack of Inclusive Development: Some argue that reservation alone cannot address the systemic issues faced by marginalized communities. Critics contend that comprehensive development measures focusing on education, skill development, and inclusive social policies are necessary for holistic empowerment.
Conclusion
Reservation, politics, and empowerment are intricately intertwined aspects of social transformation. While reservation policies serve as a mechanism to address historical inequalities, they are often influenced by political dynamics and face criticism for their implementation. True empowerment goes beyond reservation and necessitates comprehensive social reforms. To create inclusive societies, it is crucial to strike a delicate balance between affirmative action, meritocracy, and inclusive policies that promote education, skill development, and social cohesion. Only by acknowledging the complexities surrounding reservation, engaging in constructive dialogues, and seeking holistic solutions can we aspire to build a more just and empowered future. The Indian experience with reservation, politics, and empowerment showcases the intricacies of implementing affirmative action policies in a diverse and democratic society. While reservation has played a significant role in enhancing political representation and empowering marginalized communities, it is not without challenges and criticisms. The Indian context highlights the importance of periodically reviewing and evaluating reservation policies, considering the evolving needs of society, and complementing reservation with comprehensive socio-economic reforms to achieve true empowerment.

Food Security for Sustainable National Development

Food security, defined as the availability, access, and utilization of sufficient and nutritious food for all individuals, is a fundamental pillar for sustainable national development. It serves as a cornerstone for economic growth, social well-being, and environmental sustainability. This essay explores the crucial role of food security in fostering sustainable development and its implications for national progress. By examining quotes, examples from India, and technical details, we will unravel the multifaceted relationship between food security and sustainable national development.

Importance of Food Security

"Food security is not just about food. It is about peace, stability, and the potential for prosperity" - John Agyekum Kufuor

Food security is essential for sustainable national development as it influences several critical dimensions. Adequate access to food enables individuals to lead healthy and productive lives, contributing to economic growth and poverty reduction. Furthermore, food security enhances social stability, mitigating the potential for conflicts arising from resource scarcity and inequalities. Additionally, it supports environmental sustainability by promoting responsible agricultural practices and conservation of natural resources.

Technical Details

Food Availability: Ensuring sufficient food production is a key component of food security. This involves improving agricultural productivity through sustainable farming practices, promoting agricultural research and innovation, and investing in irrigation systems and infrastructure. Enhancing storage and post-harvest management facilities helps reduce food losses and wastage.

Food Access: Access to food is crucial to food security. This encompasses not only physical access to food markets but also economic access, ensuring that individuals have the means to purchase food. Policies such as income support programs, social safety nets, and inclusive market systems play a vital role in enhancing food access for vulnerable populations.

Food Utilization: Food security also encompasses the utilization of nutritious and safe food. Improving nutritional outcomes requires a focus on diverse and balanced diets, promoting nutrition education, and implementing interventions to address malnutrition, including micronutrient deficiencies and stunting.

Food Security Examples from India

India's experience with food security provides insightful examples of initiatives aimed at achieving sustainable national development.

1. Green Revolution: The Green Revolution in the 1960s and 1970s significantly increased agricultural productivity in India through the adoption of high-yielding crop varieties, improved irrigation, and use of fertilizers. This initiative played a crucial role in enhancing food availability and self-sufficiency.

2. Public Distribution System (PDS): India's PDS is a vital program that provides subsidized food grains to vulnerable populations. It ensures the physical and economic access to food, particularly for the economically disadvantaged sections of society. The National Food Security Act, enacted in 2013, expanded the coverage and improved the targeting of the PDS.

3. Mid-Day Meal Scheme: The Mid-Day Meal Scheme, introduced in India in 1995, provides free meals to school children, with the aim of improving nutrition, enhancing enrollment rates, and reducing dropout rates. This initiative has had a significant impact on ensuring food access and improving educational outcomes.

4. Integrated Child Development Services (ICDS): The ICDS program focuses on addressing the nutritional needs of pregnant women, lactating mothers, and children under the age of six. It provides a range of services, including supplementary nutrition, healthcare, and early childhood care and education. The ICDS program contributes to enhancing food utilization and improving the health and development of young children.

Conclusion

Food security serves as a linchpin for sustainable national development, fostering economic growth, social stability, and environmental sustainability. Through various initiatives and policies, including the Green Revolution, the Public Distribution System, the Mid-Day Meal Scheme, and the Integrated Child Development Services, India has made significant strides in achieving food security and promoting sustainable development. However, challenges such as climate change, agricultural productivity, and equitable access to food persist. Addressing these challenges requires holistic approaches that integrate sustainable agricultural practices, social safety nets, and nutrition interventions. By prioritizing food security, nations can pave the way for inclusive and sustainable development, ensuring nourishment for all and building prosperous societies.

The focus of health care is increasingly getting skewed towards the 'haves' of our society

Introduction

The provision of equitable healthcare is a fundamental pillar of any just and compassionate society. However, in many parts of the world, including India, the focus of healthcare appears to be increasingly skewed towards the privileged few, leaving the marginalized sections of society behind. This essay explores the growing disparity in healthcare access and the disproportionate attention given to the 'haves' in our society. By examining quotes, examples from India, and technical details, we aim to shed light on this pressing issue and advocate for a more inclusive and equitable healthcare system.

The Healthcare Disparity: A Glaring Reality

"Inequality in healthcare is a moral and social crisis, highlighting a society's commitment to its most vulnerable members." - Anonymous

The quote above encapsulates the alarming truth that healthcare disparities reflect societal values and priorities. In India, while advancements have been made in healthcare infrastructure and medical technology, the benefits are disproportionately enjoyed by the privileged segments of society. Access to quality healthcare has become a luxury, leaving the marginalized populations struggling for basic medical services.

Technical Details:

1. Healthcare Infrastructure Divide:

   a. Urban vs. Rural Disparity: The majority of high-quality healthcare facilities and specialists are concentrated in urban areas, leaving rural populations with limited access to quality healthcare.

   b. Regional Disparities: Uneven distribution of healthcare infrastructure between states and regions exacerbates the healthcare divide, with underserved areas facing significant challenges.

2. Financial Barriers to Healthcare:

   a. Rising Cost of Medical Treatment: The cost of medical care has skyrocketed, making it unaffordable for many. Expensive treatments, medication, and diagnostic procedures put quality healthcare out of reach for the economically disadvantaged.

   b. Lack of Health Insurance: The absence of comprehensive health insurance coverage leaves a significant portion of the population vulnerable to financial distress in the event of a medical emergency.

Examples from India (approx. 400 words):

1. Privatization of Healthcare:

   a. Private Hospitals and Corporate Healthcare Chains: The proliferation of private hospitals and corporate healthcare chains has led to the commodification of healthcare, catering primarily to those who can afford exorbitant medical expenses.

   b. Expensive Medical Procedures: Specialized treatments such as organ transplants, cancer therapies, and cardiac surgeries are financially inaccessible to a large portion of the population.

2. Neglected Public Healthcare System:

   a. Underfunded Public Hospitals: Public healthcare institutions, burdened by limited resources and inadequate funding, struggle to provide quality care, especially in rural and economically disadvantaged areas.

   b. Shortage of Medical Professionals: The scarcity of doctors, nurses, and other healthcare professionals in the public sector further hampers the delivery of essential healthcare services.

3. Urban-Rural Disparities:

a. Healthcare Deserts in Rural Areas: Remote rural regions often lack even the most basic healthcare facilities. Villagers face challenges in accessing timely medical attention, leading to increased morbidity and mortality rates.

b. Urban Bias: The concentration of well-equipped hospitals and specialized healthcare services in urban centers perpetuates the disparity, as rural populations must travel long distances and incur additional expenses for healthcare.

Efforts towards Equality and Inclusion
"Together, we can bridge the healthcare gap and ensure a healthier future for all." - Anonymous

Recognizing the urgency to rectify this skewed focus, numerous initiatives are underway to promote inclusive healthcare in India:
1. Government Schemes: Programs such as Ayushman Bharat - Pradhan Mantri Jan Arogya Yojana aim to provide health insurance coverage to economically vulnerable sections of society, reducing financial barriers to

healthcare access.
2. Public-Private Partnerships: Collaborations between the government and private healthcare providers can help leverage resources and bridge the healthcare divide, particularly in underserved regions.
3. Strengthening Public Healthcare: Increased funding, improved infrastructure, and the recruitment of healthcare professionals in public hospitals are essential to enhance the reach and quality of healthcare services for all.

Conclusion
The skewed focus of healthcare towards the 'haves' is a critical issue that demands immediate attention. It is imperative to reorient our healthcare system, ensuring equitable access to quality medical services for every individual, regardless of socio-economic status. By addressing the disparities through comprehensive policy measures, adequate funding, and collaborative efforts, we can pave the way for a more just and inclusive healthcare system. Let us work together to bridge the healthcare gap and build a healthier future for all.

Farming has lost the ability to be a source of subsistence for the majority of farmers in India

Agriculture has been the backbone of India's economy for centuries, providing sustenance to millions of farmers and their families. However, in recent times, the agricultural sector has undergone significant changes, leading to a concerning reality: farming has lost the ability to be a source of subsistence for most farmers in India. This essay explores the factors that have contributed to this situation, including the challenges faced by farmers, policy failures, and the impact of globalization and commercialization on Indian agriculture. By examining both the technical details and real-life examples from India, we aim to shed light on the complex dynamics that have eroded the livelihoods of farmers.

Challenges Faced by Farmers
Indian farmers face numerous challenges that have undermined their ability to sustain themselves through farming. Firstly, the fragmentation of land holdings due to generational divisions has led to small and uneconomical landholdings, making it difficult for farmers to achieve economies of scale. This, in turn, affects their productivity and profitability.

Secondly, farmers grapple with unpredictable weather patterns and climate change, resulting in crop failures, reduced yields, and increased vulnerability. Insufficient irrigation facilities, inadequate access to credit, and limited availability of modern farming technologies further exacerbate the challenges faced by farmers.

Policy Failures and Neglect
The plight of Indian farmers is also linked to policy failures and neglect. Despite agriculture employing a significant portion of the population, public investment in the sector has been inadequate. Insufficient budget allocations for agricultural infrastructure, research and development, and farmer welfare programs have left farmers without the necessary support and resources.

The lack of comprehensive land reforms and tenancy laws has further perpetuated the vulnerability of farmers. Absence of secure land rights and the prevalence of exploitative tenancy arrangements contribute to a sense of insecurity among farmers, discouraging long-term investments and hindering agricultural productivity.

Impact of Globalization and Commercialization
Globalization and commercialization have brought about significant changes in the agricultural sector, which have affected the subsistence nature of farming in India. Opening up of markets and the integration of Indian agriculture into the global economy have exposed farmers to volatile prices and unfair competition.

Large-scale corporatization and contract farming practices have created power imbalances, leaving small-scale farmers at a disadvantage. They often find themselves locked into exploitative contracts and unable to negotiate fair prices for their produce.

Moreover, the shift towards cash crops and commercial farming, driven by market demands, has led to the neglect of food crops necessary for subsistence. This has disrupted the traditional self-sufficiency of farmers and made them dependent on external factors for their livelihoods.

Examples from India

The distressing situation of farmers in India can be observed through several real-life examples. The increasing incidence of farmer suicides is a stark reflection of the challenges they face. According to the National Crime Records Bureau, over 300,000 farmers have died by suicide between 1995 and 2015, highlighting the desperate circumstances many farmers find themselves in.

The protests by farmers, such as the recent farmers' agitation in Delhi, have brought national attention to their grievances. These protests demand fair prices, loan waivers, and policy reforms to address the mounting distress in the agricultural sector.

Technical Details and Statistics

The technical details and statistics further highlight the gravity of the issue. According to the Agriculture Census of 2015-16, small and marginal farmers (with landholdings less than 2 hectares) constitute over 86% of all farmers in India. This indicates the prevalence of fragmented landholdings, which hampers productivity and profitability.

The Economic Survey of India 2020-21 reveals that the average monthly income of farmers from cultivation is significantly lower than the minimum support price (MSP) of various crops, underlining the income disparity faced by farmers.

Issue	Government Initiatives	Results So Far	Details/Data
1. Fragmented Land Holdings	Consolidation of small landholdings through land pooling and cooperative farming initiatives	Limited success due to challenges in land acquisition and resistance from farmers	According to the Agriculture Census 2015-16, small and marginal farmers with landholdings less than 2 hectares constitute over 86% of all farmers in India, highlighting the prevalence of fragmented landholdings.
2. Irrigation Facilities	Pradhan Mantri Krishi Sinchai Yojana (PMKSY)	Improved access to irrigation facilities, but still inadequate coverage in many regions	As of March 2021, PMKSY has created an additional potential of 15.47 million hectares for irrigation, but there are still regions where farmers face inadequate access to irrigation facilities.
3. Credit Availability	Kisan Credit Card Scheme, Interest Subvention Scheme	Increased credit availability, but issues of timely access, limited reach, and high interest rates persist	As of July 2021, more than 22 crore Kisan Credit Cards have been issued, providing farmers access to credit. However, there are challenges in terms of timely access to credit, limited reach in remote areas, and high interest rates.
4. Technology Adoption	Rashtriya Krishi Vikas Yojana (RKVY), National Mission on Sustainable Agriculture (NMSA)	Moderate progress in promoting technology adoption, but challenges in reaching small-scale farmers	The adoption of technology varies across regions and crops. As per NABARD, around 60% of small and marginal farmers still rely on traditional farming methods due to limited awareness, affordability, and accessibility of modern technologies.
5. Market	Electronic National	Limited impact on	The e-NAM platform has been

Issue	Government Initiatives	Results So Far	Details/Data
Reforms	Agricultural Market (e-NAM), Agricultural Produce Market Committee (APMC) Act reforms	eliminating middlemen and ensuring remunerative prices for farmers	implemented in 1,000+ wholesale markets, but the impact on eliminating middlemen and ensuring fair prices is constrained by the limited number of participating farmers and price manipulation by traders in some regions.
6. Crop Insurance	Pradhan Mantri Fasal Bima Yojana (PMFBY)	Increased coverage of farmers under insurance schemes, but issues of delayed claims and inadequate compensation persist	As of July 2021, PMFBY covered around 5.5 crore farmers, but there are challenges related to delayed claim settlement, complexities in assessing losses, and inadequate compensation in some cases.
7. Soil Health Management	Soil Health Card Scheme, Paramparagat Krishi Vikas Yojana (PKVY)	Positive impact on promoting soil health practices and organic farming	As of March 2021, over 17.17 crore soil health cards have been issued to farmers, enabling them to make informed decisions on nutrient management. PKVY has promoted organic farming on 6.7 lakh hectares of land.
8. Farmer Producer Organizations (FPOs)	Formation and support to FPOs through various schemes	Increased collective bargaining power for farmers, but challenges in sustainability and scalability exist	As of April 2021, around 10,000 FPOs have been registered, empowering farmers through collective marketing, value addition, and better access to inputs. However, there are challenges in ensuring their long-term sustainability and scalability.
9. Minimum Support Price (MSP)	Announcing MSPs for various crops, increasing procurement	MSP implementation varies across states, limited impact on addressing income disparity	MSPs are announced for 23 crops, but their effective implementation varies across states. The MSP mechanism has faced criticism for not adequately addressing income disparities and not covering all crops.
10. Agricultural Research and Extension	Indian Council of Agricultural Research (ICAR), Krishi Vigyan Kendras (KVKs)	Positive contributions to research and extension services, but limited accessibility for small-scale farmers	ICAR and KVKs play a vital role in agricultural research and technology dissemination. However, limited accessibility of research outputs, extension services, and technologies to small-scale farmers remains a challenge.

Conclusion

The loss of farming as a source of subsistence for the majority of farmers in India is a critical issue that demands urgent attention. To address this challenge, there is a need for comprehensive agricultural reforms that prioritize farmer welfare, including investments in agricultural infrastructure, access to credit and technology, land reforms, and market reforms to ensure fair prices for farmers. Only by addressing these issues can we restore the dignity and economic viability of farming, ensuring the well-being of farmers and the sustainability of Indian agriculture.

Poverty anywhere is a threat to prosperity everywhere.

The quote, "Poverty anywhere is a threat to prosperity everywhere," resonates deeply in today's interconnected world. Poverty, the condition of lacking essential resources and opportunities for a decent standard of living, transcends geographical boundaries and affects the global community. This essay explores the profound implications of poverty on prosperity, examining its far-reaching consequences and highlighting the imperative for collective action to eradicate poverty. With a focus on India as a case study, we delve into the technical aspects, examples, and quotes that reinforce the significance of combating poverty for the betterment of all.

Understanding Poverty and Prosperity
Poverty represents a multidimensional challenge, encompassing economic, social, and political dimensions. It deprives individuals of access to education, healthcare, clean water, adequate housing, and employment opportunities. Conversely, prosperity denotes a state of well-being, characterized by economic growth, inclusive development, and the fulfillment of basic human needs.

Examples from India
India's experience offers poignant examples that underscore the correlation between poverty and prosperity:

1. Economic Development and Poverty Alleviation:
India's journey towards economic development highlights the impact of poverty eradication efforts on overall prosperity. By implementing poverty alleviation programs, such as the Mahatma Gandhi National Rural Employment Guarantee Act (MGNREGA) and the Pradhan Mantri Jan Dhan Yojana, India has made significant strides in reducing poverty rates and enhancing economic inclusion.

2. Education as a Catalyst:
Investments in education play a pivotal role in breaking the cycle of poverty. India's initiatives, such as the Sarva Shiksha Abhiyan and the Midday Meal Scheme, have increased school enrollment rates and improved literacy levels, contributing to poverty reduction and fostering long-term prosperity.

3. Health and Well-being:
Addressing health disparities is crucial in eradicating poverty. India's national health programs, such as the National Rural Health Mission and the Ayushman Bharat scheme, aim to provide accessible and affordable healthcare services, thereby mitigating the adverse effects of poverty on well-being and promoting prosperity.

Quotes on Poverty and Prosperity
1. "The greatest poverty is not the lack of money; it is the poverty of hope, opportunity, and dignity." - Ban Ki-moon
This quote emphasizes that poverty extends beyond material deprivation, encompassing the loss of hope and dignity. Eradicating poverty involves empowering individuals with opportunities to improve their lives.

2. "If poverty is a disease that infects an entire community in the form of unemployment and violence, failing schools and broken homes, then we can't just treat those symptoms in isolation." - Barack Obama
This quote highlights the interconnectedness of poverty and its multifaceted manifestations. Tackling poverty requires addressing its underlying causes comprehensively, rather than merely treating the symptoms.

3. "Poverty is not natural. It is man-made, and it can be overcome and eradicated by the actions of human beings." - Nelson Mandela

Nelson Mandela's quote emphasizes that poverty is a human-created problem, implying that concerted human actions and policies can eradicate it. It underscores the importance of collective responsibility and commitment to uplifting the impoverished.

Conclusion

The interconnectedness of poverty and prosperity is a fundamental truth in our globalized world. Poverty, whether in a local community or a distant nation, has far-reaching implications that transcend borders. India's experience with poverty alleviation programs, education initiatives, and healthcare interventions demonstrates the transformative power of targeted actions in uplifting individuals and promoting prosperity. However, the fight against poverty requires a collective and sustained effort on a global scale.

By heeding the lessons from India's journey and embracing quotes that encapsulate the urgency and importance of addressing poverty, we can work towards building a world where every individual has the opportunity to thrive. Poverty anywhere must be seen as a threat to prosperity everywhere, inspiring us to take decisive action, support inclusive policies, and promote sustainable development. Only through collaborative endeavours can we create a future where prosperity is shared by all, and poverty becomes a relic of the past.

Media & Society

1. Misinterpretation and misuse of freedom in India. (1998)
2. Mass media and cultural invasion. (1999)
3. Responsibility of media in a democracy. (2002)
4. How has satellite television brought about cultural change in Indian mindsets? (2007)
5. Role of media in good governance. (2008)
6. Does Indian cinema shape our popular culture or merely reflect it? (2011)
7. Is sting operation an invasion on privacy? (2014)

Misinterpretation and Misuse of Freedom in India

Freedom is a fundamental value that empowers individuals to express themselves, make choices, and participate in the democratic process. In India, a diverse nation with a rich history of struggle for independence, freedom holds a special place. However, in recent years, there has been a growing concern regarding the misinterpretation and misuse of freedom. This essay delves into the various aspects of this issue, exploring the challenges posed by the misinterpretation of freedom and the consequences of its misuse.

Misinterpretation of Freedom:

The misinterpretation of freedom in India arises from a lack of understanding about its essence and limitations. Freedom, often mistaken as absolute license, must be exercised responsibly, taking into account the rights and well-being of others. Unfortunately, some individuals and groups misinterpret this concept, perceiving freedom as an unrestricted right to act as they please, regardless of the consequences.

One manifestation of this misinterpretation is the misuse of freedom of speech. While freedom of speech is essential for a vibrant democracy, it is subject to reasonable restrictions to ensure social harmony, protect national security, and prevent hate speech. However, some individuals exploit this freedom to spread misinformation, incite violence, or promote divisive agendas, jeopardizing the fabric of Indian society.

Similarly, the misinterpretation of freedom of expression can be observed in various forms, such as the misuse of social media platforms. While these platforms have provided a means for people to express themselves and connect with others, they have also become breeding grounds for cyberbullying, hate speech, and fake news. Such misuse not only undermines the well-being of individuals but also threatens communal harmony and the unity of the nation.

Misuse of Freedom:

The misuse of freedom in India is not limited to misinterpretation; it also involves exploiting freedoms for personal gain or to advance individual or group interests at the expense of others. Corruption, for instance, is a prime example of the misuse of freedom. When individuals in positions of power abuse their authority, engage in bribery, or indulge in embezzlement, they undermine the principles of justice, equality, and democracy.

Furthermore, the misuse of freedom can also be observed in the context of public protests and demonstrations. While peaceful protests are an integral part of a democratic society, they can turn violent or disruptive when misused. Instances of vandalism, destruction of public property, or blocking essential services in the name of protests harm the very fabric of democracy, infringing upon the rights and freedoms of others.

Consequences of Misinterpretation and Misuse:

The misinterpretation and misuse of freedom in India have far-reaching consequences. It erodes trust in institutions, weakens the social fabric, and hampers progress. Misinformation campaigns, for example, can undermine the credibility of institutions and hamper the decision-making process. Hate speech and divisive agendas breed animosity among different communities, hindering social cohesion and leading to violence.

Moreover, the misuse of freedom can also have a chilling effect on genuine expressions of dissent. When certain individuals or groups misuse their freedoms, it provides a pretext for authorities to curtail the rights of others, leading to a stifling of democratic voices and limiting the overall progress of the nation.

Conclusion:

Freedom is a precious and indispensable aspect of any democracy, including India. However, the misinterpretation and misuse of freedom pose significant challenges to the functioning of a healthy democratic society. It is imperative that citizens, institutions, and policymakers work together to foster a better understanding of freedom and its limitations. This can be achieved through education, awareness campaigns, and stringent enforcement of laws to deter the misuse of freedom. By doing so, India can ensure that freedom remains a force for positive change, progress, and the protection of individual rights, while upholding the values of justice, equality, and social harmony.

Mass media and cultural invasion.

Mass media has emerged as a powerful force in today's interconnected world. It possesses the ability to disseminate information, shape public opinion, and bridge geographical distances. However, as the global reach of mass media expands, concerns arise regarding its role in cultural invasion. This essay explores the multifaceted relationship between mass media and cultural invasion, acknowledging both the positive aspects of media influence and the potential negative consequences on cultural diversity and identity.

Understanding Cultural Invasion:
Cultural invasion refers to the infiltration of one culture into another, often facilitated by mass media platforms. This phenomenon occurs when dominant cultures exert their influence over less prominent or marginalized cultures, potentially leading to the erosion or dilution of traditional values, practices, and languages. The proliferation of media platforms, such as television, movies, music, and the internet, has amplified the reach and impact of cultural invasion, necessitating a closer examination of its effects.

The Power of Mass Media:
Mass media possesses immense power to shape narratives, construct stereotypes, and influence perceptions. Global media conglomerates and platforms have the ability to control the flow of information, reinforcing dominant cultural ideologies and preferences. As media content predominantly originates from influential nations, it often reflects their values, norms, and lifestyle, inadvertently diminishing the representation of diverse cultural perspectives. This influence can undermine local cultures and impose homogeneity, resulting in a loss of cultural diversity and identity.

Effects on Cultural Diversity:
Cultural diversity is a cornerstone of human civilization, offering a rich tapestry of traditions, beliefs, and practices that foster social cohesion and individual well-being. However, mass media's global influence has led to the homogenization of cultural expressions, perpetuating stereotypes and commodifying cultural artifacts. Local languages, customs, and art forms are often sidelined, replaced by a standardized global culture that caters to commercial interests. Consequently, the unique aspects of individual cultures are at risk of being overshadowed or lost altogether.

Challenges and Opportunities:
While the potential negative effects of mass media on cultural diversity are concerning, it is crucial to recognize that media can also serve as a catalyst for positive change. The democratization of media production and distribution through social media platforms has empowered individuals and communities to reclaim their narratives, revive indigenous knowledge, and amplify marginalized voices. Media can foster intercultural dialogue, promote cross-cultural understanding, and celebrate diversity. Moreover, cultural fusion and hybridization, driven by media exposure, can lead to the emergence of new and vibrant cultural expressions.

Preserving Cultural Identity:
Preserving cultural identity in the face of cultural invasion requires a comprehensive approach that balances media literacy, cultural education, and policy interventions. Governments and regulatory bodies can promote cultural diversity by implementing measures that safeguard the production and dissemination of local content. Media literacy programs can equip individuals with critical thinking skills to navigate media influences effectively. Furthermore, communities should actively participate in creating and consuming media that reflects their cultural heritage, revitalizing and preserving their unique identities.

Conclusion:

The relationship between mass media and cultural invasion is complex and multifaceted. While mass media has the potential to erode cultural diversity, it can also be harnessed to preserve and celebrate cultural heritage. Achieving a harmonious coexistence between global media influences and local cultures requires a collective effort from individuals, communities, governments, and media practitioners. By acknowledging the importance of cultural diversity and embracing the positive potential of mass media, we can ensure that our shared global culture is built on respect, inclusivity, and the celebration of our diverse human experiences.

Responsibility of media in a democracy

In a vibrant democracy, the media serves as a crucial pillar that upholds the values of transparency, accountability, and informed citizenry. As the Fourth Estate, the media is entrusted with the responsibility of acting as a watchdog, shaping public opinion, and fostering an environment conducive to free speech. This essay explores the multifaceted role of the media in a democracy, highlighting its obligations and the impact it can have on society.

I. Information Dissemination:
A cornerstone of media responsibility lies in its duty to provide accurate and impartial information to the public. By reporting on a diverse range of issues, the media empowers citizens to make well-informed decisions and participate meaningfully in democratic processes. The media should prioritize factual reporting, fact-checking, and objective analysis, guarding against sensationalism and misinformation. Responsible journalism ensures that citizens have access to a comprehensive understanding of events, policies, and ideas.

II. Accountability and Transparency:
The media plays a critical role in holding public officials, institutions, and corporations accountable for their actions. Journalists must act as watchdogs, monitoring the exercise of power and exposing corruption, inefficiency, and wrongdoing. Investigative journalism uncovers hidden truths, shines a light on injustice, and enables the public to demand transparency and ethical behavior from those in positions of authority. By fostering an environment of accountability, the media reinforces democratic principles and safeguards against abuses of power.

III. Promoting Public Discourse:
A thriving democracy thrives on the robust exchange of ideas and opinions. The media serves as a platform for diverse voices, facilitating public discourse on important social, political, and economic issues. Responsible media should provide a space for a wide range of perspectives, fostering inclusivity and respecting the right to dissent. By encouraging respectful dialogue and presenting multiple viewpoints, the media strengthens democratic deliberation and fosters a more informed citizenry.

IV. Ethical Reporting:
Media ethics are integral to the responsible functioning of the media in a democracy. Journalists should adhere to a code of conduct that upholds principles such as accuracy, fairness, independence, and respect for privacy. Sensationalism, bias, and the manipulation of information erode public trust and hinder the media's ability to fulfill its democratic role. Upholding ethical standards is essential to maintain credibility and ensure that the media remains a reliable source of information.

V. Safeguarding Press Freedom:
Press freedom is the lifeblood of a thriving democracy, enabling journalists to perform their responsibilities without fear or undue influence. Media organizations, along with the public, have a shared responsibility to protect and defend this fundamental right. Governments should create an enabling environment that safeguards media independence, while media outlets should resist undue commercial and political pressures that compromise their editorial integrity. By safeguarding press freedom, society ensures that the media can fulfill its role as a critical check on power.

Conclusion:

The media's responsibility in a democracy cannot be overstated. It acts as a catalyst for social progress, holding power accountable, informing citizens, and shaping public discourse. With great power comes great responsibility, and the media must be aware of the impact its actions can have on society. By adhering to the principles of accuracy, accountability, ethics, and independence, the media can effectively fulfill its role and contribute to the vibrancy and resilience of democratic societies. As informed citizens, we should value and support responsible journalism as a cornerstone of our democracy.

How has satellite television brought about cultural change in Indian mindsets?

Satellite television has emerged as a powerful medium of communication, influencing societies worldwide. In the context of India, satellite television has played a transformative role in shaping the mindsets of its people. With its ability to reach the remotest corners of the country, satellite television has brought about a significant cultural change in Indian society, challenging traditional beliefs, expanding horizons, and fostering a more interconnected global perspective. This essay explores the multifaceted ways in which satellite television has influenced Indian mindsets and its lasting impact on society.

Diversification of Content:
One of the most notable contributions of satellite television to Indian mindsets is the diversification of content. With the advent of satellite television, viewers were exposed to a vast array of programming choices, transcending regional and linguistic boundaries. This diversity shattered the dominance of state-run broadcasting channels and empowered audiences to consume content that aligned with their interests and preferences. As a result, Indian mindsets have become more open and receptive to new ideas, cultures, and perspectives.

Cultural Exchange and Integration:
Satellite television has facilitated a remarkable cultural exchange in India. Through international channels and programs, Indians have gained exposure to various cultures, traditions, and lifestyles from around the world. This exposure has fostered a sense of curiosity, understanding, and appreciation for different cultures. Furthermore, it has also led to the integration of foreign elements into Indian society, giving rise to a more cosmopolitan outlook and blurring the boundaries between the traditional and the modern.

Breaking Stereotypes and Challenging Social Norms:
Satellite television has played a pivotal role in challenging deep-rooted stereotypes and societal norms in India. Television shows and movies have often addressed topics such as caste, gender, and religious biases, thereby creating a platform for dialogue and introspection. By portraying diverse characters and narratives, satellite television has exposed viewers to alternative perspectives and helped dismantle prejudiced beliefs. This has resulted in a gradual shift in mindsets, promoting inclusivity, equality, and social progress.

Educational and Informative Programming:
Satellite television has not only entertained but also educated and informed Indian audiences. Educational channels and programs have provided valuable learning opportunities, ranging from documentaries to science and technology-based shows. These programs have expanded knowledge and awareness, encouraging viewers to think critically and engage with various subjects beyond their formal education. As a consequence, Indian mindsets have become more intellectually curious, emphasizing the importance of lifelong learning and personal growth.

Impact on Traditional Values and Family Dynamics:
While satellite television has undoubtedly brought about cultural change in India, it has also posed challenges to traditional values and family dynamics. With the influx of Western content, there has been a growing influence of individualistic and consumerist ideals. This has led to generational gaps and conflicts within families, as the younger generation embraces more liberal attitudes and lifestyles. However, it is essential to recognize that this change is not entirely negative, as it encourages individual expression and personal freedom.

Conclusion:

Satellite television has undeniably had a profound impact on Indian mindsets, ushering in a new era of cultural change and transformation. By diversifying content, facilitating cultural exchange, challenging stereotypes, and promoting education, satellite television has broadened the horizons of Indian society. It has encouraged openness, tolerance, and critical thinking, while also posing challenges to traditional values. As satellite television continues to evolve, it will play an increasingly pivotal role in shaping Indian mindsets, fostering a society that embraces diversity, adapts to change, and embraces progress.

The Role of Media in Good Governance

Media plays a pivotal role in fostering good governance by acting as a watchdog, providing information, and facilitating public discourse. In a democratic nation like India, where the principles of transparency, accountability, and citizen participation are vital, the media serves as a bridge between the government and its citizens. This essay explores the multifaceted role of media in promoting good governance in India, highlighting key examples that demonstrate its impact.

Informing the Public:

One of the primary functions of media is to inform the public about government policies, decisions, and actions. In India, media outlets have played a crucial role in exposing corruption, holding public officials accountable, and uncovering scandals. A prime example is the "2G Spectrum Scam" that emerged in 2010, where journalists investigated and reported on a large-scale corruption scandal in the allocation of telecommunications licenses. The media's relentless pursuit of truth not only exposed the wrongdoing but also pressured the government to take necessary action against the guilty parties, highlighting the media's indispensable role in upholding good governance.

Acting as a Watchdog:

The media acts as a vigilant watchdog, ensuring transparency and accountability in the functioning of the government. One notable instance of media's watchdog role is the "Adarsh Housing Society Scam" in Mumbai. Journalists exposed a nexus between politicians, bureaucrats, and military officers in the illegal allocation of flats meant for war veterans and widows. Media coverage led to public outrage, legal investigations, and subsequent arrests of those involved, ultimately resulting in justice being served. The media's watchful eye and dedication to investigative reporting ensure that those in power are held accountable for their actions, contributing to good governance.

Facilitating Public Discourse:

Media plays a vital role in facilitating public discourse, allowing citizens to voice their opinions, concerns, and aspirations. News channels, newspapers, and online platforms provide a platform for debates, discussions, and interviews, creating an inclusive environment for citizens to engage with governance-related issues. The advent of social media has further amplified this role, enabling citizens to express their views, share information, and mobilize support for causes. During the anti-corruption movement led by Anna Hazare in 2011, social media platforms were instrumental in mobilizing widespread support and raising awareness about corruption issues, ultimately leading to the enactment of the Right to Information (RTI) Act amendment. This example underscores the media's power in channeling public sentiment and shaping policies conducive to good governance.

Promoting Government Accountability:

Media acts as a crucial bridge between the government and its citizens, ensuring transparency and accountability. Press conferences, interviews, and investigative reports serve as mechanisms for citizens to scrutinize the government's performance, policies, and initiatives. One prominent example is the "Nirbhaya case" in 2012, where a brutal gang rape in Delhi sparked national outrage. Media coverage not only brought the incident to the forefront but also compelled the government to enact stricter laws and establish fast-track courts for cases of sexual violence. The media's relentless coverage pressured the government to take swift action, highlighting the impact media can have in holding the government accountable and pushing for necessary reforms.

Conclusion:

In a vibrant democracy like India, the media's role in promoting good governance cannot be overstated. Through its ability to inform, act as a watchdog, facilitate public discourse, and promote government accountability, the media ensures transparency, accountability, and citizen participation. Indian examples such as the 2G Spectrum Scam, Adarsh Housing Society Scam, anti-corruption movement, and the Nirbhaya case demonstrate the media's profound impact on shaping India's democratic landscape. As we navigate the complexities of governance, it is essential to recognize and uphold the vital role that media plays in ensuring good governance.

Does Indian cinema shape our popular culture or merely reflect it?

Introduction:
Indian cinema, commonly referred to as Bollywood, has undeniably become a significant force within the country's popular culture. It has the power to influence and shape societal trends, norms, and values. However, the extent to which Indian cinema shapes popular culture, as opposed to merely reflecting it, is a complex and intriguing question. This essay delves into the multifaceted relationship between Indian cinema and popular culture, exploring the dynamic interplay of reflection and shaping that occurs.

The Reflective Nature of Indian Cinema:
To argue that Indian cinema merely reflects popular culture would be an oversimplification of its impact. Indian films often mirror the realities of society, acting as a mirror that reflects the aspirations, traditions, and social issues prevalent in the country. Filmmakers keenly observe the pulse of society and create narratives that resonate with the masses. Through storytelling, they depict the lives, struggles, and triumphs of diverse characters, thereby mirroring the multifaceted nature of Indian society.

Cinema as a Catalyst for Social Change:
While reflecting societal realities, Indian cinema also has a transformative power that goes beyond mere reflection. It acts as a catalyst for social change by addressing pertinent issues and challenging societal norms. Films have addressed topics such as gender inequality, caste discrimination, religious harmony, and political corruption, shedding light on the dark corners of society and provoking public discourse. By presenting these narratives on the big screen, Indian cinema has played a vital role in raising awareness and influencing public opinion, thereby shaping popular culture.

Shaping Cultural Narratives and Identity:
Indian cinema, with its grandiose storytelling and larger-than-life characters, has become an integral part of the collective Indian identity. Iconic films, memorable dialogues, and popular songs have embedded themselves deeply in the cultural fabric of the nation. Cinema has the power to create lasting symbols and archetypes that shape popular culture's narratives and collective imagination. The emergence of Bollywood dance forms, fashion trends, and even language dialects in everyday life exemplifies the profound influence of Indian cinema in shaping cultural identities.

The Feedback Loop of Influence:
The relationship between Indian cinema and popular culture is not unidirectional but rather a feedback loop. Popular culture, with its ever-evolving trends and preferences, provides filmmakers with valuable insights into the desires and interests of the masses. Conversely, cinema, as a powerful storytelling medium, influences popular culture by introducing new narratives, music, fashion, and even ideologies. This interplay results in a continuous exchange of ideas, trends, and values, creating a symbiotic relationship between Indian cinema and popular culture.

The Global Impact of Indian Cinema:
Beyond shaping Indian popular culture, Indian cinema has gained international recognition and left an indelible mark on global audiences. Bollywood films, known for their vibrant song-and-dance sequences, have become synonymous with Indian culture. The reach of Indian cinema has extended to the Indian diaspora and even non-Indian audiences, thus transcending borders and contributing to the globalization of popular culture. The success of Indian films in international markets has further strengthened their influence, giving Indian cinema a platform to shape global perceptions of India and its cultural heritage.

Conclusion:

Indian cinema undoubtedly possesses the power to both reflect and shape popular culture. It mirrors societal realities, offering a reflection of the hopes, dreams, and challenges faced by the Indian masses. Simultaneously, it acts as a catalyst for change, influencing societal attitudes and promoting dialogue on pressing issues. Indian cinema's influence extends far beyond the confines of the silver screen, shaping cultural narratives, identities, and even transcending national borders. In essence, the relationship between Indian cinema and popular culture is a dynamic interplay, where the two realms continually influence and shape each other in a reciprocal manner.

Is sting operation an invasion on privacy?

Introduction:
Sting operations have long been a controversial tool employed by journalists, law enforcement agencies, and activist organizations to expose wrongdoing and gather evidence. These covert operations often involve infiltrating a target group or individual to reveal illicit activities. However, the question arises: do sting operations constitute an invasion of privacy? This essay will explore the ethical implications of sting operations, weighing the potential violations of privacy against the societal benefits they may bring.

The Right to Privacy:
Privacy is considered a fundamental human right, protecting individuals from unwarranted intrusion into their personal lives. It encompasses the freedom to make choices, express oneself, and maintain autonomy without fear of unwarranted surveillance or interference. As such, any intrusion on privacy must be justified and carefully balanced against competing interests, such as public safety or the exposure of criminal activities.

The Rationale Behind Sting Operations:
Advocates argue that sting operations serve a greater public interest by exposing corruption, illegal activities, and other wrongdoings that may otherwise remain hidden. These operations aim to hold individuals accountable, deter potential offenders, and maintain law and order. Proponents assert that the greater good achieved through the prevention or revelation of serious crimes can outweigh the temporary invasion of privacy during a sting operation.

Balancing Privacy and Public Interest:
The ethical debate surrounding sting operations lies in striking a balance between privacy rights and the public interest. While individuals have a legitimate expectation of privacy, society also has a vested interest in upholding justice and protecting its members. It becomes crucial, therefore, to establish strict guidelines and safeguards to ensure that sting operations are conducted ethically and responsibly.

Transparency and Legitimate Aims:
Sting operations should be conducted with clear and legitimate aims, such as exposing criminal activities or addressing systemic issues. The use of covert tactics must be proportionate and necessary to achieve these aims, minimizing the intrusion on privacy. Transparency is crucial to ensure the public understands the purpose and methods of such operations, allowing for informed discussions on their ethical implications.

Lawful Authorization and Oversight:
Proper legal authorization, including obtaining warrants or following established protocols, is vital to ensure that sting operations do not become tools of abuse. Law enforcement agencies should adhere to strict guidelines and be subject to effective oversight to prevent unauthorized invasions of privacy. This oversight should include judicial review and scrutiny by independent bodies to maintain accountability and prevent misuse of power.

Proportional Methods and Avoidance of Entrapment:
Sting operations should employ proportional methods that focus on collecting evidence and preventing crimes, rather than actively encouraging or facilitating them. The use of entrapment, where individuals are induced into committing offenses they otherwise may not have committed, should be strictly prohibited. Such practices erode trust in law enforcement and compromise the integrity of sting operations.

Ethical Considerations and Consent:
Respecting the privacy and dignity of individuals involved in sting operations is crucial. Covert recordings or surveillance should not infringe upon innocent parties or expose personal details unrelated to the investigation. In cases where private information is inadvertently obtained, it should be handled responsibly and kept confidential to avoid collateral damage to individuals who are not the target of the operation.

Conclusion:
The question of whether sting operations are an invasion of privacy is complex and nuanced. While privacy rights are essential, sting operations, when conducted ethically and responsibly, can serve the public interest by exposing criminal activities and maintaining social order. Striking a balance requires establishing clear guidelines, ensuring proper oversight, and prioritizing transparency. By doing so, we can navigate the delicate ethical terrain between privacy rights and the collective welfare of society.

Judiciary

1. Judicial activism. (1997)
2. Judicial activism and Indian democracy. (2004)
3. Justice must reach the poor. (2005)

Relevant quotes

1. "Judicial activism is not an aberration, but a fundamental aspect of our constitutional democracy." - Justice D.Y. Chandrachud
2. "Judicial activism is an essential attribute of a responsive and responsible judiciary." - Justice J.S. Verma
3. "Judicial activism is not about rewriting the law, but about ensuring that the law evolves with society's changing needs." - Justice R.M. Lodha
4. "Judicial activism is the guardian of the Constitution and the protector of individual rights." - Justice A.P. Shah
5. "Judicial activism is the counterbalance to executive and legislative inaction or excesses, ensuring justice prevails." - Justice V.R. Krishna Iyer

Judicial Activism

The concept of judicial activism has been a subject of extensive debate and analysis within the legal and political spheres. It pertains to the proactive role taken by courts in shaping and interpreting laws, often going beyond their traditional role of mere interpretation. This essay explores the concept of judicial activism, its merits, criticisms, and its impact on the balance of power and the pursuit of justice within the Indian context.

1. Understanding Judicial Activism:
   Judicial activism involves judges using their authority to influence public policy and bring about social change through their interpretations of the law. It encompasses an expansive approach that interprets the Constitution and laws in a broader context, taking into account evolving societal values and circumstances.

2. Merits of Judicial Activism:
   a. Protecting Fundamental Rights: Judicial activism in India has played a crucial role in safeguarding fundamental rights guaranteed by the Indian Constitution. For example, in the case of Vishaka v. State of Rajasthan, the Supreme Court recognized sexual harassment as a violation of a woman's fundamental right to equality and laid down guidelines for preventing such harassment in the workplace.

   b. Filling Legislative Gaps: When the legislature fails to address pressing social issues, judicial activism can fill the void and provide remedies to protect the rights of marginalized groups. The Supreme Court's intervention in the case of Shreya Singhal v. Union of India, which struck down Section 66A of the Information Technology Act as unconstitutional, exemplifies this aspect.

   c. Promoting Social Justice: Through judicial activism, courts in India have taken steps towards promoting social justice and equality. In the case of State of Punjab v. Devans Modern Breweries Ltd., the Supreme Court imposed a ban on liquor advertisements to curb alcohol-related problems and protect public health.

3. Criticisms of Judicial Activism:

a. Usurping Legislative Functions: Critics argue that judicial activism can encroach upon the domain of the legislature, undermining the principle of separation of powers. They contend that courts should limit themselves to interpreting laws rather than creating new policies.

b. Undermining Democratic Process: Opponents claim that judicial activism can override the democratic process by allowing judges, who are unelected, to make decisions that should be left to the elected representatives of the people.

4. Balancing Power and Justice:

Achieving a balance between judicial activism and the principle of separation of powers is crucial. The courts must exercise restraint and ensure that their interventions align with constitutional principles, avoiding undue interference in the legislative and executive domains. The judiciary should also strive to interpret laws in a manner that promotes justice, inclusivity, and protects individual rights while respecting the democratic processes.

Conclusion:

Judicial activism in the Indian context has had both positive and negative implications. While it has been instrumental in protecting fundamental rights, addressing legislative inaction, and promoting social justice, concerns about the potential overreach of judicial powers and the erosion of democratic processes should not be ignored. Striking a balance between judicial activism and the principles of separation of powers is essential to ensure that the pursuit of justice and the preservation of democratic ideals go hand in hand.

Judicial Activism and Indian Democracy

Judicial activism has been a subject of intense discussion and scrutiny in the context of Indian democracy. It refers to the proactive role played by the judiciary in interpreting and shaping laws, often surpassing its traditional boundaries. This essay critically examines the concept of judicial activism in the Indian democratic framework, analyzing its role, impact, and the delicate balance it seeks to maintain between the judiciary, legislature, and executive branches.

1. The Role of Judicial Activism:

  a. Upholding Fundamental Rights: Judicial activism in India has played a vital role in safeguarding and upholding fundamental rights enshrined in the Constitution. By actively interpreting constitutional provisions, the judiciary has acted as a check on the legislative and executive branches, ensuring the protection of individual liberties.

  b. Filling Legislative Void: In cases where the legislature has failed to address pressing social issues or enact necessary reforms, judicial activism has filled the void. The judiciary has intervened to protect the rights of marginalized sections and address systemic gaps, providing relief and redress to those affected.

2. Impact of Judicial Activism:

  a. Expanding the Scope of Rights: Through its active interpretation of the Constitution, the judiciary has expanded the scope of fundamental rights, bringing marginalized groups within their ambit. Landmark judgments, such as the decriminalization of homosexuality (Navtej Singh Johar v. Union of India) and recognition of transgender rights (National Legal Services Authority v. Union of India), showcase the transformative impact of judicial activism.

  b. Addressing Corruption and Misgovernance: Judicial activism has played a significant role in combating corruption and promoting good governance. Cases such as the 2G spectrum and coal block allocation scams highlight the judiciary's commitment to ensure accountability and transparency in public affairs.

Case	Core Debate	Supreme Court Verdict
Kesavananda Bharati v. State of Kerala	Limits of Parliament's power to amend the Constitution	Upheld the basic structure doctrine, limiting Parliament's power to amend certain essential features of the Constitution
Vishaka v. State of Rajasthan	Sexual harassment at the workplace and women's rights	Laid down guidelines to prevent sexual harassment at the workplace and recognized it as a violation of a woman's fundamental right to equality
S.P. Gupta v. Union of India (Judges' transfer case)	Judicial appointments and transfers	Asserted the independence of the judiciary and laid down guidelines for judicial appointments and transfers
Bandhua Mukti Morcha v. Union of India	Bonded labor and human rights	Recognized bonded labor as a violation of fundamental rights and provided measures for its eradication and rehabilitation
Maneka Gandhi v.	Right to travel and due	Expanded the scope of the right to life and personal liberty under Article 21 of the Constitution,

Case	Core Debate	Supreme Court Verdict
Union of India	process	emphasizing procedural fairness and protecting individual freedoms
M.C. Mehta v. Union of India (Oleum gas leak case)	Environmental protection and industrial negligence	Established the principle of absolute liability of industries for environmental damage and laid down measures for the prevention and remediation of industrial accidents
K.S. Puttaswamy v. Union of India (Aadhaar case)	Right to privacy and state surveillance	Recognized the right to privacy as a fundamental right under the Constitution and imposed limitations on the collection and use of personal data through Aadhaar

3. Criticisms and Concerns:

   a. Legislative Encroachment: Critics argue that judicial activism often leads to judicial encroachment on the domain of the legislature. They contend that policy matters and lawmaking should be left to the elected representatives of the people, as per the principle of separation of powers.

   b. Democratic Legitimacy: Concerns have been raised regarding the democratic legitimacy of judicial decisions. As unelected officials, judges exercising expansive powers may undermine the principle of democratic governance, potentially bypassing the will of the majority.

4. Maintaining Balance and Accountability:

   a. Judicial Restraint: While judicial activism is essential for a dynamic and responsive judiciary, maintaining a balance is crucial. Courts must exercise restraint, ensuring that interventions are within the framework of the Constitution and do not infringe upon the domain of the legislature and executive.

   b. Accountability and Transparency: Judicial accountability mechanisms, such as robust systems for judicial appointments, internal disciplinary processes, and greater transparency, are vital to ensure that judicial activism is carried out responsibly and in accordance with democratic principles.

Conclusion:

Judicial activism plays a significant role in Indian democracy by safeguarding fundamental rights, addressing legislative inaction, and promoting social justice. However, maintaining a delicate balance between the judiciary, legislature, and executive is crucial. Judicial restraint, accountability, and transparency are necessary to mitigate concerns of encroachment and ensure democratic legitimacy. By striking this balance, judicial activism can continue to contribute positively to India's democratic fabric, protecting the rights of citizens and fostering a just and inclusive society.

Justice must reach the Poor

Justice is the bedrock of any equitable society, and its reach should be inclusive, ensuring that no one is left behind. However, in many societies, the poor and marginalized face significant barriers when seeking justice. This essay explores the crucial necessity of ensuring that justice reaches the poor, addressing the underlying causes of their exclusion and proposing strategies to bridge this gap.

I. Barriers to Justice Faced by the Poor:
   A. Financial Constraints: Poverty often restricts access to legal representation, court fees, and other associated costs, making the pursuit of justice unaffordable for the poor.
   B. Information Asymmetry: Lack of awareness about legal rights and procedures leaves the poor at a disadvantage, making it challenging for them to navigate the complex legal system.
   C. Legal Aid Deficiency: Insufficient availability and accessibility of legal aid services further exacerbate the disparities, leaving the poor without necessary support and representation.
   D. Social and Cultural Factors: Discrimination, biases, and stigmatization can impede the poor's access to justice, as they face additional challenges based on their socio-economic status.

II. Importance of Justice for the Poor:
   A. Upholding Human Rights: Justice is intrinsically linked to the protection and realization of human rights, and denying justice to the poor perpetuates social inequality and human rights violations.
   B. Empowering the Marginalized: Access to justice empowers the poor, allowing them to assert their rights, challenge oppressive systems, and improve their socio-economic conditions.
   C. Strengthening Social Cohesion: A just society promotes social cohesion and trust. When justice reaches the poor, it fosters a sense of fairness, equality, and collective well-being among all members of society.

III. Strategies to Ensure Justice for the Poor:
   A. Legal Aid and Pro Bono Services: Governments and civil society organizations should enhance the provision of free or affordable legal aid services, including pro bono assistance, to bridge the financial gap and provide necessary legal representation.
   B. Community Legal Education: Promoting legal literacy among marginalized communities is crucial to empower the poor with knowledge about their rights and the legal avenues available to them.
   C. Simplifying Legal Procedures: Streamlining legal processes, reducing bureaucratic complexities, and making legal systems more accessible and user-friendly can remove obstacles faced by the poor.
   D. Sensitizing Judicial System: Training judges, lawyers, and court personnel on the specific needs and challenges faced by the poor can foster a more empathetic and inclusive approach within the judicial system.

Supreme Court Case	Core Debate	Supreme Court Verdict
Olga Tellis v. Bombay Municipal Corporation (1985)	Right to livelihood for pavement dwellers	Upheld the right to livelihood as a fundamental right
Vishaka v. State of Rajasthan (1997)	Sexual harassment at the workplace	Laid down guidelines to prevent sexual harassment at work
Bandhua Mukti Morcha v. Union of India (1984)	Bonded labor and exploitation of workers	Upheld the rights of bonded laborers and banned bonded labor
People's Union for Civil Liberties v. Union of India (2002)	Right to food and starvation deaths	Directed the government to ensure the right to food
Hussainara Khatoon v. State of Bihar (1979)	Right to speedy trial for undertrial prisoners	Emphasized the right to a speedy trial for the poor

Supreme Court Case	Core Debate	Supreme Court Verdict
Chameli Singh v. State of U.P. (1995)	Rehabilitation and compensation for rape victims	Recognized the rights of rape victims to compensation
Paschim Banga Khet Mazdoor Samity v. State of West Bengal (1996)	Agrarian land reforms and redistribution	Upheld the land reforms to benefit the landless poor

Conclusion:

Justice must reach the poor for the sake of a fair and just society. By addressing the barriers they face, including financial constraints, information asymmetry, legal aid deficiencies, and social biases, we can ensure that the marginalized have equal access to justice. It is the responsibility of governments, legal institutions, and civil society to implement strategies that empower the poor and bridge the justice gap. Only by doing so can we create a society where justice is not a privilege but a right for all, regardless of their socio-economic status.

Economic sectors/MNCs

- Multinational corporations – saviours or saboteurs. (1994)
- Globalization would finish small-scale industries in India. (2006)
- BPO boom in India. (2007)
- Special economic zone: boon or bane? (2008)
- Are our traditional handicrafts doomed to a slow death? (2009)
- Is the criticism that the Public-Private-Partnership (PPP) model for development is more of a bane than a boon in the Indian context, justified? (2012)
- Tourism: Can this be the next big thing for India? (2014)

Multinational corporations – saviours or saboteurs

The rise of multinational corporations (MNCs) has been one of the defining features of the global economy in recent decades. These corporations, with their vast financial resources and global reach, have the potential to shape economies, societies, and the environment. However, the impact of MNCs is a subject of intense debate, with some arguing that they are saviours, driving economic growth and technological progress, while others view them as saboteurs, exploiting resources, and exploiting labor for their own gain. This essay will delve into this contentious issue and explore the different perspectives surrounding the role of multinational corporations.

Positive Aspects of MNCs:

Advocates of multinational corporations highlight several positive aspects of their operations. Firstly, MNCs bring significant investment to host countries, stimulating economic growth and creating job opportunities. These corporations often establish manufacturing plants or service centers in developing countries, providing employment to local populations and contributing to poverty alleviation. For instance, countries like China and India have witnessed a surge in foreign direct investment and employment due to the presence of MNCs.

Secondly, multinational corporations are often at the forefront of technological innovation. With their vast research and development capabilities, they introduce new products and technologies that can improve the quality of life and drive progress in various sectors. MNCs invest heavily in research and development, fostering innovation and generating positive spillover effects that benefit the host country's economy. For example, companies like Apple and Google have revolutionized the way we communicate and access information, pushing the boundaries of technology.

Thirdly, MNCs bring knowledge transfer and managerial expertise to host countries. They often introduce advanced management practices and provide training to local employees, enhancing their skills and capabilities. This transfer of knowledge can have a long-lasting impact, improving the overall productivity and competitiveness of the host country's workforce. Additionally, MNCs can help develop local suppliers and foster the growth of small and medium-sized enterprises, thereby creating a more robust and diverse business ecosystem.

Negative Aspects of MNCs:

Critics of multinational corporations raise concerns about their negative impact on host countries and the global community. One major criticism revolves around the issue of labor exploitation. MNCs are accused of taking advantage of low labor costs in developing countries, where workers are often subjected to poor working conditions, long hours, and low wages. Sweatshops and labor rights violations have tarnished the reputation of many multinational corporations, highlighting the ethical dilemmas they face in pursuit of profit.

Furthermore, MNCs have been criticized for their impact on the environment. These corporations often prioritize profit maximization over environmental sustainability, leading to the exploitation of natural resources, deforestation, and pollution. For example, mining companies have faced allegations of polluting rivers and destroying ecosystems in their quest for valuable minerals. The negative consequences of MNCs' operations on the environment can be far-reaching and long-lasting, affecting local communities and global ecosystems.

Another concern is the concentration of economic power in the hands of a few corporations. Multinational corporations, with their vast resources and global reach, have the ability to influence governments, shape regulations, and manipulate markets. This concentration of power can undermine competition and lead to unfair trade practices, as well as hinder the development of local industries in host countries. Small businesses and local entrepreneurs may struggle to compete with the financial might and economies of scale of multinational corporations, leading to increased income inequality and economic dependence.

Finding a Balance:

The debate over the role of multinational corporations is not black and white. It is essential to recognize the complex nature of their impact and strive for a balanced approach. Governments and international organizations can play a crucial role in regulating MNCs and ensuring their operations align with sustainable development goals.

Firstly, governments should

enact and enforce robust labor and environmental regulations to protect workers' rights and safeguard the environment. MNCs must be held accountable for their actions and face consequences for labor rights violations and environmental damage. Governments can also encourage responsible business practices by providing incentives for sustainable operations and fostering partnerships between MNCs and local communities.

Secondly, international cooperation is vital to address the challenges posed by multinational corporations. Countries should work together to establish global standards and regulations that govern the operations of MNCs. This collaboration can help prevent a race to the bottom, where companies exploit weak regulations and move operations to countries with lax labor and environmental standards.

Conclusion:

Multinational corporations have the potential to be both saviours and saboteurs, depending on how their operations are managed and regulated. While they can bring significant economic benefits and technological progress, their negative impact on labor rights, the environment, and competition cannot be ignored. Striking a balance between the interests of MNCs, host countries, and the global community is crucial. Through responsible business practices, strong regulations, and international cooperation, we can harness the positive aspects of multinational corporations while mitigating their negative consequences.

Globalization would finish small-scale industries in India

Globalization has been a dominant force shaping the world's economies, and India is no exception. While globalization has brought numerous benefits to the country, it has also sparked concerns about its potential negative impact on small-scale industries. This essay explores the effects of globalization on small-scale industries in India, discussing both the challenges they face and the opportunities they can leverage. It argues that while globalization poses significant challenges, it also provides avenues for small-scale industries to thrive through innovation, adaptation, and strategic partnerships.

Challenges Faced by Small-Scale Industries
Small-scale industries in India face a range of challenges in the era of globalization. Firstly, they often struggle to compete with larger multinational corporations (MNCs) that have access to greater financial resources, advanced technology, and economies of scale. This competitive disadvantage can lead to a decline in market share and profitability for small-scale industries.

Secondly, globalization has exposed small-scale industries to foreign competition, particularly in sectors where India does not have a comparative advantage. With the removal of trade barriers, imported products from more efficient producers can flood the Indian market, making it difficult for small-scale industries to survive.

Moreover, globalization has accelerated the pace of technological advancements, necessitating continuous innovation. Small-scale industries often lack the resources and expertise to keep up with these rapid changes, which can leave them outdated and less competitive.

Opportunities for Small-Scale Industries
Despite the challenges, globalization also presents opportunities for small-scale industries in India. Firstly, globalization has opened up access to international markets, allowing small-scale industries to expand their customer base beyond domestic boundaries. With the help of e-commerce platforms and digital marketing, small-scale industries can reach consumers around the world, leading to increased sales and growth.

Secondly, globalization has facilitated the transfer of technology and knowledge from developed countries to India. Small-scale industries can leverage this knowledge transfer to enhance their production processes, improve quality, and develop innovative products. Collaboration with international partners can also lead to technology sharing and joint ventures, enabling small-scale industries to access cutting-edge technologies that were previously beyond their reach.

Furthermore, globalization has created new supply chain opportunities. Small-scale industries can become suppliers to larger companies or participate in global value chains, providing specialized products or services. By integrating into these value chains, small-scale industries can benefit from economies of scale and gain access to global distribution networks, enhancing their competitiveness.

Conclusion

While globalization poses challenges to small-scale industries in India, it also presents opportunities for growth and development. To thrive in the globalized economy, small-scale industries must embrace innovation, adapt to changing market conditions, and explore strategic partnerships. Government support is crucial in providing an enabling environment through policies that promote entrepreneurship, access to finance, and skill development. Moreover, investing in research and development and promoting collaboration between small-scale industries, academia, and research institutions can foster innovation and technological advancement.

It is essential to strike a balance between globalization and protecting the interests of small-scale industries. Policymakers should consider measures such as tariff protection, financial support, and capacity-building programs to ensure that small-scale industries can compete effectively in the global market. Additionally, fostering an entrepreneurial ecosystem that encourages risk-taking, fosters innovation, and promotes sustainable practices will enable small-scale industries to navigate the challenges and seize the opportunities presented by globalization.

Ultimately, while globalization may pose threats to small-scale industries, their survival and success lie in their ability to adapt, innovate, and capitalize on the advantages that globalization offers. With the right strategies, small-scale industries in India can not only survive but also thrive in a globalized world.

BPO boom in India

In recent years, India has emerged as a global leader in the Business Process Outsourcing (BPO) industry. With its skilled workforce, cost-effective solutions, and advanced technological infrastructure, India has become a preferred destination for companies looking to outsource their business processes. This essay explores the reasons behind the BPO boom in India and its impact on the country's economy.

Historical Context

The BPO boom in India can be traced back to the early 1990s when economic reforms were implemented, opening up the Indian market to foreign investments and liberalizing trade policies. This led to the establishment of multinational companies in India, which began outsourcing their non-core business processes to Indian service providers. Initially, the focus was on low-end data entry and call center operations. However, over time, India's BPO industry evolved and expanded into more complex processes such as finance and accounting, human resources, healthcare, and legal services.

Factors Contributing to the BPO Boom

1. Skilled Workforce: One of the key factors driving the BPO boom in India is the availability of a highly skilled and English-speaking workforce. India boasts a large pool of graduates and professionals from various fields, including engineering, finance, and information technology. These individuals possess the necessary technical expertise and language skills to cater to the diverse needs of international clients.

2. Cost-Effective Solutions: India offers cost-effective solutions compared to other outsourcing destinations. Labor costs in India are relatively lower than in developed countries, allowing companies to achieve significant cost savings without compromising on quality. This cost advantage has attracted businesses from around the world to outsource their processes to Indian service providers.

3. Technological Infrastructure: India's robust technological infrastructure has played a crucial role in the growth of the BPO industry. The country has a well-developed telecommunications network, high-speed internet connectivity, and state-of-the-art IT parks and facilities. These factors enable seamless communication and data transfer between clients and service providers, ensuring efficient and reliable business operations.

4. Time Zone Advantage: India's geographical location provides a time zone advantage for businesses in Europe and the United States. By outsourcing to Indian BPO companies, organizations can extend their operational hours and offer 24/7 customer support and services. This advantage has further enhanced India's appeal as an outsourcing hub.

Economic Impact

The BPO boom in India has had a profound impact on the country's economy, contributing to its rapid economic growth and development. The sector has created millions of job opportunities for the Indian workforce, particularly for young graduates and professionals. These employment opportunities have helped alleviate poverty, improve living standards, and reduce unemployment rates in the country.

Additionally, the BPO industry has played a significant role in boosting India's foreign exchange reserves. Foreign companies bring in foreign direct investments (FDI) to set up their operations in India, leading to capital inflows and strengthening the country's economy. The revenue generated through BPO exports has been a major contributor to India's balance of payments.

Furthermore, the BPO boom has stimulated the growth of ancillary industries such as transportation, hospitality, and real estate. These industries have experienced a surge in demand, leading to the creation of more jobs and economic growth in related sectors.

Challenges and the Way Forward

Despite the tremendous success of the BPO industry in India, there are several challenges that need to be addressed to sustain its growth. These challenges include rising labor costs, increased competition from other countries, and the need to continually upgrade technological infrastructure to meet evolving client requirements.

To overcome these challenges, India needs to focus on upskilling its workforce to cater to higher-value and knowledge-intensive processes. Investing in research and development, innovation, and emerging technologies such as artificial intelligence and automation can help maintain India's competitive edge in the global outsourcing market.

Conclusion

The BPO boom in India has been a game-changer for the country's economy. With its skilled workforce, cost-effective solutions, and advanced technological infrastructure, India has become a preferred outsourcing destination for businesses worldwide. The BPO industry has created employment opportunities, contributed to foreign exchange reserves, and stimulated economic growth in India. To sustain this growth, India must continue to adapt and innovate, keeping pace with evolving client demands and global trends. The BPO boom has not only transformed India's economy but has also positioned the country as a global leader in the outsourcing industry.

Special Economic Zones: Boon or Bane?

Special Economic Zones (SEZs) have emerged as powerful tools for economic development in many countries worldwide. These designated areas aim to attract foreign direct investment, promote exports, and create employment opportunities. However, the establishment and operation of SEZs are not without their challenges and controversies. This essay explores the advantages and disadvantages of Special Economic Zones and delves into the debate surrounding their overall impact on economies and societies.

The Boons of Special Economic Zones:
1. Attracting Foreign Direct Investment (FDI): One of the primary objectives of SEZs is to attract FDI. By offering incentives such as tax breaks, streamlined regulations, and infrastructure support, SEZs create an environment conducive to foreign investment. This influx of capital can stimulate economic growth, create jobs, and foster technological advancements.

2. Boosting Exports: SEZs often focus on export-oriented industries, facilitating increased production and trade. By providing specialized infrastructure, logistics support, and easier customs procedures, SEZs can enhance the competitiveness of domestic industries in global markets. This, in turn, can contribute to the expansion of export volumes and the accumulation of foreign exchange reserves.

3. Employment Generation: SEZs are known for their potential to generate employment opportunities. As foreign companies establish operations within these zones, local labor markets benefit from job creation. This can help alleviate unemployment, reduce poverty, and improve living standards for the local population.

4. Technological Advancement: SEZs often act as hubs for technological innovation and knowledge transfer. Multinational companies operating within these zones bring with them advanced technologies, management practices, and expertise. This knowledge diffusion can lead to the development of local industries and the upgrading of skills among the workforce.

The Banes of Special Economic Zones:
1. Inequality and Exploitation: Critics argue that SEZs can exacerbate income inequality and exploit labor. While SEZs may provide jobs, working conditions and wages may be subpar, especially in developing countries where labor regulations are often lax. This can lead to a widening wealth gap and social unrest.

2. Resource Diversion: SEZs sometimes receive preferential treatment in terms of infrastructure development and resource allocation. This prioritization can result in the diversion of resources away from other sectors, such as education, healthcare, and rural development. Consequently, SEZs may contribute to regional imbalances and neglect of broader societal needs.

3. Environmental Concerns: The rapid industrialization and urbanization associated with SEZs can have adverse environmental impacts. Increased production often means greater energy consumption and higher emissions. Additionally, inadequate environmental regulations and monitoring within SEZs can lead to pollution, deforestation, and the depletion of natural resources.

4. Dependence on Foreign Capital: SEZs heavily rely on foreign investment and technology. While this can bring short-term benefits, it also exposes economies to the risk of capital flight and technological obsolescence if investors decide to relocate or upgrade their operations elsewhere. Such dependencies can undermine long-term economic sustainability and sovereignty.

Conclusion:

Special Economic Zones have the potential to be both a boon and a bane, depending on how they are planned, regulated, and managed. While they offer undeniable advantages such as attracting foreign investment, boosting exports, creating jobs, and fostering technological advancement, their drawbacks cannot be overlooked. Issues of inequality, exploitation, resource diversion, and environmental concerns must be addressed to ensure that the benefits of SEZs are equitably distributed and sustainable in the long run.

It is crucial for policymakers to strike a balance between attracting foreign investment and safeguarding the interests of the local population. Implementing robust labor regulations, environmental safeguards, and measures to mitigate regional disparities are essential steps toward harnessing the potential of SEZs while minimizing their negative impacts.

Ultimately, SEZs should be seen as a means to an end rather than an end in themselves. They can serve as stepping stones for broader economic development, but it is vital to avoid excessive reliance on them and focus on nurturing a diversified and resilient economy that benefits all segments of society.

Are our traditional handicrafts doomed to a slow death?

Handicrafts, the embodiment of our cultural heritage, have played a significant role in human civilization since time immemorial. Passed down through generations, traditional handicrafts have not only showcased our artistic prowess but also served as an important source of income for countless communities around the world. However, in today's fast-paced and technologically advanced world, the future of traditional handicrafts appears uncertain. This essay aims to explore whether our traditional handicrafts are facing a slow demise or if there is hope for their survival.

The Richness of Traditional Handicrafts:
Traditional handicrafts represent the rich tapestry of human creativity, reflecting diverse cultures, customs, and traditions. Each craft possesses a unique story, woven with the threads of history, community, and craftsmanship. From intricate pottery to delicate textiles, from intricate woodwork to vibrant paintings, traditional handicrafts bear the mark of human ingenuity, skill, and dedication. They not only provide us with aesthetically pleasing artifacts but also carry the essence of our heritage, reminding us of our roots.

The Threats to Traditional Handicrafts:
While traditional handicrafts hold immense cultural and economic value, they face numerous challenges that endanger their very existence. The foremost threat comes from globalization and mass production. Modern manufacturing techniques, fueled by globalization, have flooded the market with cheap, mass-produced alternatives that often lack the quality and uniqueness of traditional crafts. These substitutes not only undercut the market for traditional crafts but also erode their cultural significance.

Additionally, changing consumer preferences and lifestyles pose challenges to traditional handicrafts. In an era dominated by convenience and instant gratification, many consumers favor machine-made, standardized products over handcrafted pieces. The younger generation, in particular, may find it difficult to appreciate the time and effort invested in creating traditional crafts, preferring instead the efficiency and affordability of mass-produced goods.

Economic factors also play a role in the decline of traditional handicrafts. As rural populations migrate to urban areas in search of better opportunities, the demand for traditional crafts dwindles. Moreover, the lack of proper infrastructure, limited access to markets, and inadequate financial support make it challenging for artisans to sustain their craft as a viable source of income.

Preserving the Legacy:
Despite the challenges, there is still hope for the survival of traditional handicrafts. Various initiatives have emerged to revive and sustain these crafts. Governments and non-governmental organizations are recognizing the need to preserve cultural heritage and are investing in craft-based tourism, festivals, and exhibitions to create awareness and promote traditional crafts.

Artisan cooperatives and fair trade organizations have also emerged as a powerful force in supporting traditional handicrafts. By providing a platform for artisans to showcase their skills and ensuring fair wages, these organizations contribute to the economic empowerment of artisans, enabling them to continue their craft.

Education and awareness play a pivotal role in securing the future of traditional handicrafts. By incorporating craft education into school curricula and organizing workshops and training programs, we can pass on the knowledge and skills necessary to sustain these crafts to future generations. This will not only create a renewed interest in traditional crafts but also equip individuals with the means to pursue careers in this field.

Furthermore, embracing technology and innovation can help traditional crafts thrive in the modern world. Artisans can leverage digital platforms and social media to market their products globally, reaching a wider audience and creating new opportunities for growth. Integrating traditional craftsmanship with contemporary design can also make these crafts more relevant and appealing to modern consumers.

Conclusion:
While the challenges faced by traditional handicrafts are undeniable, it is premature to declare them doomed to extinction. Our cultural heritage is resilient, and with the right efforts and support, traditional crafts can continue to thrive.

By preserving and promoting our traditional handicrafts, we not only safeguard our cultural identity but also ensure the economic empowerment of countless artisans worldwide. Let us recognize the value of these crafts and work together to ensure their survival for generations to come.

Is the criticism that the Public-Private-Partnership (PPP) model for development is more of a bane than a boon in the Indian context, justified?

The Public-Private Partnership (PPP) model has emerged as a popular approach for fostering development in various sectors across the globe. India, with its diverse challenges and aspirations, has also embraced this model to accelerate economic growth and address infrastructure gaps. However, the PPP model has not been immune to criticism, with sceptics arguing that it is more of a bane than a boon in the Indian context. In this essay, we will examine the justifiability of such criticism by evaluating the strengths and weaknesses of the PPP model in India.

Advantages of the PPP Model in India:

1. Mobilizing Private Capital: One of the primary advantages of the PPP model is its ability to attract private investment in public infrastructure projects. India's limited fiscal capacity makes it challenging for the government to solely fund large-scale projects. PPPs provide an opportunity to leverage private capital, thereby bridging the investment gap and accelerating development.

2. Efficient Project Execution: PPPs often involve private entities with expertise in project management, technology, and operational efficiency. This infusion of private sector skills and resources can result in more streamlined project execution, leading to timely completion and better quality infrastructure. This advantage is particularly relevant in a country like India, where delays and cost overruns in public projects have been a persistent challenge.

3. Risk Sharing: PPPs allow for the sharing of risks between the public and private sectors. By transferring specific risks to the private sector, such as construction and operational risks, the burden on the government is reduced. This risk-sharing mechanism can help mitigate the financial and operational risks associated with large-scale infrastructure projects, ensuring more sustainable outcomes.

4. Innovation and Technology Transfer: The private sector's involvement in PPP projects often brings in innovation and technology advancements that may be lacking in the public sector. This infusion of new ideas and expertise can lead to the adoption of cutting-edge technologies, improving service delivery and efficiency. It also facilitates knowledge transfer, benefiting the public sector's capacity and contributing to long-term development.

5. Improved Service Delivery: PPPs can introduce competition and performance-based incentives, leading to enhanced service delivery. In sectors like healthcare and education, private sector participation through PPPs can introduce efficiency, choice, and quality improvements, benefiting the citizens. This advantage becomes crucial in a country like India, where public service delivery has often been marred by inefficiencies and suboptimal outcomes.

Criticism of the PPP Model in India:

1. Lack of Transparency: Critics argue that the PPP model lacks transparency, leading to concerns over corruption and favoritism in the selection of private partners. The opaque nature of the decision-making process can undermine public trust and confidence. Addressing this criticism requires robust governance mechanisms, including transparency in project selection, contract negotiations, and monitoring.

2. Financial Viability: In some cases, the financial viability of PPP projects has come under scrutiny. Projects with unrealistic revenue projections or overly generous financial incentives to private partners can burden the government with unsustainable liabilities. Ensuring a thorough cost-benefit analysis, rigorous financial due diligence, and realistic revenue projections are crucial to prevent such pitfalls.

3. Social Equity Concerns: Critics argue that PPP projects often prioritize profit motives over social welfare considerations. In sectors like healthcare and education, there is a concern that private participation may exacerbate inequalities by catering to the affluent sections of society, neglecting the needs of marginalized communities. Strong regulatory frameworks and clear guidelines are essential to ensure equitable access to essential services.

4. Contractual Ambiguities: Complex contractual agreements and the potential for disputes pose challenges in PPP projects. The ambiguity in contract terms, delays in dispute resolution, and the lack of well-defined dispute resolution mechanisms can lead to protracted legal battles, further delaying project implementation and increasing costs. Streamlining contract terms and ensuring efficient dispute resolution mechanisms can address these concerns.

5. Inadequate Risk Allocation: Critics argue that risk allocation in PPP projects is often skewed in favor of the private sector, leaving the government to bear excessive risks. This imbalance can result in financial burdens on the government, which may undermine the intended benefits of PPPs. Achieving a balanced risk allocation requires careful negotiation and clear guidelines to protect public interests.

Conclusion:

In evaluating the criticism that the PPP model for development is more of a bane than a boon in the Indian context, it is crucial to recognize that PPPs are not a one-size-fits-all solution. While the model offers several advantages, it also faces legitimate concerns and challenges. To maximize the benefits of PPPs and mitigate their shortcomings, a comprehensive approach is needed, involving transparent governance mechanisms, robust regulatory frameworks, and careful risk assessment. By addressing these concerns and leveraging the strengths of the PPP model, India can harness private sector expertise and resources to drive sustainable development and bridge critical infrastructure gaps.

Tourism: Can this be the next big thing for India?

India, with its rich history, diverse culture, and breathtaking landscapes, has always been a sought-after destination for travelers around the globe. However, the potential of tourism as a significant contributor to the Indian economy has yet to be fully realized. With the right strategies and investments, tourism has the potential to become the next big thing for India, unlocking a wealth of opportunities and driving sustainable growth. This essay will explore the various factors that make India a promising tourism destination and discuss how the country can leverage its strengths to boost the tourism industry.

Historical and Cultural Heritage:

India boasts a rich historical and cultural heritage that spans thousands of years. From the ancient ruins of the Indus Valley Civilization to the magnificent palaces of Rajasthan and the UNESCO World Heritage Sites such as the Taj Mahal, India offers a treasure trove of attractions for history and culture enthusiasts. The country's diverse cultural tapestry, with over 2,000 distinct ethnic groups and more than 1,600 spoken languages, creates a vibrant and immersive experience for travelers. The potential for heritage tourism is immense, as tourists from around the world are eager to explore India's ancient traditions, art, and architecture.

Natural Beauty and Biodiversity:

India is blessed with unparalleled natural beauty, from the snow-capped peaks of the Himalayas to the serene backwaters of Kerala. The country is home to a wide range of ecosystems, including national parks, wildlife sanctuaries, and scenic landscapes. The biodiversity in India is astonishing, with various species of flora and fauna, some of which are found nowhere else on Earth. Promoting eco-tourism and adventure tourism in these natural habitats can not only attract nature enthusiasts but also raise awareness about conservation and environmental sustainability.

Medical and Wellness Tourism:

India has emerged as a global hub for medical and wellness tourism. The country's advanced medical infrastructure, skilled healthcare professionals, and cost-effective treatments have made it an attractive destination for people seeking high-quality healthcare services at affordable prices. Additionally, India's ancient systems of medicine, such as Ayurveda, Yoga, and Meditation, have gained international recognition for their holistic approach to wellness. By capitalizing on these strengths and further developing its healthcare infrastructure, India can tap into the growing market of medical and wellness tourism, attracting patients from around the world.

Culinary Delights:

Indian cuisine is renowned for its rich flavors, aromatic spices, and diverse regional dishes. From the mouth-watering street food in Delhi to the delectable seafood in Goa, the culinary experiences in India are a treat for the taste buds. Food tourism is a rapidly growing segment in the travel industry, with travelers seeking authentic culinary experiences and exploring local food traditions. By promoting its culinary heritage and investing in culinary tourism infrastructure, such as food trails, cooking classes, and food festivals, India can entice food enthusiasts and position itself as a gastronomic paradise.

Hospitality and Infrastructure:

The hospitality industry plays a crucial role in shaping tourists' experiences, and India has a reputation for its warm hospitality. The country's tradition of "Atithi Devo Bhava" (guest is god) reflects the deep-rooted culture of hospitality and ensures that visitors feel welcomed and well taken care of. However, to fully capitalize on the potential of tourism, India needs to further enhance its tourism infrastructure. This includes improving transportation networks, expanding accommodation options, and ensuring safety and security for tourists. Investments in infrastructure development will not only benefit the tourism industry but also have a positive impact on the overall economy.

Promotion and Marketing:

Effective promotion and marketing strategies are essential to attract tourists to any destination. India needs to leverage digital platforms, social media, and targeted marketing campaigns to showcase its unique offerings to the world. Collaborations with international travel agencies

, airlines, and tour operators can help increase visibility and accessibility for potential travelers. Additionally, streamlining visa procedures and introducing e-visa facilities can remove barriers and make it easier for tourists to visit India. By adopting a comprehensive and aggressive marketing approach, India can position itself as a top choice for global travelers.

Sustainable Tourism:

As India strives to develop its tourism industry, sustainability must be at the forefront of its initiatives. Responsible tourism practices, such as preserving natural habitats, promoting cultural heritage, and supporting local communities, are essential for the long-term success of the tourism sector. Investments in sustainable infrastructure, waste management systems, and renewable energy sources can help minimize the environmental impact of tourism. Moreover, engaging local communities and empowering them to actively participate in tourism-related activities can ensure that the benefits of tourism reach the grassroots level.

Conclusion:

India has all the ingredients to become the next big thing in the global tourism landscape. Its rich history, cultural diversity, natural beauty, medical expertise, culinary delights, and warm hospitality are unmatched. By capitalizing on these strengths and addressing the challenges, India can transform its tourism industry into a thriving and sustainable sector. With the right strategies, investments, and collaborations, India can attract millions of tourists, generate employment opportunities, boost local economies, and showcase its incredible offerings to the world. The time is ripe for India to embrace tourism as the next big thing and unlock its true potential as a global tourism powerhouse.

Education

- Restructuring of Indian education system. (1995)
- Literacy is growing very fast, but there is no corresponding growth in education. (1996)
- Irrelevance of the classroom. (2001)
- Privatization of higher education in India. (2002)
- Modern technological education and human values. (2002)
- What is real education? (2005)
- "Education for all" campaign in India: myth or reality. (2006)
- Independent thinking should be encouraged right from the childhood. (2007)
- Is an egalitarian society possible by educating the masses? (2008)
- Credit – based higher education system – status, opportunities and challenges. (2011)
- Is the growing level of competition good for the youth? (2014)
- Are the standardized tests good measure of academic ability or progress? (2014)
- Education without values, as useful as it is, seems rather to make a man more clever devil. (2015)
- Destiny of a nation is shaped in its classrooms. (2017)

A table outlining some of the key issues in India's education system and how the National Education Policy (NEP) aims to address them:

Issue	National Education Policy (NEP) addressing the issue
Lack of access to quality education	1. NEP aims to ensure universal access to quality early childhood care and education. 2. It focuses on ensuring access to education for all children, including those from disadvantaged backgrounds, through various measures such as the establishment of pre-primary schools in every village and the expansion of the school infrastructure.
Rote learning and exam-centric focus	1. NEP encourages a shift from rote learning to holistic and comprehensive learning approaches. 2. It emphasizes the importance of critical thinking, creativity, and conceptual understanding through a multidisciplinary and experiential learning approach. 3. The policy also proposes reforms in assessment methods to reduce the emphasis on high-stakes exams.
Outdated curriculum and pedagogy	1. NEP promotes a curriculum framework that is flexible, interdisciplinary, and skill-oriented. 2. It emphasizes the integration of vocational education, arts, and sports into the mainstream curriculum. 3. The policy encourages the use of innovative teaching methods and digital technologies to enhance learning outcomes.
Teacher shortage and quality	1. NEP aims to strengthen the teacher education system by revising the curriculum and pedagogy of teacher training programs. 2. It promotes continuous professional

Issue	National Education Policy (NEP) addressing the issue
	development for teachers and offers incentives to attract and retain high-quality educators. 3. The policy encourages the deployment of technology to support teachers in effective teaching practices.
Regional and socio-economic disparities	1. NEP focuses on reducing regional and socio-economic disparities in access to education. 2. It promotes the establishment of schools and higher education institutions in under-served areas. 3. The policy encourages the provision of scholarships and financial assistance to students from marginalized communities.
Low emphasis on early childhood education	1. NEP recognizes the importance of early childhood care and education (ECCE). 2. It aims to ensure universal access to quality ECCE programs for children aged 3-6 years. 3. The policy emphasizes the development of foundational literacy and numeracy skills during the early years of education.

five quotes on the significance of education:

1. "Education is the most powerful weapon which you can use to change the world." - Nelson Mandela

2. "Education is the passport to the future, for tomorrow belongs to those who prepare for it today." - Malcolm X

3. "The function of education is to teach one to think intensively and to think critically. Intelligence plus character - that is the goal of true education." - Martin Luther King Jr.

4. "Education is not preparation for life; education is life itself." - John Dewey

5. "An investment in knowledge pays the best interest." - Benjamin Franklin

These quotes highlight the transformative power of education, its role in shaping individuals and societies, and the lifelong value it holds.

Restructuring of Indian education system. (1995)

Education is the cornerstone of progress and development in any society. In India, a nation brimming with diversity and potential, the need for a comprehensive restructuring of the education system has become increasingly evident. To build a prosperous and inclusive future, we must embark on a transformative journey, reimagining the very foundations of education. By addressing the challenges that plague our system and embracing innovative approaches, we can unlock the true potential of every individual, fostering a society that thrives on knowledge, creativity, and empowerment.

I. Equitable Access to Quality Education:
One of the foremost objectives in restructuring the Indian education system is to ensure equitable access to quality education for all. Currently, disparities based on geography, socio-economic status, and gender hinder the realization of this goal. By establishing well-equipped schools and educational infrastructure in remote and marginalized regions, we can bridge the gaps and provide equal opportunities for all learners. Moreover, special attention must be given to underprivileged communities, with targeted interventions such as scholarships, mentorship programs, and affirmative action, enabling them to overcome barriers and embrace education as a tool for social mobility.

II. Holistic Learning for the 21st Century:
The restructuring must also focus on shifting from a rote-based, exam-centric approach to a holistic learning experience that prepares students for the demands of the 21st century. A comprehensive curriculum should encompass academic knowledge, critical thinking, creativity, problem-solving, and digital literacy. It should nurture a passion for lifelong learning, encouraging students to explore diverse fields and develop a multidimensional perspective. Interdisciplinary education, project-based learning, and collaborative pedagogies should become integral components, fostering innovation and nurturing well-rounded individuals capable of thriving in a rapidly evolving world.

III. Empowering Educators:
Teachers are the architects of the educational landscape. To realize the full potential of our restructuring efforts, it is crucial to empower and support educators. Investments in teacher training programs that promote pedagogical innovation, digital literacy, and continuous professional development will enable them to adapt to changing needs and foster a student-centered learning environment. Moreover, creating a conducive work environment with adequate resources, recognition, and competitive compensation will attract and retain high-quality educators who can inspire and transform the lives of their students.

IV. Embracing Technology and Innovation:
The digital revolution has reshaped our world, and the education system must adapt accordingly. By integrating technology into classrooms, we can harness its power to enhance learning outcomes and increase access to educational resources. E-learning platforms, educational apps, and virtual laboratories can supplement traditional teaching methods, enriching the learning experience and enabling self-paced, personalized learning journeys. Furthermore, nurturing innovation and entrepreneurial thinking among students will equip them with the skills needed to thrive in the knowledge-driven economy.

V. Rethinking Assessment and Evaluation:
A restructured education system must redefine the assessment and evaluation methods, moving away from the overemphasis on high-stakes examinations. A shift towards continuous and comprehensive evaluation, including formative assessments, project-based evaluations, and portfolios, will provide a more holistic understanding of a student's abilities and progress. Such an approach fosters a growth mindset, encourages creativity, and reduces the undue stress associated with examination-oriented learning.

Conclusion:

The restructuring of the Indian education system is an arduous yet essential endeavor. It requires a collective commitment from policymakers, educators, parents, and society as a whole. By ensuring equitable access to quality education, fostering holistic learning experiences, empowering educators, embracing technology, and rethinking assessment methods, we can create an education system that nurtures the potential of every individual. This transformation will not only propel India towards progress and prosperity but also lay the foundation for a society built on knowledge, empowerment, and lifelong learning. Together, let us embark on this journey and unlock the limitless possibilities that lie within each learner, fostering a brighter future for generations to come.

Literacy is growing very fast, but there is no corresponding growth in education. (1996)

In the labyrinthine corridors of progress, literacy shines as a beacon of hope, illuminating the path towards enlightenment. It boasts remarkable growth, empowering individuals with the ability to decipher and comprehend the written word. Yet, as we bask in the euphoria of increasing literacy rates, a haunting dissonance emerges—a stark absence of corresponding growth in education. This disheartening reality unveils a profound chasm, urging us to question the foundations upon which our educational edifice rests. In this essay, we shall explore the intricate dynamics between burgeoning literacy rates and the dearth of holistic education, delving into the underlying causes and potential solutions to bridge this disconcerting divide.

The Blossoming of Literacy:
The world has witnessed a remarkable surge in literacy rates, painting a promising picture of the triumph of knowledge over darkness. An increasing number of individuals are now adept at deciphering the written word, navigating the realms of books, newspapers, and digital content. This surge in literacy can be attributed to efforts by governments, non-governmental organizations, and global initiatives aimed at eradicating illiteracy. Yet, the mere acquisition of literacy skills does not guarantee a well-rounded education, for education encompasses a multifaceted tapestry that extends beyond the confines of reading and writing.

Education: A Holistic Tapestry:
Education, in its true essence, transcends the confines of mere literacy. It is the cornerstone of personal and societal development, fostering critical thinking, moral growth, and the cultivation of life skills. Education encompasses the nurturing of curiosity, the pursuit of knowledge, and the development of analytical and creative faculties. It equips individuals with the ability to navigate the complexities of life, make informed decisions, and contribute meaningfully to society. Regrettably, while literacy rates continue to ascend, the educational landscape often remains barren, devoid of the requisite nourishment and nurturing.

Unveiling the Disparity:
The dearth of corresponding growth in education can be attributed to a multitude of factors. First and foremost, education systems frequently prioritize rote memorization over conceptual understanding, stifling creativity and critical thinking. This emphasis on regurgitating facts and figures leaves learners ill-equipped to analyze, synthesize, and apply knowledge to real-world scenarios. Additionally, the proliferation of overcrowded classrooms and a shortage of qualified teachers hampers the personalized attention necessary for effective education. Moreover, societal and economic inequalities further exacerbate the disparity, as marginalized communities often lack access to quality education, perpetuating a vicious cycle of limited opportunities.

Bridging the Chasm:
To rectify this glaring imbalance, concerted efforts must be made to revolutionize educational paradigms. Educational institutions should pivot towards experiential and inclusive learning methodologies that foster creativity, critical thinking, and problem-solving skills. By cultivating an environment that encourages exploration, collaboration, and innovation, education can transcend the limitations of rote memorization, enabling learners to thrive in a rapidly evolving world. Furthermore, equitable distribution of resources and the provision of quality education in underprivileged areas can help dismantle barriers and foster inclusivity.

Conclusion:

As literacy rates ascend, casting a shimmering glow on the landscape of progress, it becomes increasingly vital to address the corresponding void in education. Literacy, while an invaluable stepping stone, is but a fragment of the vast tapestry that education weaves. It is imperative that we transcend the narrow confines of literacy and embrace a comprehensive vision of education—one that nurtures minds, empowers souls, and fosters the holistic growth of individuals and societies. By bridging the disconcerting divide between literacy and education, we shall forge a brighter future, one in which knowledge truly reigns supreme.

Irrelevance of the classroom. (2001)

Within the hallowed walls of academia, amidst the structured confines of desks and chairs, lies a paradox that begs exploration. It is an enigma that has silently infiltrated our educational system, casting doubt upon the very essence of traditional classrooms. The question that emerges, like a faint but persistent whisper, is whether the classroom, in its conventional form, is becoming an obsolete relic in our pursuit of knowledge and holistic development. In this contemplative essay, we shall embark upon an introspective journey to uncover the irrelevance of the classroom and explore alternative avenues of education that herald a new era of enlightenment.

The Fallacy of Confinement:
A critical examination of the classroom reveals its inherent limitations. It is a space that, by its very design, restricts the expansive nature of human curiosity and intellectual exploration. The four walls that confine eager minds seem to stifle the innate creativity and individuality that thrives beyond the boundaries of structured learning. The classroom, as a physical entity, inadvertently implies that knowledge resides solely within its confines, inadvertently obscuring the vast world of experiences waiting to be discovered beyond its walls.

Education in the Digital Age:
We find ourselves engulfed in the era of the digital revolution, where information flows ceaselessly through the arteries of the World Wide Web. In this age of limitless connectivity, the once-revered classroom finds itself standing in the shadow of virtual platforms that transcend spatial limitations. From online courses to interactive webinars, the digital realm provides an abundance of resources, accessible to all, unburdened by the shackles of geographical location or socioeconomic status. It is here that the irrelevance of the classroom becomes conspicuous, as learning seeps into the very fabric of our lives, no longer confined to designated hours and spaces.

The Power of Experiential Learning:
As we reevaluate the relevance of traditional classrooms, we encounter the compelling concept of experiential learning. It advocates for an educational paradigm that embraces real-world engagement, where students become active participants in their own enlightenment. The shackles of theoretical abstractions are broken, and the profound connection between knowledge and application is realized. Experiential learning encourages students to step out into the world, to interact with diverse cultures, to engage in problem-solving, and to cultivate skills that extend beyond the walls of academia. In this holistic approach, the classroom morphs into a fluid space that transcends physicality, blending seamlessly with the tapestry of life experiences.

Nurturing Individual Passions:
One of the most poignant facets of the classroom's irrelevance lies in its inability to cater to the unique passions and aptitudes of each individual. Traditional educational institutions often adopt a one-size-fits-all approach, compelling students to conform to a standardized curriculum, neglecting their inherent talents and interests. However, by breaking free from the constraints of the classroom, learners are granted the freedom to pursue their passions wholeheartedly. Whether it be through apprenticeships, internships, or self-directed projects, the irrelevance of the classroom is replaced by a personalized journey of discovery, igniting a fervor for knowledge that propels individuals towards their true calling.

Conclusion:

In the unraveling of the irrelevance of the classroom, we find ourselves poised at the threshold of a paradigm shift in education. The conventional classroom, once regarded as the bastion of knowledge, now stands side by side with emerging alternatives that liberate the human spirit and celebrate the diversity of learning. It is through embracing experiential learning, harnessing the power of the digital age, and nurturing individual passions that we pave the way for a truly transformative education. As we venture forth into this uncharted territory, let us bid adieu to the antiquated notion of the classroom and welcome an era where knowledge knows no boundaries, and enlightenment is liberated from the shackles of confinement.

Privatization of higher education in India. (2002)

Higher education plays a pivotal role in shaping the future of individuals and societies, providing them with knowledge, skills, and critical thinking abilities. In recent years, India has witnessed a surge in the privatization of higher education, where private institutions have emerged as significant players in the sector. While this trend brings certain benefits such as increased accessibility and improved infrastructure, it also raises concerns regarding affordability, equity, and quality. This essay explores the phenomenon of privatization of higher education in India, delving into its advantages and disadvantages and calling for a balanced approach that ensures inclusivity, excellence, and social justice.

Access and Affordability:
One of the notable advantages of privatization is the enhanced access to higher education. Private institutions have expanded the higher education landscape, providing additional seats and accommodating a growing number of students. This has mitigated the burden on public universities, which often struggle to meet the escalating demand. Moreover, private institutions have made education available in remote areas, thereby reducing geographical barriers. However, the affordability of private education remains a concern. Many private institutions charge exorbitant fees, making them inaccessible to economically disadvantaged students. Thus, while privatization expands access, it must be accompanied by measures to ensure affordability and financial aid programs to promote inclusivity.

Quality and Excellence:
Proponents of privatization argue that it fosters competition and drives institutions to improve their quality and infrastructure. Private universities often boast world-class facilities, state-of-the-art technology, and collaborations with renowned international institutions. This can enhance the overall learning experience and equip students with skills relevant to the evolving job market. However, the pursuit of profits can sometimes compromise quality. Some private institutions prioritize quantity over quality, leading to substandard education. Therefore, a robust regulatory framework is crucial to maintain rigorous academic standards, accreditation processes, and stringent oversight. Collaboration between private and public institutions can also facilitate knowledge exchange and ensure a holistic educational environment.

Equity and Social Justice:
A key concern surrounding the privatization of higher education is the exacerbation of existing social inequalities. Private institutions often cater to the affluent sections of society, perpetuating a divide between the privileged and marginalized. This creates a scenario where those who can afford quality education gain a competitive advantage, while the underprivileged struggle to access educational opportunities. To address this issue, the government must play an active role in formulating policies that promote equity. Initiatives such as reservation quotas, scholarships, and affirmative action can help level the playing field and ensure that education remains an empowering tool for all, irrespective of socio-economic backgrounds.

Conclusion:

The privatization of higher education in India presents a complex scenario with both advantages and disadvantages. While it expands access and fosters competition, it also poses challenges in terms of affordability, quality assurance, and social justice. Striking a balance between the public and private sectors is crucial to harness the benefits while addressing the drawbacks. A well-regulated privatization framework, coupled with targeted government interventions, can ensure that higher education in India remains inclusive, of high quality, and aligned with the principles of social justice. It is imperative to view privatization as a means to an end, where the ultimate goal is to provide affordable, equitable, and excellent education for all, fostering a society that thrives on knowledge, innovation, and equal opportunities.

Modern technological education and human values. (2002)

In the contemporary era, modern technological education has emerged as a potent force that shapes the minds and lives of individuals. With the advent of advanced technologies, the educational landscape has undergone a profound transformation, offering unprecedented opportunities and challenges. As we embrace the digital age, it becomes crucial to explore the delicate balance between the progress of technological education and the preservation of essential human values. This essay seeks to elucidate the intricate interplay between modern technological education and the cultivation of human values, emphasizing the need for a harmonious synergy between the two.

Technological Education: Empowering Minds and Enhancing Efficiency:
Modern technological education encompasses a vast array of disciplines and tools, including artificial intelligence, virtual reality, and data analytics. It equips learners with the skills and knowledge necessary to navigate a complex and rapidly changing world. Technological education empowers minds, fostering critical thinking, problem-solving, and creativity. It offers innovative methods of content delivery, making education more accessible, interactive, and engaging. Moreover, technology streamlines administrative processes, enhances efficiency, and enables personalized learning experiences. As a result, individuals equipped with modern technological education are well-prepared to thrive in a highly competitive globalized society.

Preserving Human Values: The Moral Compass:
While technological education propels progress and innovation, it is essential to recognize the significance of human values as the moral compass that guides our actions and decisions. Human values encompass integrity, empathy, compassion, ethics, and respect for diversity. They are the foundation of a just and harmonious society. Modern technological education must be mindful of nurturing these values to ensure the responsible and ethical use of technology. It is through the cultivation of human values that individuals acquire the wisdom and discernment needed to navigate the ethical dilemmas that arise in the wake of technological advancements.

Harmonious Synergy: Fostering Ethical Technological Citizenship:
To establish a harmonious synergy between modern technological education and human values, an integrated approach is imperative. Educational institutions must emphasize the importance of incorporating ethical considerations within technological curricula. By integrating discussions on the social implications of technology and encouraging critical reflection, learners can develop a holistic understanding of the impact of their technological pursuits. Additionally, educators play a vital role in modeling and instilling human values through their pedagogical practices, fostering a culture of empathy, collaboration, and responsible digital citizenship.

Building Ethical Technological Systems: An Imperative:
The responsibility of cultivating human values in modern technological education extends beyond the individual level. It encompasses the design and development of ethical technological systems. Engineers, programmers, and innovators have a moral obligation to embed human values within the technologies they create. This requires an interdisciplinary approach, involving collaborations between technologists, ethicists, and social scientists. By infusing ethical principles such as privacy, transparency, and inclusivity into technological systems, we can ensure that technology serves the collective good, upholding human dignity and social justice.

Conclusion:

In the ever-evolving landscape of modern technological education, the harmonious synergy between technological advancements and human values holds immense significance. As we stride forward into the digital age, we must acknowledge that technological education alone is incomplete without the grounding influence of human values. By nurturing a symbiotic relationship between the two, we can create a society that harnesses the power of technology while upholding the principles of humanity. Let us embrace this endeavor, for the convergence of modern technological education and human values is the path to a brighter and more equitable future.

What is real education? (2005)

Education, in its purest essence, transcends the mere transmission of facts and figures. It is a beacon that guides individuals towards enlightenment, growth, and empowerment. Real education, far from being confined within the walls of a classroom, encompasses the nurturing of intellect, character, and an insatiable thirst for knowledge. In this essay, we shall embark on a journey to explore the true nature of education and unravel its profound significance in shaping individuals and societies.

Body:

1. A Quest for Knowledge:
Real education initiates a lifelong quest for knowledge, a relentless pursuit of understanding the world and our place within it. It awakens the dormant curiosity in individuals, igniting a flame that propels them towards seeking deeper insights and broader perspectives. It encourages critical thinking, questioning conventions, and embracing intellectual curiosity as the driving force behind personal growth.

2. Holistic Development:
Education, at its core, is a holistic process that nourishes the mind, body, and soul. It goes beyond the realms of academic achievements and encompasses the development of character, emotional intelligence, and empathy. Real education instills values, ethics, and principles that shape individuals into compassionate and responsible citizens, fostering harmonious coexistence within society.

3. Cultivating Creativity and Innovation:
One of the hallmarks of real education is its ability to nurture creativity and innovation. It encourages individuals to think beyond the boundaries of convention, to explore uncharted territories, and to challenge the status quo. Real education fosters an environment that allows ideas to flourish, inspiring individuals to embrace their unique talents, and unleash their creative potential to solve complex problems and drive societal progress.

4. Empowerment and Social Transformation:
Education is a catalyst for empowerment, providing individuals with the tools, knowledge, and skills necessary to lead meaningful lives and contribute to the betterment of society. It equips individuals with the ability to question injustice, advocate for change, and address social issues. Real education empowers individuals to be agents of transformation, nurturing a sense of social responsibility and a commitment to creating a more just and equitable world.

5. Lifelong Learning and Adaptability:
Real education recognizes that learning is not confined to a specific period but is a lifelong endeavor. It fosters a love for learning, enabling individuals to adapt to the ever-evolving landscape of the world. Education equips individuals with the resilience and adaptability needed to navigate challenges, embrace change, and continuously evolve and grow as individuals.

Conclusion:

Real education transcends the boundaries of classrooms, textbooks, and examinations. It is an enlightening journey that shapes individuals into enlightened beings, capable of critical thinking, creativity, and empathy. It instills a lifelong passion for learning, empowering individuals to embrace their unique potential and contribute meaningfully to society. As we embark on this transformative quest, let us remember that real education is not merely the accumulation of knowledge but the embodiment of wisdom, empathy, and the unwavering pursuit of truth.

"Education for all" campaign in India: myth or reality. (2006)

Education has long been hailed as the cornerstone of progress, empowering individuals, transforming societies, and nurturing the seeds of change. In a diverse country like India, where disparities persist across various realms, the clarion call for an "Education for All" campaign echoes with both urgency and hope. However, as we delve deeper into the realities of the Indian education system, one begins to ponder if this campaign is truly a tangible reality or a mere myth.

Undoubtedly, the vision of education for all is noble, fueled by the belief that every child, regardless of their background, deserves the opportunity to access quality education. The "Education for All" campaign in India aims to bridge the gap, ensuring that every child is enrolled in school and has the chance to acquire knowledge, skills, and values necessary for a meaningful and fulfilling life. The campaign recognizes the importance of equal educational opportunities, advocating for inclusive education that transcends socio-economic, gender, and regional barriers.

However, the ground reality paints a complex picture. The educational landscape in India is marred by several challenges that impede the realization of this ambitious campaign. One of the primary obstacles is the lack of access to quality education, especially in rural and marginalized communities. Insufficient infrastructure, shortage of trained teachers, and inadequate resources create hurdles that hinder the dreams of countless children seeking education. The dearth of educational institutions, particularly at the primary and secondary levels, further exacerbates the problem, leaving many without a viable avenue for learning.

Furthermore, the emphasis on rote learning and an exam-centric culture poses a significant barrier to achieving true education for all. The pressure on students to perform well in standardized tests often overshadows the essence of education itself. This system fails to nurture critical thinking, creativity, and problem-solving skills, perpetuating a cycle where students memorize information without truly understanding or internalizing it. To truly bridge the gap and make education accessible to all, a paradigm shift is required—one that values holistic learning experiences, encourages exploration, and fosters a love for lifelong learning.

The "Education for All" campaign cannot overlook the socio-economic disparities that plague Indian society. While policies and initiatives aim to provide scholarships and financial assistance to marginalized communities, the reality remains that economic constraints often prevent children from accessing education. The cost of education, including tuition fees, textbooks, and additional expenses, becomes an insurmountable hurdle for families struggling to make ends meet. True inclusivity demands a multi-pronged approach, including targeted interventions to address economic disparities and ensure that financial burdens do not hinder a child's right to education.

Despite these challenges, it is important to acknowledge the progress made in recent years. India has witnessed significant improvements in terms of increased enrollment rates, especially at the primary level. Government initiatives such as the Right to Education Act and the Midday Meal Scheme have played a crucial role in expanding access to education, particularly for marginalized sections of society. These steps provide a glimmer of hope, reminding us that the dream of education for all is not entirely elusive.

To transform the "Education for All" campaign from myth to reality, concerted efforts are needed on multiple fronts. First and foremost, there must be a commitment from all stakeholders, including policymakers, educators, parents, and communities, to prioritize education as a fundamental right. Adequate funding must be allocated to improve infrastructure, enhance teacher training programs, and provide necessary resources to schools across the country. Simultaneously, there is a need to reform the curriculum, adopting innovative teaching methods that foster critical thinking, creativity, and skills relevant to the evolving world.

Furthermore, a comprehensive approach is required to address the socio-economic disparities that hinder access to education. Targeted interventions, scholarships, and financial assistance programs can

make a significant difference, ensuring that economic constraints do not become barriers to learning. Collaboration between the government, non-governmental organizations, and civil society is crucial to channel resources, knowledge, and expertise toward the common goal of education for all.

In conclusion, the "Education for All" campaign in India stands at the intersection of myth and reality. While challenges persist and disparities linger, it is important to remember that progress is not linear. With concerted efforts, unwavering commitment, and a transformative vision, the dream of education for all can become a tangible reality. Let us not be deterred by the hurdles but rather fueled by the conviction that every child, regardless of their circumstances, deserves the key that unlocks the doors of knowledge and opportunity—education.

Independent thinking should be encouraged right from the childhood. (2007)

Independent thinking, the ability to form opinions and make decisions based on personal judgment and critical analysis, is an invaluable skill in today's rapidly changing world. The cultivation of independent thinking from childhood is a topic of great significance. This essay argues that fostering independent thinking in children is crucial for their intellectual, emotional, and social development. By encouraging children to think independently, we empower them to become active participants in society, capable of adapting to new challenges, contributing innovative ideas, and shaping a better future.

Development of Critical Thinking Skills

From an early age, children possess natural curiosity and an innate desire to explore the world around them. By nurturing independent thinking, we harness and enhance these qualities. Independent thinking encourages children to question, analyze, and evaluate information, enabling them to develop critical thinking skills. By presenting diverse perspectives and encouraging open dialogue, children learn to examine ideas from multiple angles, identify biases, and make informed judgments. This ability to think critically equips them to distinguish between fact and fiction, challenge conventional wisdom, and make reasoned decisions.

Enhancement of Creativity and Problem-Solving Abilities

Independent thinking serves as a catalyst for creativity and problem-solving. When children are encouraged to think independently, they are more likely to generate novel ideas and explore alternative solutions. By fostering an environment that values imagination and originality, we inspire children to think beyond the boundaries of traditional thinking. They learn to approach challenges with a fresh perspective, envision innovative solutions, and embrace failure as an opportunity for growth. Independent thinking nurtures resilience and adaptability, empowering children to overcome obstacles and find creative ways to address complex problems throughout their lives.

Empowerment of Individual Identity and Confidence

Encouraging independent thinking from childhood fosters the development of a strong individual identity. By allowing children to explore their own interests, values, and beliefs, we promote self-awareness and self-expression. When children are free to think independently, their unique perspectives and talents can flourish. This process enhances their self-confidence and enables them to assert their opinions and engage in constructive debates. By valuing their individuality, children learn to appreciate diverse perspectives and cultivate empathy, creating a foundation for healthy interpersonal relationships and a more inclusive society.

Preparation for Active Citizenship

Independent thinking is fundamental to responsible citizenship. In a democratic society, the ability to critically evaluate information, analyze societal issues, and make informed decisions is essential. By instilling independent thinking in children, we prepare them to become active and engaged citizens who contribute positively to their communities. Independent thinkers are more likely to challenge societal norms, advocate for justice, and seek innovative solutions to pressing problems. They become agents of positive change, capable of influencing public discourse and shaping the future of their societies.

Cultivation of Lifelong Learning

Independent thinking is closely intertwined with a passion for lifelong learning. When children are encouraged to think independently, they develop an intrinsic motivation to seek knowledge and expand their understanding of the world. They become enthusiastic learners, driven by curiosity and a thirst for new experiences. Independent thinkers are more likely to pursue education beyond formal schooling, explore diverse fields of knowledge, and engage in continuous personal and professional development. By cultivating a love for learning from childhood, we equip individuals to adapt to the evolving demands of the modern world and contribute meaningfully to society.

Conclusion

Independent thinking is a vital skill that should be nurtured right from childhood. By fostering critical thinking, creativity, and problem-solving abilities, we empower children to navigate the complexities of the world with confidence and resilience. Independent thinkers are more likely to become active citizens, challenge societal norms, and shape a better future for all. As parents, educators, and society at large, it is our responsibility to create an environment that encourages independent thinking, embracing diversity of thought, and valuing the power of individual ideas. By doing so, we unlock the full potential of our children, enabling them to become independent thinkers who contribute positively to society and make lasting impact.

Is an egalitarian society possible by educating the masses? (2008)

The concept of an egalitarian society, where all individuals have equal rights and opportunities, has long been a topic of discussion and aspiration. Education, as a powerful tool for social progress, has been seen as a potential means to achieve this vision. This essay explores the question of whether an egalitarian society is possible by educating the masses. By examining the relationship between education, social equality, and the challenges inherent in achieving egalitarianism, we can better understand the potential and limitations of education as a catalyst for social change.

Education as a Path to Equality

Education plays a crucial role in promoting social equality. By providing individuals with knowledge, skills, and critical thinking abilities, education empowers them to challenge existing power structures and demand equal opportunities. Education fosters social mobility by enabling individuals from disadvantaged backgrounds to acquire the tools necessary to improve their circumstances. Moreover, education cultivates values such as empathy, tolerance, and respect, which are essential for fostering an egalitarian society.

Access to Education: A Prerequisite

For education to be a driving force in fostering equality, it must be accessible to all members of society. Unfortunately, access to quality education remains unequal in many parts of the world. Socioeconomic disparities, gender inequality, and geographic location are among the factors that limit access to education. Additionally, discrimination based on race, ethnicity, and other forms of identity can hinder marginalized groups from receiving equitable educational opportunities. Therefore, creating an egalitarian society through education necessitates addressing these barriers and striving for inclusive educational policies and practices.

Challenges and Limitations

While education can contribute significantly to social progress, it is not a panacea for all societal issues. There are inherent challenges and limitations to consider when discussing the potential of education in achieving an egalitarian society.

1. Structural Inequalities: Education alone cannot eradicate deeply ingrained structural inequalities within society. Factors such as wealth disparities, institutional biases, and systemic discrimination create barriers that educational systems alone cannot overcome. To achieve true egalitarianism, a comprehensive approach addressing social, economic, and political structures is necessary.

2. Quality of Education: Simply expanding access to education does not guarantee equality. The quality of education is equally important. Inadequate funding, overcrowded classrooms, and underqualified teachers can perpetuate disparities and hinder the transformative potential of education. Therefore, investing in quality education that fosters critical thinking, creativity, and social skills is crucial.

3. Social Reproduction: Education systems are not immune to social reproduction, whereby existing social inequalities are perpetuated across generations. Socioeconomic background, cultural capital, and family support continue to influence educational outcomes. Breaking this cycle requires addressing the wider social determinants of educational success and providing targeted support to marginalized communities.

Beyond Education: A Holistic Approach

While education is a powerful tool for promoting equality, achieving an egalitarian society requires a comprehensive, multi-faceted approach. Combining education with policies that address wealth distribution, healthcare, employment opportunities, and social welfare is essential. By addressing structural inequalities and promoting social justice, society can create an environment in which education can flourish and contribute to the goal of egalitarianism.

Conclusion

Education undoubtedly plays a pivotal role in striving for an egalitarian society. By empowering individuals, fostering critical thinking, and promoting inclusive values, education has the potential to challenge existing power dynamics and create a more equal world. However, education alone cannot address all the complexities and structural barriers that perpetuate inequality. A comprehensive approach that includes educational reforms alongside broader social and economic transformations is necessary to foster genuine egalitarianism. By recognizing the limitations and challenges while leveraging the transformative power of education, societies can move closer to achieving a more equitable and just future.

Credit – based higher education system – status, opportunities and challenges. (2011)

India's higher education landscape has witnessed significant transformations in recent decades, with the adoption of a credit-based system being one of the key changes. The credit-based higher education system emphasizes the accumulation and transfer of credits, providing students with greater flexibility and personalized learning pathways. This essay explores the status, opportunities, and challenges associated with the credit-based higher education system in India.

Status of Credit-Based Higher Education System:
The credit-based system was introduced in India as part of the National Policy on Education in 1986 and subsequently implemented across universities and colleges. Currently, most Indian higher education institutions have embraced the credit-based system, aligning themselves with international standards. This shift has led to the restructuring of curriculum, incorporating a credit framework based on the workload and learning outcomes of each course.

Opportunities in Credit-Based Higher Education:
1. Flexibility and Choice: The credit-based system enables students to choose from a diverse range of courses, tailor their academic journey according to their interests, and explore interdisciplinary subjects. This flexibility encourages a holistic and well-rounded education experience.

2. Enhanced Mobility: The credit-based system facilitates credit transfer between institutions, enabling students to switch institutions or pursue courses across different universities. This promotes collaboration and exchange of knowledge, enhancing the overall quality of education.

3. Lifelong Learning: The credit-based system encourages a culture of lifelong learning by recognizing and accrediting prior learning experiences, such as vocational training or work experience. This recognition empowers individuals to continually upskill and reskill, adapting to evolving industry demands.

4. Skill Development: The credit-based system provides opportunities for the integration of skill-based courses, fostering the development of industry-relevant skills alongside academic knowledge. This prepares students for the demands of the job market, bridging the gap between academia and industry.

Challenges in Credit-Based Higher Education:
1. Standardization and Quality Assurance: Ensuring the consistency and quality of credit-based programs across institutions remains a challenge. Effective mechanisms for curriculum design, evaluation, and accreditation are necessary to maintain uniform standards and avoid discrepancies.

2. Faculty Training and Evaluation: Implementing the credit-based system requires adequately trained faculty who can design and deliver courses aligned with the credit framework. Faculty development programs should focus on promoting learner-centered approaches and assessment methods that accurately measure student learning outcomes.

3. Infrastructure and Technological Readiness: Successful implementation of the credit-based system necessitates robust infrastructure, including digital platforms, learning management systems, and online resources. Ensuring equitable access to these resources across institutions, particularly in rural areas, is crucial.

4. Student Support Mechanisms: The credit-based system demands strong academic advising and student support services to guide students in selecting appropriate courses, managing credit loads, and addressing academic challenges. Adequate counseling and mentoring frameworks are essential to facilitate student success.

Conclusion:
The credit-based higher education system in India presents significant opportunities for students, institutions, and the overall education ecosystem. Its emphasis on flexibility, mobility, and skill development aligns with the changing dynamics of the global workforce. However, addressing challenges related to standardization, faculty training, infrastructure, and student support is crucial for the successful implementation and sustainability of the credit-based system. By embracing these opportunities and proactively mitigating challenges, India can further strengthen its higher education system, equipping students with the necessary knowledge and skills to thrive in a rapidly evolving world.

Is the growing level of competition good for the youth? (2014)

Competition has become an integral aspect of modern society, permeating various domains such as education, sports, and the job market. The youth, in particular, find themselves increasingly exposed to a heightened level of competition. While some argue that competition fosters essential skills and personal growth, others contend that it can have detrimental effects on the well-being and development of young individuals. This essay aims to explore the implications of the growing level of competition for the youth, considering both its potential benefits and drawbacks.

I. Competition and Skill Development:
One of the primary arguments in favor of the growing level of competition among the youth is its potential to foster skill development. Competitive environments often push individuals to strive for excellence, promoting the acquisition of knowledge, proficiency, and discipline. For example, in academic settings, competition can motivate students to study harder, acquire deeper subject knowledge, and develop critical thinking skills. Similarly, in sports or other extracurricular activities, competition can enhance physical abilities, teamwork, and the pursuit of personal goals.

II. Personal Growth and Resilience:
Competition can also contribute to personal growth and resilience in young individuals. When faced with challenging situations, such as competing for top grades or securing a desired job, youth are often pushed out of their comfort zones. This exposure to adversity can foster resilience, as they learn to cope with failures, setbacks, and rejection. The experience gained through competition can develop important life skills, such as goal-setting, time management, and adaptability, which are valuable for future endeavors.

III. Mental Health and Well-being:
On the other hand, the growing level of competition can have negative consequences for the mental health and well-being of young individuals. The pressure to constantly excel and outperform peers can lead to increased stress, anxiety, and burnout. The emphasis on competition as the primary measure of success may foster a sense of inadequacy or low self-esteem in those who cannot meet the perceived standards. Moreover, the relentless pursuit of success may overshadow other aspects of life, such as social relationships and personal fulfillment, leading to an imbalanced lifestyle.

IV. Inequality and Exclusion:
Another concern associated with excessive competition is the exacerbation of inequality and exclusion among the youth. Not all individuals have equal access to resources, opportunities, or support systems necessary to thrive in competitive environments. Socioeconomic disparities can significantly hinder the ability of some young individuals to participate on an equal footing. Moreover, intense competition may foster a cutthroat mentality, undermining collaboration and empathy, and promoting unhealthy rivalries and unethical behavior.

V. Balancing Competition and Collaboration:
While competition can offer numerous benefits, it is crucial to strike a balance with collaboration and cooperation. Encouraging young individuals to compete in healthy, fair, and supportive environments can help harness the positive aspects of competition while mitigating its negative consequences. Emphasizing collaboration alongside competition can foster teamwork, empathy, and a sense of community, allowing youth to develop both individual skills and the ability to work effectively with others.

Conclusion:

The growing level of competition among the youth is a multifaceted issue with both advantages and drawbacks. While competition can foster skill development and personal growth, its potential negative effects on mental health, well-being, inequality, and exclusion should not be overlooked. To maximize the benefits and minimize the harms, it is imperative to create supportive environments that strike a balance between competition and collaboration, ensuring that young individuals have equal access to resources and opportunities. By doing so, we can create a more inclusive and nurturing society that promotes the holistic development of our youth.

Are the standardized tests good measure of academic ability or progress? (2014)

Standardized tests have long been used as a benchmark for evaluating academic ability and measuring progress in education systems around the world. These tests aim to provide an objective assessment of students' knowledge, skills, and potential. However, the validity and reliability of standardized tests as a comprehensive measure of academic ability and progress have been a topic of debate among scholars, educators, and policymakers. This essay critically examines the strengths and limitations of standardized tests in accurately assessing academic ability and progress.

I. The Value of Standardized Tests:
A. Objective Measurement: Standardized tests provide a standardized format and scoring rubric, ensuring consistent evaluation across diverse populations and educational institutions. This objectivity helps eliminate biases and variations in grading, making comparisons between students and schools more reliable.
B. Accountability and Quality Assurance: Standardized tests play a crucial role in holding educational institutions accountable for their performance and ensuring the delivery of quality education. They provide valuable data for policymakers to identify areas of improvement and allocate resources effectively.
C. College Admissions: Standardized tests, such as the SAT and ACT, are often used as a key criterion for college admissions. They provide a standardized benchmark for universities to assess a large number of applicants fairly, especially when other aspects of students' profiles may be subjective or challenging to compare.

II. Limitations of Standardized Tests:
A. Narrow Assessment of Skills: Standardized tests typically focus on assessing a narrow range of skills, such as reading comprehension, mathematical proficiency, and analytical reasoning. They often neglect other essential skills like creativity, critical thinking, problem-solving, and social-emotional intelligence, which are equally important for academic success and real-world application.
B. Cultural and Socioeconomic Bias: Standardized tests can be culturally and socioeconomically biased, as they may reflect the experiences and knowledge of specific groups or regions. Students from disadvantaged backgrounds or non-native English speakers may face disadvantages due to unfamiliar contexts or language barriers, leading to an inaccurate assessment of their true abilities.
C. Teaching to the Test: The emphasis placed on standardized tests may result in a narrow and superficial teaching approach, focusing on test-specific content and strategies rather than fostering a deep understanding of the subject matter. This teaching-to-the-test phenomenon limits the development of critical thinking, problem-solving skills, and creativity.
D. Test Anxiety and Stress: Standardized tests can generate significant anxiety and stress among students, potentially impairing their performance and hindering the accurate reflection of their true abilities. This emotional burden may disproportionately affect certain individuals, leading to an inaccurate measurement of academic progress.

III. The Need for a Holistic Approach:
A. Multiple Measures of Assessment: To address the limitations of standardized tests, educators and policymakers should incorporate multiple measures of assessment, including project-based assignments, portfolios, and performance evaluations. This holistic approach can provide a more comprehensive understanding of students' abilities, strengths, and areas for improvement.
B. Contextualized Assessments: Recognizing the importance of cultural diversity and socioeconomic factors, assessments should be designed to consider different contexts and allow for flexible evaluation methods. This approach can help mitigate bias and provide a more accurate reflection of students' abilities.

C. Longitudinal Tracking: Rather than relying solely on one-time standardized tests, longitudinal tracking of student progress can offer a more comprehensive view of their academic growth over time. This approach considers the individual's progress, strengths, and weaknesses, facilitating personalized interventions and support.

Conclusion:
Standardized tests have their merits as a tool for measuring academic ability and progress, providing an objective and standardized assessment. However, their limitations in assessing a broad range of skills, potential biases, and negative impact on teaching and student well-being cannot be ignored. A more comprehensive and holistic approach to assessment, considering multiple measures and contexts, is crucial to obtaining a more accurate understanding of students' academic abilities and progress. By embracing a multifaceted evaluation system, education systems can better foster the development of well-rounded individuals equipped for success in both academia and the real world.

Education without values, as useful as it is, seems rather to make a man more clever devil. (2015)

Education plays a crucial role in shaping individuals and societies, equipping individuals with knowledge, skills, and critical thinking abilities. However, the statement "Education without values, as useful as it is, seems rather to make a man more clever devil" prompts us to explore the potential consequences of an education system devoid of moral and ethical values. This essay aims to delve into the notion that while education can be beneficial, its effectiveness in fostering true human development is compromised without the incorporation of values.

The Role of Education

Education is a powerful tool that imparts knowledge, promotes cognitive development, and equips individuals with skills required for personal growth and societal progress. It opens doors to employment opportunities, enhances economic development, and cultivates critical thinking. Through education, individuals gain the ability to analyze, evaluate, and make informed decisions. However, the extent to which education contributes to the overall well-being of individuals and societies depends on the values it instills.

Values in Education

Values are the fundamental principles that guide human behavior, shape character, and foster positive social interactions. They encompass virtues such as honesty, empathy, respect, and integrity. Education, in its true essence, should go beyond the transmission of facts and knowledge and actively instill these values in learners. When values are incorporated into education, it nurtures moral reasoning, empathy, and social responsibility.

Education as a Double-Edged Sword

Education without values can potentially lead to adverse consequences. While it enhances cognitive abilities and intellectual prowess, it may lack the guiding principles necessary for responsible and ethical decision-making. Without a solid moral foundation, knowledge alone can be misused, leading individuals to employ their cleverness for personal gain or malicious purposes. History is replete with instances of highly educated individuals who have perpetrated atrocities, demonstrating the dark side of education divorced from values.

Enhancing Cleverness: The Devil Within

Education without values can inadvertently promote selfishness and manipulation. A person who is clever but lacks moral grounding may exploit others, manipulate situations for personal gain, and engage in deceitful practices. Cleverness, when unchecked by values, becomes a tool for achieving personal objectives at the expense of others' well-being. This can lead to a society where intelligence is revered but moral principles are neglected, breeding a culture of cunning individuals who prioritize self-interest over the common good.

The Need for Values-Based Education

Values-based education ensures that the pursuit of knowledge is intertwined with moral and ethical growth. By integrating values into the curriculum, educators can foster compassion, empathy, and social responsibility. Students are encouraged to think critically, consider the consequences of their actions, and develop a sense of ethics. Through values-based education, individuals become more than just clever; they become responsible citizens committed to building a just and equitable society.

Conclusion

Education, when divorced from values, runs the risk of making individuals clever devils who exploit their intelligence for personal gain without considering the well-being of others. Cleverness, in the absence of values, can lead to the erosion of moral principles and societal harmony. To foster genuine human development, education must incorporate values that promote empathy, integrity, and social responsibility. Only then can education truly fulfill its transformative potential by producing individuals who are not only knowledgeable but also virtuous and compassionate members of society.

Destiny of a nation is shaped in its classrooms. (2017)

Education has long been regarded as the cornerstone of a prosperous and progressive society. The destiny of a nation is intricately tied to the quality of education it provides to its citizens. In this context, classrooms play a pivotal role as the nurturing ground for knowledge, values, and skills. The impact of education extends far beyond academic achievements; it encompasses the development of individuals as responsible citizens, critical thinkers, and contributors to the nation's growth. This essay explores how classrooms, as the primary settings for formal education, play a vital role in shaping the destiny of a nation.

Body:

1. Education as the Foundation of National Development:
Education is widely acknowledged as a critical catalyst for national development. It equips individuals with the necessary tools to contribute to society, fosters economic growth, promotes social mobility, and enhances democratic values. Classrooms serve as the primary vehicles for imparting knowledge, enabling students to develop skills and competencies that are vital for their personal growth and the progress of their nation.

2. Fostering Human Capital:
Classrooms are the birthplace of human capital, the collective knowledge, skills, and capabilities of individuals. The quality of education received within classrooms directly impacts the development of this human capital. A nation that invests in a robust and inclusive education system can harness the potential of its citizens, leading to advancements in science, technology, arts, governance, and various other spheres. Classrooms provide a nurturing environment where students can acquire knowledge, develop critical thinking abilities, and cultivate the skills necessary to thrive in a rapidly evolving world.

3. Inculcating Values and Citizenship:
Beyond academic knowledge, classrooms also serve as spaces to instill values and shape the character of individuals. Education should go beyond simply equipping students with subject-specific knowledge; it should also foster empathy, ethical behavior, and a sense of responsibility towards one's nation and fellow citizens. Through classroom interactions, discussions, and extracurricular activities, students learn the importance of tolerance, respect, and civic engagement. A nation's destiny is shaped by citizens who are well-rounded and possess a strong moral compass, which can be nurtured in classrooms.

4. Promoting Social Cohesion and Equality:
Classrooms are where individuals from diverse backgrounds come together, fostering social cohesion and promoting equality. Education serves as a leveling platform, allowing students from various socio-economic, ethnic, and cultural backgrounds to interact and learn from each other. Inclusive classrooms help break down barriers and prejudices, creating a more harmonious society. By providing equal opportunities and resources to all students, classrooms can counteract the perpetuation of inequality, ensuring a more equitable destiny for the nation.

5. The Role of Teachers:

Teachers are central to the classroom experience and play a pivotal role in shaping the destiny of a nation. They are not only disseminators of knowledge but also mentors, role models, and facilitators of learning. Skilled and passionate teachers can inspire students, foster their curiosity, and guide them towards personal growth and academic excellence. Well-supported teachers with adequate training and resources can transform classrooms into vibrant hubs of intellectual exploration, creativity, and critical thinking, thereby shaping the future destiny of their nation.

Conclusion:

The destiny of a nation is indeed shaped in its classrooms. The quality of education provided within these classrooms directly influences the development of human capital, the inculcation of values, and the promotion of social cohesion and equality. Through inclusive and holistic education, classrooms have the power to nurture responsible citizens who possess the knowledge, skills, and ethical values necessary for the nation's progress. Therefore, it is imperative for policymakers and stakeholders to prioritize investments in education, ensuring that classrooms become spaces that empower individuals and lay the foundation for a prosperous and harmonious future.

Printed in Great Britain
by Amazon